Under ✦ a
Blue Flag
~ A Novel ~

Under a
Blue Flag
~ A Novel ~

DANIEL
PUTKOWSKI

HAWSER
PRESS

ISBN 978-0-9815959-2-4

FIRST HAWSER PRESS TRADE PAPERBACK EDITION FEBRUARY 2011
10 9 8 7 6 5 4 3 2 1

danielputkowski.com

FOR
CARLOTTA

Give them a reason to live and rules to survive.

ALSO BY
DANIEL PUTKOWSKI

An Island Away

Bonk's Bar

Universal Coverage

AUTHOR'S NOTE

Under a Blue Flag is a continuation of the events which began in my novel, *An Island Away*. As with any sequel, the reader is encouraged to explore the first installment in order to fully enjoy the second.

"I AM NOT YOUR FATHER, but you are my son."

So it was that Hernán Revilla stood beside the body of Captain Nathan Beck, who had been the only father he'd known and who had promised one day to tell him the facts of how he came to be a stepson. Hernán knew there was a story to be told, the one about his mother and Captain Beck. Over the years he'd heard whispers, saw packages sent, and understood that none of the loyal crew would betray their master. However, Captain Beck passed to the next world without having fulfilled his promise in this one, leaving Hernán to discover his birthright, whatever it may be, on his own.

First, there was a funeral to be held at a spot more than a hundred miles east of the Delaware Bay. The crew assembled on the stern deck of Beck's massive salvage tug *Tenacious*, where his wrapped body lay on a plank of polished teak. A chaplain from the Seaman's Church Institute of Philadelphia administered the service, the same man who presided over the launch ceremony for *Tenacious* eight years ago.

As sometimes happens in this part of the Atlantic, a high-pressure system dominated the weather, rendering the ocean flat calm and the sky a faultless blue. Only the chaplain's steady voice broke the silence as he intoned the service from memory. Then came the moment when the men on both sides of the plank moved in unison. As they raised the edge, each of them remembered the man who had been their captain, who had led them through the perils of the sea, who had trusted them as they trusted him.

Hernán was one of the four whose hands touched that piece of wood. Although he was only six years old when he first met Captain Beck, he remembered every detail about the day. He had flown from Bogotá, Colombia, to the island of Aruba under the watchful eye of a concerned flight attendant who stayed with him through immigration and customs. Then he saw his mother on the other side of a glass door. Like any boy who hadn't seen his mother in many months, he ran for her open arms. She clutched him so hard his ribs ached. Just past her, he noticed a serious-looking man standing only a few feet away.

"This is Captain Beck," his mother said. "Thanks to him, we can be together."

The time with his mother spanned only several months, ending on a breezy night when she kissed him good-bye and sent him with the man who had quickly become his guardian. That was fifteen years ago.

The weight in Hernán's hands suddenly decreased as Beck's body slid toward the water. A moment later, a gentle splash lapped *Tenacious'* hull. In short order, the plank was stowed while the chaplain offered his personal condolences and best wishes. When his official duties were complete, he was helped onto the launch that would take him back to shore.

One by one, the crew returned to work, leaving Hernán alone to contemplate his future. He was now master and owner of *Tenacious*, free to sail anywhere in the world with water deep enough to float her keel. At his disposal were her crew of twelve and her eight thousand horsepower. Together, they hauled dead ships off rocks, towed oil rigs into position, and led the way for less robust vessels through storms, ice, and minefields. It was his turn to give the orders, an honor he earned as much as he inherited.

"Captain?" Syd, the chief engineer, asked.

Hernán raised his eyes from the water through which Beck had passed. The whole world surrounded him, but there was one place he had to go before any other.

"South," he said. "South by east."

2

LUIS INHERITED A PIECE OF PARADISE. The place had a ramshackle look, a dusty patina, and sometimes an odd smell, but for him, it was home. Others called it a barroom. With it came several vehicles, a house by the water in the near-by village of Savaneta, and an aged cat named Screwball. Although his name wasn't on the deeds to these assets, his uncle made Luis the custodian of tradition and enforcer of customs by entrusting him with the memories, secrets, and rusty keys necessary to accomplish the task.

In the same manner as its founder, Luis sat on the veranda above the World Famous Charlie's Bar with the heart of San Nicolaas, Aruba, sprawling to the north, south, and east. To the west sat the oil refinery that gave the town its joy and pain, which, depending upon one's perspective, might be the same thing.

The only pain Luis felt on this particular night came from his legs. He'd been dancing for hours in a hotel ballroom on the other side of the island where ten thousand tourists a week found their version of a tropical heaven. High- and low-rise hotels, miles of beaches, dozens of restaurants, swanky night-clubs, and shopping malls appealed to all types of travelers, especially those from colder climates. Luis enjoyed his evenings there, particularly the live music, which was hard to come by in San Nicolaas these days.

While it lacked glamour, San Nicolaas was the place where he belonged. It was a little worse for the wear, but her buildings still stood, her people worked more often than not, and no one complained about the way things were as much as they hoped for better.

In that frame of mind, Luis looked over the parapet at the street below. The thoroughfare fronted eleven bars, two cloth-ing stores, two hair salons, one junk shop, two pharmacies, two banks, a few offices, and a Western Union agent. No one other than himself actually lived on Main Street. Then again, there were residents of a certain type. Those eleven bars each housed four young women employed as hostesses according to their work permits. This convenient term masked the more intimate activities for which they were paid. Therefore, Main Street's population included Luis and forty-four women, a ratio he believed was nearly perfect, not that he frequently indulged in that form of entertainment. Still, if he was in the mood and wanted to improve his odds, he need only stroll a few blocks from Main Street to one of the nineteen other bars to see what was on offer, which was precisely what a fair number of men were doing at the moment.

Luis learned a good many things from his uncle, includ-ing how to read the street from this covered porch located one flight of stairs above it all. Charlie knew how to differentiate between a wild crowd and a destructive one, a few guys having a good time and a gang looking for a fight. He also appreciated the value of free-spending tourists over cheap refinery workers. He instructed Luis in the mystical arts of barkeeping, which weren't so cryptic as they were pragmatic.

"Be a friend, not a mentor. Avoid politics, religion, and other men's wives," Charlie had said. "Unless business is slow. Then pick one to start a fight, and you'll have a crowd in no time."

Thankfully, Luis hadn't started any fights since his uncle brought him to the island. Just the same, he did his share of tourist wrangling. Like Charlie before him, he poured free drinks for any woman brave enough to sit at the bar topless. He also danced a wicked salsa or merengue with a lady who caught his eye and many who just needed to get on their feet. Anyone who asked received an informative briefing on how to experience San Nicolaas to the fullest without getting into trouble with either the law or their emotions. Many of the counseled forgot the key points, however, only to find themselves in Police Chief Calenda's custody, or miserably heartbroken, or both. He couldn't help but laugh at this predicament, which could never be scripted. It happened on its own, in full view of anyone who cared to watch, including those involved, none of whom understood that in pursuit of their desires they might be fine entertainment for others.

A flicker of light caught his attention, and Luis shifted his gaze from the refinery back to Main Street. The neon sign at China Clipper switched off. He didn't need to look at his watch to know it was 2 AM, closing time at that bar. The owner, Rafael Montoya, stepped out the door, rebuffed a trio of men who wanted him to remain open, and proceeded to close the metal gate that secured the building. This was standard procedure in

San Nicolaas. Then Montoya dropped his keys, picked them up, struggled with the lock, and dropped them again. Stooping to recover the ring, he toppled onto the sidewalk where he remained.

Just as Luis was about to trot down the block to see if the man had a heart attack or another medical calamity, Montoya regained his footing. He hung onto the gate with one hand while attempting to work the lock with the other.

Looking back at Screwball, Luis said, "He's drunk."

Screwball issued a gaping yawn to indicate his feelings on the matter.

It took several tries, but Montoya finally locked the gate. His next move took him across the street but not without difficulty. The curb presented a problem, as did a car, which would have been understandable had it been moving. He glanced off the fender, gave the finger to a driver who wasn't there, and made it to the other side.

Any bar owner with brains never consumed his own booze or sampled his own merchandise. "There are better ways to go broke or kill yourself," Charlie had noted. "Make it an adventure or a good headline."

At least Montoya wasn't spending the night with one of the girls from China Clipper. It wasn't unheard of, but it was foul play in the realm of San Nicolaas social politics. Luis didn't know Montoya as the type to take girls home no matter where they worked. Not that this was a problem, so long as he paid her rate within the Zone of Tolerance, which began at the head of Main Street, stretched to the refinery wall, and spanned the three blocks between Rodgerstraat and Helfrichstraat. To exchange money for carnal pleasure anywhere else broke the law, and then Chief Calenda or one of his fellow officers would have to administer an uncomfortable punishment to both client and hostess.

It appeared Montoya was bent on having an adventure after all, because he meandered down the block when he should have been on the phone for a ride home. Or, he could have slept in his car a few hours until he was sober enough to make it on his own. Instead, he loped around the corner to answer the call of self-destruction.

Fortunately, he was smart enough to stay out of Minchi's. A formidable bouncer worked there, a nice guy who would put up with drunkenness but had a hair trigger for belligerence. There were other reasons for Montoya to stay away from that location, but they were far enough in the past that soon no one would remember. As Luis turned his back on the street, the sound of Charlie's voice filled his head.

"A burning fuse eventually finds the bomb."

It was too late to discuss the issue with his uncle's ghost. The oversized recliner that he kept on the veranda during the dry season pulled away the last of his strength. Letting his head settle back on the cushion, he stared up at the night sky. Screwball mounted the armrest, relaxed onto his paws, and muttered a quiet purr.

Dozing off, Luis couldn't help but dream about Minchi's owner. She was a woman, not a chica. She had her pick of the men the way the men thought they had the pick of the girls. Given the chance, he wouldn't mind a fair amount of her time, a semi-permanent arrangement perhaps, but Charlie regularly advised him to find someone else.

"She's bound for a place none of us can reach."

Of course, Charlie never mentioned when, which gave plenty of men, including Luis, false hope that they might have the chance to join her there.

3

NOT A MILE FROM WHERE LUIS DRIFTED OFF, there stood another man thinking of the same woman. His name was Garrett Turner. He worked at the refinery, and he fell for none of the illusions about which Charlie had warned. He expected to get what he paid for, nothing more, which is the way he viewed every aspect of life, including the women in San Nicolaas. At the same time, he accepted nothing less because he believed a deal was a deal and the parties to it should honor their commitment, including himself. It was how he lived and worked.

Part of his compensation package at the refinery granted Turner one of the few remaining homes that were part of the original Lago Colony at Seroe Colorado on the southeast tip of the island. An ironic view was Bungalow 58's best feature. To the southeast stretched a sweeping hook of sand known as Rodgers Beach, while to the northwest squatted the refinery complex. Turner appreciated the proximity of work and play. In twenty years traveling the world in the employ of oil companies he'd not seen another place like it.

However, he had experienced plenty of towns similar to San Nicolaas. Its combination of necessity and vice commonly abutted industrial complexes, which made sense considering the relationship the two halves shared. One provided gainful employment while the other offered a slew of opportunities to dispose of wages earned. Similarly, the type of people who worked there — temporary contractors, apprentice tradesmen, and itinerate managers like himself — were happy to spend in ways that gentle society preferred not to acknowledge. Such was the difference between San Nicolaas and Oranjestaad, two towns barely ten miles apart on a small island, and yet they might have been on separate planets. It didn't matter to Turner what anyone thought about San Nicolaas. He found the barmen to be honest, the female company agreeable, and the walk to town a good form of exercise.

As he passed through the refinery, beneath its tangle of pipes, around its many smokestacks, and over a few of its obsolete pieces, he thought how the facility was generally declining. A more sympathetic man might have worried about such an observation, but Turner thought of himself as a mercenary. He did his job, did it well, but owned no stock in the company. Nor did he doubt his ability to find a similar job working for a similar outfit in a similar place. It happened before. It would happen again. His loyalty lay with himself. He was a single man with a valid passport and a pocket bulging with money thanks to his skills wrangling men and machines. He spoke three languages, too. If the company furloughed him or a better offer came along, his bag would be packed in less than an hour. Nothing belonging to him arrived on the island that didn't do so in his suitcase. It could very easily leave the same way. He learned long ago not to acquire things that didn't fit through the door of an airplane.

Not that Turner was in any hurry to leave Aruba. He liked the island, plain and simple, especially because he worked in places much worse, where getting a cold beer was a matter of running the gauntlet as opposed to avoiding the potholes. Furthermore, there was this woman in town that he'd taken a liking to, and she was reason enough to ignore the mail and phone calls from people trying to lure him down the career highway.

Just this week he declined a serious offer for a position in Argentina. It came with a handsome signing bonus, travel expenses, and a company car. He almost jumped at it when Bill Fenner, the recruiter who haunted him, mentioned the salary, nearly ten percent more than he was currently earning. He refused for three general reasons: Aruba was comfortable, relatively stress free, and there was that woman, the one he was going to see tonight. Had he met someone like her earlier in his life things might have turned out differently. As it was, he knew better than to invest in romantic notions, but he wasn't afraid to make the most of a good thing while it lasted.

The refinery's main gate opened into San Nicolaas. Through it once passed more than eight thousand workers. At present, Turner was one of perhaps a quarter that number, and at this early hour of the morning he strolled through alone. A few yards away, he spotted Chief Calenda parking his car in the lot of an unfinished hotel that marked the east end of Main Street.

"*Bon nochi*, Mr. Turner," Calenda greeted him. "On your way to see José?"

"Among other things," Turner replied.

"A short stop on life's long journey," Calenda remarked.

"I'm well on my way," said Turner.

"In San Nicolaas you don't have far to go," continued Calenda.

"A few blocks one way or the other, depending on what you're looking for."

Adjusting his cap, Calenda asked, "Have you found what you're looking for, Mr. Turner?"

"For the moment," came the reply.

"Only that long?" pressed Calenda, who knew that Turner regularly visited one woman and none other.

"I'll let you know."

Calenda resisted the urge to pursue the subject. His curiosity, the thing that made him a fine policeman, was sometimes a liability in personal conversation. Besides, Turner wasn't the first man to pretend innocence or ignorance. The challenge was figuring out which it was, or if it was something else entirely. In this case, the answer didn't matter as Turner behaved himself within the limits of the Zone of Tolerance and was thus exempt from Calenda's professional ministrations.

"Enjoy yourself," Calenda said and set off to make his rounds.

At Black & White Bar, Turner received full value for his money in terms of drinks and social interaction, both provided by the bartender. José was an expert at interrupting Turner's usual afterwork thoughts, which centered on that woman working a few doors away. A chat with him was a value-enhancing proposition in that it cost nothing extra and diverted Turner from spending more time with a certain lady than he budgeted.

Lately, José had a new tack in his conversation, one that focused on two purebred dogs he purchased. He made the mistake of letting them into his air-conditioned bedroom. Now they wouldn't sleep anywhere else, which meant he had to leave the cooling system on all day long or they would scratch the bottom of his door to splinters.

"How's the electric bill?" Turner joked as he took his regular seat at the bar.

"These dogs cost more than a sad girlfriend," José moaned.

"Trade them in for a nice chica," suggested Turner.

"Then my wife gets everything."

"So you're better off with the dogs."

"My kids, let me tell you, I think God is punishing me with them. They feed the dogs Vienna sausages, and I come home to diarrhea all over the rugs."

This tragedy Turner acknowledged with a guffaw. "You should have taken a lesson from Kenny. He married one of the girls, moved to Colombia, and lives happily ever after."

José rolled his eyes. "Kenny outlived Coco the Red to become the oldest bartender in San Nicolaas before he found the right one. You think I want to wait that long?"

"The way things are going at the refinery," Turner continued, "soon there will be hotels from Rodgers Beach to Savaneta, and you'll be serving strawberry daiquiris to divorcées and coeds."

"In that case I better lose some weight," José said rubbing his protruding belly. "What about the turnaround?" he asked next, referring to the periodic shutdown of the refinery when major maintenance projects were done.

"More likely you'll lose thirty pounds."

"It's overdue, no?"

"Yes, and there are no plans to restart Unit Two," Turner explained, thinking that he might have made a mistake by not taking the offer Bill Fenner made. It was always better to take another job while you still had one.

José pulled a bottle of Balashi from the cooler, snapped off the cap, and poured it into Turner's glass. "I guess there's room for a cruise ship at those piers," he said with a wave toward the refinery.

"Plenty of room," Turner agreed. "Just get rid of everything else."

"What about us?" José protested. "Without guys like you, we'll be out of business."

Turner sorted some bills from his pocket as he said, "You don't know how to make a strawberry daiquiri, do you?"

"I'd rather clean up dog crap."

"Money's money," countered Turner. "What's the difference if you get it from a guy in coveralls or a chick in a bikini?"

"Good point."

The door in the back wall opened. Two of José's girls and their clients entered the room. They sat at the far end of the bar where José served them a round of drinks.

Turner checked his watch, saw it was nearly 3 AM, and scooped his money off the bar. After downing the last of his beer, he took his leave. He wasn't a few steps out the door when another familiar face appeared from the alley that separated Black & White from the next block.

"Just in time," Frankie said, holding his wrist to look at an imaginary watch. The town's most reliable choller, as vagabonds were known in Aruba, Frankie earned his way by begging florins, dollars, Euros, and any other currency, including food, drinks, and discarded clothing, that passersby might be willing to give him. None of these gifts included a set of teeth, which he desperately needed. In fact, the only good teeth in his head came courtesy of Samito, and these stuck out like goal posts on a muddy field.

"What time would that be?" Turner replied without slowing down.

"The time that Mr. Turner leaves Black & White Bar for Minchi's," Frankie answered.

"Very observant," Turner said.

"Nothing escapes my perfect vision or my ears, which can hear a rat fart at a hundred meters."

"Those fangs of yours don't look like they could chew a slice of wet bread," countered Turner.

Frankie lowered his head. "Every man has his limitations," he murmured.

"You'll have to find a job for those eyes and ears," mocked Turner.

"Hah! I already have one. The town spy is what I am. Finder of facts."

"How much does that pay?"

"A florin, a guilder, one in the same if you want me looking out for you," Frankie replied.

"I'll take my chances," Turner said, reaching for the door to Minchi's.

"Then you're on your own," proclaimed Frankie, "in a place of mystery and intrigue!" He pivoted on his worn-out heel and shuffled back into the ally where soon the trash from the corner restaurant would be at the curb.

For all Frankie's drama, there was nothing exotic about Turner, who lived a mostly solitary life. The men that worked for him and those for whom he worked were nothing more than employees and employers. The loose bonds he formed with them rarely extended beyond a beer after work or small talk at the lunch table. He liked it that way because he knew his assignments were permanently temporary. It was a tedious burden to keep track of friends when moving from place to place. Why bother when there were new people to meet at the next stop?

That's how it was with the woman at Minchi's. He could have paid the fine, or *molta* as it was called in Spanish, and spent the entire night with her. However, Turner didn't see that as a good deal in either financial or emotional terms. After an hour between the sheets and a bit of conversation, he was ready to sleep. Not that he didn't appreciate quality time. He did, especially with this woman. Her companionship felt easy, like it would never end without being wearisome the way it frequently was with hired women after the initial charm wore thin. Why else would he have picked her and none other in the past twelve months?

Turner stepped into Minchi's Bar anticipating foul looks from the other three girls working there who thought him mean-spirited for not sharing some of his wealth with them. He wasn't disappointed. Two of them hardly glanced his way as they settled their nightly account with the bartender, Pablo. Turner watched as he counted out the chips deposited into a plastic cup for every vino they coaxed from potential clients that night. The third, a crafty blonde named Angela, stood before a mirror against the far wall.

Turner caught Angela staring at him in the mirror. She had a body old men lusted for but an attitude that required a young man's tolerance. He was neither, which meant Angela had no hope of seeing any money from his pocket. Despite this reality, she took his diffidence to be a challenge, never passing up an opportunity to solicit him. Then again, maybe she was simply sharpening her skills.

In two quick steps, Angela was leaning against Turner's right side, marking him with a combination of perfume and makeup.

Polite as he was, Turner offered a slack smile, then nodded to Pablo that he'd like a beer. Angela held on, brushing her hair against his neck.

"¿Un vino para mí, señor?" she asked.

This was how the process started for a man who wanted to spend half an hour of private time with the girl. Two wines had to be purchased, and then the bartender would slide the key to the girl's room across the bar. Turner had no interest in going upstairs with this girl, and therefore did not want to buy her a vino. Besides, it was closing time.

"Sorry," he said, "I'm here to visit my friend."

"I know. The refinery's assistant superintendent only deals with the boss."

"That's right," Turner said without looking at her.

Not to be put off, Angela pressed on. "If you won't share a vino with me, tell me something."

"If I can."

"You always come for her. Tell me why."

Turner felt as if he were being interviewed for his next job. The problem wasn't that he didn't have an answer; it was that he had hundreds of them. Which one to pick?

"Aren't I pretty?" Angela asked.

"Of course."

"What a body I have, too."

Reflexively, Turner let his eyes follow the curves of her figure the way any male of the species would.

"If you want to chat, we could talk about music, travel, a little about soccer."

Conversation was a big part of it, admitted Turner with a silent nod.

"You've been with her a long time. Aren't you bored?"

It was a brash question for a person recently out of her teens and it was asked of a man who dated her boss. *Provocative,* thought Turner, the way a clever safety inspector might attack a recalcitrant operator.

"You go to a restaurant, the beach, maybe overnight to a hotel, then what?" Angela wanted to know. "Don't men always want something different?"

She might have studied rhetoric the way she fired off these questions. Whatever her education, Turner had his answer, which was that he liked this woman, part and parcel. Still, he wasn't going to discuss it with another chica, no matter what her qualifications.

"Some other time," he said dismissively and looked to Teo, the bar's bouncer, for a rescue.

Teo mouthed the words "ten minutes" with a finger pointed toward the ceiling.

"*¡Perfecto!*" chided Angela, who intercepted the message. "You can share a vino with me."

Chafed by Angela's persistence, Turner glared at her, only to get a wry smile in return. Then he remembered that subtracting a five florin vino from his salary was like taking a bucket of sand off the beach. He laughed at himself, ordered a vino, and settled onto a comfortable stool. The other two girls, perturbed by Angela's maneuver, left the room in a huff.

In a practiced way, Angela sipped from her flute without taking her eyes off him. "I would like to own a place like this someday," she began.

"Then what?" Turner said, mimicking her earlier retort.

"Then I'd be like her. The boss. Collecting for the casa, sitting in the passenger seat while Teo drove me to the salon, entertaining the clients I like, and turning down the ones I don't. That's the life."

From his own experience, Turner believed it was better to be number two on the pecking order: nearly as much authority and pay for much less responsibility than number one. He considered trying to explain that, then decided against it. If Angela wanted to be the queen bee, he wished her all the luck in the world. If José didn't want to make daiquiris, he might sell his bar to her.

"As soon as I figure out how she holds on to men like you," she whispered.

The door banged open, and Pablo let out a groan. He didn't mind Turner lingering past closing time, but less generous tippers were unwelcome. Then he saw who it was. Rafael Montoya. He was piss drunk, too, which meant Teo might have to throw him in the street.

Montoya weaved his way up to the bar, leered at Angela, and slapped his hand in front of Pablo. "Tequila!" he demanded.

"We're closed," Pablo said evenly in an attempt not to provoke him.

"Closed? I see a man there, a *puta* there, and you are right here with nothing to do. Tequila!"

"I'll call you a taxi," Teo offered.

"A taxi? My car is across the street. I want tequila!"

No one moved.

Fixating on Angela, Montoya said, "Don't waste your time with him. He's in love with your boss."

Angela pretended not to hear him.

"Has he given you a florin yet?" demanded Montoya.

"Let me buy you that shot of tequila," Turner put in.

Stiffening, Montoya slurred, "You know the difference between a rich man and a poor man? A poor man has to be patient. A rich man can do what he wants when he wants to do it."

Turner raised his glass to that bit of philosophical rambling. Teo was less impressed.

"Have a drink in peace or find your way out," the bouncer said.

Suddenly lucid, Montoya calmly pointed at the ceiling and replied, "Tell her not to worry about the rent."

"The rent?" Teo queried.

"Yes, the rent. Tell her next month is free."

At first, Teo thought Montoya was talking about Minchi's, which didn't make any sense because his boss paid only the mortgage to the bank. Then it struck him that Montoya was talking about her house. Montoya owned it and received the rent money, which Teo personally delivered, a few days early each month.

"I'll let her know," Teo said.

"A rich man does what he wants," repeated Montoya and left the building.

"I guess he doesn't want that tequila after all," Turner joked.

Everyone laughed but Angela who added, "Not the type of rich man I'm looking for."

Just then, her boss, and the subject of Montoya's notice, entered the room looking bright-eyed and excited, as if it was the beginning of the night, not the end. She wrapped her arms around Turner, greeting him like a favorite uncle with a kiss to his cheek. Then she stepped behind the bar where she casually told Pablo that he and Teo were free to go.

Teo took her aside for a moment to explain about Montoya, but she assured him everything was fine even as she scanned the ledger where the girls' activities were logged. This took only a few seconds, after which she drew a fresh beer from the cooler for Turner and refilled Angela's vino.

"Do you mind if I have something myself?" she asked.

So easygoing was the inquiry, as if she didn't want to interrupt them, that neither Angela nor Turner knew who she was asking. They replied in unison, "Please, join us," and "Por qué no."

On their common insistence, she poured a glass of Baileys with ice and joined their conversation by saying, "It's been hot. We could use some rain."

And there she was, a lady sharing drinks with her friends, not a chica pestering her client or a woman worried about her landlord. Anyone who saw these three sitting at the bar would have assumed nothing else. Even Angela, who knew better, was amazed at how only a short time ago her boss had ushered a client down the stairs and out the back door. The metal gate to the street had hardly clanged shut when she hurried up to her room where she showered, reapplied her makeup, and pulled on a fresh dress. However, when she came through the door, she was relaxed and pleased to join a little get-together. Where did she find the energy? And that drunken man, wasn't she worried about him?

Angela caught herself staring and switched her gaze to her glass. She listened while Turner commented on the weather, a few things at the refinery, and how he was sad to release some employees. Then her boss saw that the vino was nearly empty.

"Would you like a Baileys?" she asked.

Technically, the bar was closed. Still, this was a grand gesture, one that was forbidden during regular hours when the girls were only permitted to drink vino or water. It was also a test. As much as Angela wanted the drink and to study her boss in action, she knew it was time to go. True to form, the lady in charge was only being polite. Excusing herself delicately, Angela headed for her room, where she would review everything that happened in the past several minutes. She might even rehearse in front of the mirror. Didn't the best actresses practice their lines?

Peeking back at them from the doorway, Angela heard Turner say, "You look great, Luz," and then the clink of their glasses coming together.

IN HER LIFE AS A PROSTITUTE, men tested Luz. They would ask for or demand things, not only sexually but intangibles, like discretion or sympathy. Sometimes it was as simple as the comfort of a quiet moment. She gave them these, but never immediately or for free. Everything had a price, either overtly stated or subtly implied. The cost was not always discussed because in her life much was left unsaid, and thereby interpreted through imperfect signals. The message was frequently confused, misinterpreted, or lost entirely. Nonetheless, she ultimately got what she wanted or what others agreed to give her. The tricky part was knowing what to give and how much to take. Once in a while she made a painful mistake, which meant losing a client or more.

Luz struggled to decode Garrett Turner. He came to her room several times a week and used her body in the most rudimentary of ways. He was neither creative nor passionate, simply mechanical, as if he was testing a piece of equipment that might fail if not regularly used. Afterward, he would remain in her room for an hour or so, sometimes dozing off, other times staring out the window at the refinery flares and chatting. Usually, he did not depart until just before dawn, when the streets were devoid of everyone including Frankie.

She assumed he was like many of the men who worked on the other side of the wall: lonely, disconnected from home, and/or unsatisfied by a wife or girlfriend. However, it was impossible to gain any insight into his thoughts. Over the past several months, she raised the price three times in an effort to at least hear a complaint. It never came. Apparently, money was unimportant or maybe he was falling in love. She preferred the former, knowing eventually the matter would be clear.

Whatever his inclinations, Turner disclosed none of them this night. He enjoyed his usual activities, then took a seat by the window.

"Your competitor across the street drinks a little too much," he began.

"He's not the only one in San Nicolaas," observed Luz.

"He's a generous drunk, too. Said your rent is free next month."

Teo had told her this, and Luz attributed it to Montoya being out of his mind. She'd been living in a house he owned for fifteen years, paying her rent early without fail. Why would he suddenly give her a free month? Then again, it didn't have to make sense. Stupidity and drunkenness were born of the same mother.

"Maybe he's going to throw you out," Turner suggested.

Luz screwed up her face. "*Nada de nada,*" she said because in San Nicolaas of all places, nothing was for nothing. If Montoya truly was forgiving the rent, he would be looking for compensation in another form.

"You could always live with me," Turner suggested. "Bungalow 58 has a beautiful view."

She recalled the scene but didn't mention she'd been a guest of the previous occupant.

"Angela admires you," continued Turner.

This was no secret. Whatever Luz did, she felt Angela's eyes upon her.

"She's ambitious, too."

Ambition was a requirement to succeed in San Nicolaas, she could have told him. She'd seen lazy girls try to operate on good looks and sexy ones attempt to hustle clients with clever ploys. An average-looking, slightly heavy girl made twice as much when she focused on the assembly-line nature of the work, and that required an aggressive mentality. Time was a scarce resource. Getting a man upstairs as quickly as possible was crucial to maximizing profit. Similarly, the act had to be completed expeditiously in order to return to the bar to snare the next client. All this had to be done under the illusion that the man was the most important one in the world. The most ambitious girls serviced as many as eight clients a night and perhaps several more in the afternoon.

There was another method, one Luz honed over the years. It was a niche business, which meant there were only enough clients to support two or three girls. The key was to land men like Garrett Turner who wanted more than a teenager's release. They preferred a total experience, which was akin to the magic of a first date, a honeymoon, and happily-ever-after all rolled into one. With a few men of this type, a girl could live very well in San Nicolaas and send plenty of money to her family in Colombia. That Angela aspired to this level on her first visit to

Aruba was a good indication of her future.

"Angela does very well," Luz said without commenting on her co-workers, Maria and Julia, who were less successful.

"A guy in the purchasing department says he's had a good time with her."

Personal recommendations were another critical component to a girl's earning potential. The most enlightened clients were not possessive, and often preferred their favorite chica to service friends as opposed to strangers. A bigger contradiction Luz could not imagine because any man's regular girlfriend was off limits to his pals, except in San Nicolaas where she could be a common possession.

The girls did not enjoy the same flexibility in sharing the men. While Luz was pleased to hear good things about Angela, she was not ready to release Garrett Turner. She had three clients left, and he would be the first to go, but not yet. Already she had the day marked on a calendar in her mind. It was next week, after she sold Minchi's and before her son returned to Aruba. In the meantime, she would not fool away the money he paid for pleasant company.

"Is there anything new at the refinery?" Luz inquired to change the subject.

Looking at the smokestacks framed by the window, Turner said, "The turnaround has been canceled. Some guys from headquarters will be making a visit to discuss the situation."

This news focused her attention. A turnaround meant new contractors, huge sums spent with local businesses, and a steady crowd at Minchi's. What made its termination most relevant was her pending sale of the bar. If the buyer heard about this, he might let the deal evaporate.

"Angela is going to have trouble finding an Americano like me," Turner said to Luz's consternation.

"You told me she already has one in the purchasing department," she said by way of distraction, hoping Turner would reveal more details about the refinery.

"And *you* have the assistant superintendent," Turner noted, thinking about his salary versus the purchasing clerk's. The room in which he sat was more tastefully decorated than any expensive hotel in which he stayed. The furniture was solid wood, the bed linens crisp, the bathroom practically a spa. Flowers on a corner table offered their faint scent to the room without marking those who had been in it the way perfume would. Next to them burned a votive candle before the picture of a saint and a small offertory containing several coins.

Carefully, Luz said, "I'm grateful to have you."

Turner looked away from the window. His hostess wore an expensive silk slip, one of half a dozen he'd seen, which left him calculating how much a woman like her was worth and if it was possible that her understudy, Angela, might be able to buy a bar of her own.

"You're welcome," he said.

Deciding that the only way to get more information from Turner was to keep him in her room, Luz shifted on the bed to reveal her thighs. She got half the reaction she wanted. Turner came to her, but only to kiss her cheek. He said nothing more about the refinery before he left.

From the same window through which Turner had watched the refinery, Luz peered down at the sidewalk. She waited for him to move out of sight. Five minutes later, Chief Calenda walked up Main Street. This was her cue to go home. She could have just as easily slept here, above the bar. While she worked in the manner of the other three girls, she felt a need to remain apart as much as possible. She had been in their position and understood the necessity of being away from the boss, to be free of her potentially critical eye, and to gossip amongst themselves.

The walk to her house, the one she rented from Montoya, took only a few minutes during which not even the stray dogs molested her. Already the sky lightened with the coming dawn. A fleeting thought of Montoya's drunken visit to Minchi's passed through her mind. She dismissed it again for what it was, the ramblings of a drunk. It was probably a prelude to increasing the rate.

She entered a cool kitchen where she switched on the kettle to make a cup of tea. While the water boiled, she changed into a pair of pajamas, her fifth outfit of the day.

Returning to the kitchen, she passed one of the two magnificent paintings in the house. It covered the entire wall of her living room. The lighthouse at California Point on the northwest part of the island stood on the far side. A cascade of sand dunes flowed down to the sea where they were met by a surging ocean. It was realistic enough to hear the sound of those waves.

The mural had been painted by a famous artist, Andrés Cortés, when he was only eighteen. He had technically been her husband, a marriage of convenience arranged by her former boss. For the privilege of this union, which gave her and her son legal status as Dutch citizens living in Aruba, Luz paid $300 per month for two years. Then there was a quiet divorce when her former husband was halfway through art school in Amsterdam, not that there was much for him to learn.

Andrés Cortés was a prodigy who would soon be anointed the master of New Dutch Realism, a genre that currently fetched record prices. In spite of his skill or maybe because of it, he needed money to remain in Amsterdam, one of the most expensive cities in the world. His only tangible asset was Minchi's. In her role as manager, Luz sent him monthly payments, but he wanted a lump sum, enough to buy a small studio where he could paint without worrying about increasing rent and complaining neighbors. For that reason, he sold the bar to Luz, who arranged her own financing with the help of her most amiable client, Herr Diedrik, an attorney with important connections on and off the island.

If Luz wanted to, she could have wrecked Andrés' career. If she had failed to make her regular payments during those first two years, if she had skimmed the profits from the bar, he might not have been able to support himself. Furthermore, at any time since, she might have revealed that he had been married to a prostitute who managed a barroom brothel he had inherited with some difficulty from his father. Money from that brothel had flowed to his local account before finding its way to Holland.

Had she been a woman of lesser character, she could have been an expensive nuisance after Andrés became famous. She might have extorted him with threats of going to the tabloids or at least badgered him for enough money to live a comfortable life without having to rent her body. But that's not who she was. Her clients paid for her services, among which none counted for more than privacy. She learned early in her tenure at Minchi's that a kept secret paid better than any crime, and selling one was more dangerous than smoking in bed. The majority of men who confided in her were less sophisticated than those familiar with modern art. They lusted after the female form in the flesh, not pretty pictures that hung on the wall. Yet, they were granted her discretion as much as the pleasure of her body.

These days, Luz seldom visited the other painting, the one in the back bedroom. Covering an entire wall and part of the ceiling, too, this one featured the coast of Renaissance-era Holland, complete with windmills standing like sentinels along a dyke that stretched into the distance. What struck her most about this painting, and what kept her away from it, was the boy standing on the dyke. It evoked memories of her only son, Hernán, the one she'd sent away.

Had it been a mistake?

This was the question she frequently asked herself. If he had stayed on the island, sooner or later he would have discovered his mother's profession. If she had left him with her mother and sister in Colombia, he might have grown up distant and bitter like them, or dead like her father, or disappeared like her brother who had been caught stealing. These were her biggest concerns at the time and comforting justification when doubts or regret clouded her thinking. She gave him the chance to have a life few people from her station could ever dream of. As for what he made of it, she had a good idea that he exceeded her expectations thanks to a series of letters and photographs that came every year.

Her famous ex-husband, the one who painted the walls, was due on the island next week. It was a homecoming of sorts for Andrés, complete with a ballroom gala at the Marina Hotel in Oranjestaad. Invitees would dine and dance among his latest works, none of which had been seen by the public.

With the sun casting its first rays through the blinds, Luz recalled the day Andrés whitewashed the walls.

"It's only primer," he'd said.

How bright that paint was! And the smell, it almost made her ill.

Having finished her tea, she rinsed the cup and set it on the drain board. Just then, her cell phone chimed. She knew the caller before opening the handset. Only desperate clients and Carlotta called at this hour. Luz ignored the former and always spoke with the latter. She'd known the woman since her first days in Aruba and owed much of her business success to Carlotta, who had been a fixture in San Nicolaas for four decades.

Like Luz, Carlotta had started as a San Nicolaas prostitute. She became the owner of Bar Sayonara thanks to her common-law marriage to the owner, an affable fellow named Max. Upon Max's death, she took over Sayonara, managing it until finally retiring and returning to her native Colombia. Together, she and Luz purchased a home on the edge of Barrio El Prado in Barranquilla, a rapidly improving city on Colombia's Caribbean coast.

"You're up early," Luz said to her dearest friend.

"How much can an old woman sleep?" Carlotta replied. "The workmen come early, and I make them stay late."

Their house needed a complete renovation, a project Carlotta was overseeing.

"These men," she scoffed, "if they would curse less and work more, you would have a beautiful place to vacation."

It wasn't vacation Luz was thinking of when she agreed to invest in the house. Her son was a mariner, and it was wise to live close to the sea. Barranquilla was a port city frequented by commercial vessels and cruise ships. Hernán and Captain Beck could certainly dock their tugboat in the harbor, too. Therefore, she partnered with Carlotta to secure a place for herself beyond Aruba's shores.

Luz felt sorry for the workmen in Barranquilla. Carlotta was probably walking through the house holding up color swatches, pieces of tile, and lengths of fabric. The woman exhibited the manners of a queen and demanded that kind of respect from those around her. Luz was more flexible but appreciated her friend's sensibility.

"They start in the bathroom today," Carlotta was saying. "Hopefully, they'll be finished in a couple weeks."

"I'm sure they will."

"Have you heard from *el Capitán?*"

"No."

"Well, he told you the end of September. Things over here will be ready."

"*Gracias,*" Luz said.

"Get some sleep and call me with good news."

Retiring to her bedroom, Luz pushed her face deep into a pillow. She recalled how Hernán had been transfixed by the finished painting the first time he entered his room. Had he seen himself as the boy looking out from the dyke? She fell asleep, content that soon she could ask him.

THE SWEET ODOR OF FRESH ENAMEL reminded Hernán Revilla of a specific moment in his childhood. His mother held his hand, ushering him over the threshold of her home in Aruba, telling him he had a room of his own. He'd never had his own room; he always slept with her or his uncle.

He was not afraid to be in this strange house, not in the least. The trip to Aruba on an airplane made him feel differently about himself. Bogotá was far away. He'd said good-bye to his grandmother and aunt. Then there was that man, *el Capitán*, as his mother called him, standing nearby. Hernán understood the term *captain*. He knew it was used by the police and the military and was a high rank. Again, he felt no fear. If anything, he wanted to show he was ready for some serious or dangerous task that might be in the offing on this island to which his mother had brought him.

Before he could settle on the idea, he was standing in the room his mother had been talking about. At first, he thought the view was some kind of trick, as if there was a giant movie screen draped on the far wall. Seeing that nothing moved, he determined it was a painting. Then the smell caught up to his thoughts.

"Don't touch it," his mother said. "It's new."

He wouldn't disappoint her, not in front of *el Capitán*. The detail amazed him, and he smiled at the birds circling in the upper corner.

Now, on the bow of *Tenacious*, he had a different sight before him. While a pair of deckhands touched up the paint around the forward bits, Hernán looked at the ocean. The placid waters of the funeral had been replaced by a long, rolling swell. A storm was out there, probably more than five hundred miles away. It was pushing this sea at them, giving the tug a gentle pitch, like a horse walking on soft ground. No matter. *Tenacious* stretched nearly a football field in length, drew twenty-two feet, and her reinforced bow smashed a yard of ice like a hammer through plate glass. As for storms, she and her crew had been through the worst of them because it was frequently her job to rescue the victims of such torment.

To this life he'd come as a boy, brought to it by Captain Beck during those few months in Aruba. In Bogotá, he liked to play soccer with his friends in a vacant lot down the street from his house. He enjoyed a few games in his new Aruban neighborhood, but they were dull compared to the excitement of the boats to which Captain Beck took him. There always seemed to be a point to what the boats were doing, something important as opposed to simply a score, which was nothing but a number scratched in the dirt.

Furthermore, there was Beck's hand on his shoulder, telling him in oddly accented Spanish, *"Poco a poco, a la derecha,"* as Hernán steered the boat to the right. It took them to destinations with other boats and sometimes ships. Men were there, too, men like Beck, men who put their hands out for Hernán to shake, who greeted him as a member of the crew, or saluted him as if he were an admiral. How could soccer compete? He hadn't touched a ball since.

He forgot about life in Colombia. Memories of his grand-mother, aunt, and uncle faded, replaced by new ones of times with Beck and his crew aboard their launch *Huntress* or the tug *Kathryn*. Syd, the chief engineer, constructed a sturdy box on which Hernán stood high enough to see from the wheelhouse windows. Because all the controls were on the console, it didn't matter where his feet were.

The power, the noise, the surging energy of *Kathryn* as she nudged against the massive tankers calling at the refinery in San Nicolaas excited him. Hernán absorbed the confidence Beck showed when approaching these beasts. At first, he felt a tingling fear that the ships would run them over. After all, they loomed like massive thunderclouds waiting to strike. Yet, Beck went in close, ran alongside them as Tony, the lead deck-hand, caught lines lowered from high above. Wouldn't they be dragged along like a fallen cowboy whose foot was stuck in the stirrup? Not at all, he soon learned. *Kathryn* put her bow against the ship's hull. She pushed, gently at first, but increas-ingly harder, until a stream of gases blew from her stacks like a volcano and a wicked cauldron of seawater churned at her stern. Every man aboard seemed attentive, but none of them afraid. Hernán quickly assumed their posture, mimicking their stances as well as their urgency as they darted about to loosen lines or make them fast.

During those first weeks in Aruba he experienced life in a

complete family. Instead of supper with his grandmother and aunt, always a dour ritual, there was his mother and Captain Beck at the table, who sat opposite each other with Hernán between them.

"You talk too much," his grandmother used to say. "Why don't you save it up for your mother?"

In Aruba, he did just that, relating every detail of his day until she pointed at his plate.

"Don't let your food get cold," she would remind him.

There were rules in the house, ones very similar to those on the tugboat. They lent structure to home life, a concept he hadn't experienced in Bogotá. No hats at the table. Rooms, tools, and toys were kept clean and organized. Don't wait to be asked to help. Keep the TV volume low. If the captain has something to say, be quiet and listen. These were easy for Hernán to adopt because anyone in Beck's presence followed them to the letter, including his mother.

In the evening, his mother would kiss him good-bye before leaving to work at a restaurant. If *el Capitán* needed to be aboard his boat late into the night, a woman named Donna came to the house. In the morning, he would leave early with Beck, both of them putting on their shoes outside so as not to make any noise. Having worked late, his mother was usually sleeping.

A more normal life Hernán never had. However, like the previous interludes when his mother came home to Bogotá, the period in Aruba ended abruptly and without warning. He departed the island aboard *Kathryn*. On the night he left, his mother remained at the dock, dressed in clothes that he thought inappropriate for the boat. The hug she gave him lasted longer than any he'd ever had, including the one at the airport. He thought that strange. And why did she pack his clothes in a little suitcase? Wouldn't he return after a ship was docked or a barge shifted? His mother said something about Captain Beck bringing him back to her, but his young mind figured, of course, he would. Why mention it? And why was she crying? He clambered up to the wheelhouse where his special perch awaited.

Only a boy of that age could have misunderstood the significance of the moment. The next morning he awoke to a view of unblemished ocean. No refinery flares poked the sky. No desert island hills loomed in the distance. No ship waited for their assistance. Ramirez, Syd's assistant engineer, told him they were headed to a city called Philadelphia.

Now, staring up from the deck of *Tenacious*, Hernán smiled at this memory.

"In for a blow," Tony said as he tapped closed the lid on his can of paint.

"The update from Fleet Weather will be on the computer soon," Hernán replied.

Tony jabbed a thumb over his shoulder. "That sea's telling me all I need to know."

Looking at the swell, Hernán nodded his head. He'd had his share of weather, good and bad. His first voyage north, the one that took him nonstop from Aruba to Philadelphia, had been uneventful. His first months in that city proved otherwise.

Kathryn arrived in a place not unlike San Nicolaas, at least as it was seen from the water. There were oil refineries nearby, tankers on the river, and the smell of industry hung in the air. The crew shared a joyous homecoming with their families, leaving the dock for their homes and much-deserved vacations. No one was there for Captain Beck and Hernán.

They went to a narrow brick home of a type Hernán had never seen. Here, he met a woman, one who looked nothing like his mother. She wore long skirts and crisp blouses, reminding him of a nun. He learned her full name only later: Nicole Reston. However, as a boy, he heard her referred to only as Nicole by Captain Beck.

Having not yet learned English, Hernán missed the details of their conversation that day. The tone was clear, and it was not always pleasant. He stared out the second-story window at the skyscrapers in the distance while Beck and Nicole talked in the garage below.

"What are you going to do with him?" Nicole began.

"He'll be my son," Beck answered.

"He's not your son. He can't be."

"Why not?"

"Because he has a family of his own. He belongs with them."

"His mother asked me to raise him," Beck said. "I promised her I would."

"What kind of woman would do such a thing?"

"One who understands her place in the world."

The conversation almost stopped there. Beck hurtled up the stairs, stumbling at the top where he struck his shin. Bursting into the room, he rubbed his leg for a few minutes before unpacking the articles from his seabag. Moments later, Nicole entered through the same door. She avoided Beck, instead, moving close to Hernán. She gently turned him from the window to look at his face.

"You're a handsome boy," she said.

Not understanding, Hernán looked shyly at his feet.

This lanky woman, who was at least a head taller than his mother, stooped down so that he couldn't avoid her gaze. She smiled and spoke to Beck.

"He doesn't speak English, does he?" she asked.

"He's learning," Beck told her.

"Really, Nate," Nicole pleaded as she rose.

At the sound of this name, Hernán looked over his shoulder at the man who'd brought him here. To this point he'd been *el Capitán*. Now there was a new, clipped term used in the same voice Hernán's aunt used when speaking to his mother. This could only mean she was someone close to Beck. Was she the captain's sister?

"You can't have him here," Nicole was saying. "Where will he go to school?"

These pleading questions fell on Hernán like the sadly sincere prayers his grandmother used to mutter from time to time. The only difference was he knew the words his grandmother said but had no idea about the meaning of Nicole's lament.

"He'll start school next year after he learns some English," Beck said. "Until then, he goes with me."

"On the boat?"

"There's no better place. Ramirez speaks Spanish and mine is passable. We'll give him a head start."

"Have you thought about this, Nate? Do you know what you're doing?"

At this point, his seabag was empty. Beck carried the bag to a closet where he hung it on a peg.

"I'll be his father," he said.

"He needs a mother," she countered.

"He already has one."

The exchange ended there, but Hernán was to see Nicole again a few months later. In between, he was back aboard a boat, this one named *Marlena*. It was slightly smaller than *Kathryn*, but she had a similar design. The crew returned from their vacations, settled into new bunks, and straightened out the galley.

Only a few days went by before a stack of books showed up. With these books came lessons, mostly informal, in English. Beck and Ramirez switched back and forth between English and Spanish whenever they spoke to their youngest crew member. A second chair was rigged beside the captain's station in the wheelhouse. This one was reserved exclusively for Hernán. Here he sat with a book on his lap as the boat lumbered up and down the river.

"*Digame en inglés,*" Beck would say, pointing at a page in the heavily illustrated primers.

This command was repeated by every member of the crew. It was a challenging game for a boy of his age, but he played it with all his wits. He wanted to understand what they were talking about. He wanted to be part of the crew, to be able to do what the captain asked, to help Syd with his tools, and to ask when he would see his mother again.

They rarely left the harbor. The days passed in a series of short trips between piers, sometimes towing barges, sometimes not. A ship might be helped to the dock or a few hours idled away waiting for the next job. In the wheelhouse, Hernán listened to Beck talk on the radio, call orders from the window to Tony on deck, and converse on a cell phone.

One night, Hernán had stretched out on the bench at the rear of the wheelhouse and fallen asleep. The dim red light on the chart table and the green glow of the radar display cast spooky shadows around the room. Awakened by the sound of the radio, Hernán opened his eyes to a scene that might have been taken from the hell his grandmother had warned him about. Unconsciously, he began to weep, fearing that his adventure with Captain Beck had been nothing but a long dream, one that was now over. He'd done something wrong and had been banished to a dungeon.

"*Está bien,*" Captain Beck said to him. "*Todo está bien.*"

Beck's voice reassured him that he'd not been dreaming. Nor was he in the hell his grandmother feared. He was in the real world where the devil had better be wary of Captain Beck who audaciously roamed the water.

Content with the answers given, he made himself comfortable and promptly fell asleep again.

Andy, *Tenacious'* new first mate, rounded the deck bearing a sheet of paper. He'd been promoted from second mate to first upon Beck's death. His replacement had yet to be secured. Given that they were on more of a repositioning cruise than a salvage job, it meant that he and Hernán split the day into four, six hour segments.

"Low pressure and getting lower," Andy said, handing over the report from Fleet Weather.

"How low?"

"Tropical depression low."

This meant waves to twenty feet. For a moment, Hernán thought of diverting to the west for a stop at Wilmington, North Carolina, but then reconsidered. *Tenacious* and her men stood into taller seas before. They would continue to Bermuda.

"Ask Syd to keep the keel heavy," Hernán said. "I'll be standing midnight to six."

Andy smiled. He liked weather. The odds improved that some vessel would need their assistance, and that meant salvage money. Just the same, they suffered a spot of bad luck with the death of Captain Beck, and it was probably better to exercise caution until a good omen balanced the scale.

Hernán, on the other hand, was still mulling over that time he'd fallen asleep as a boy in *Marlena's* wheelhouse. The next morning they were back at the dock. Ramirez's wife, Carmela, brought groceries for the galley. The last thing she handed her husband was a small, clear plastic box.

"*Para el Capitán*," Hernán heard her say.

Ramirez studied the box.

"Someone has to look over him," his wife said.

"Look over him?" questioned Ramirez.

"Yes. He has a boy now. They both need protection."

Later that night, after he and Ramirez finished an English lesson, Hernán got the rest of the story.

"My wife ordered this from Our Lady of Guadalupe in Mexico City," Ramirez began, placing the plastic box on the table. "Our Lady of Guadalupe is a magnificent cathedral, the most holy place in all of Mexico."

Taking it into his hands, Hernán examined the object within. It was the kind of medal many people wore in Colombia. This one was gold. On its face was the image of a winged angel bearing a sword in one hand and scales in the other.

"That's Saint Michael," said Ramirez, "the protector."

"The protector?"

"My wife is giving this medal to Captain Beck so Saint

Michael will watch over him."

Hernán didn't think Beck needed the protection of anyone. He steered the boat, gave the orders, and was universally respected. Who would dare confront him?

"Saint Michael will protect Captain Beck the way he protects you."

Sitting there, listening to Ramirez and looking at the medal, Hernán realized he was separated from his mother again, the way he had been twice before. Later, he tried to concentrate on his lessons, but little by little he became distracted by thoughts of her. Whenever he dredged up the courage to ask, Beck and the crew were on the move. At last, he couldn't focus on the words in the books. He folded his arms over them and wouldn't budge.

"*¿Qué pasó?*" Ramirez asked.

"*Nada,*" was the only reply Hernán would utter. He refused to cry, not in front of them. They might make fun of him the way the older kids did when he fell playing one day. For a few days he recovered, only to slip into a depression again when he and Beck left the boat for the narrow brick house.

Nicole was there. They ate with none of the friendly chatter at the table the way a meal passed in Aruba. Hernán felt the same tension as when his uncle disappeared for reasons his grandmother wouldn't say. He didn't like Nicole's piercing gaze, either. It made him uncomfortable, as if he had grease on his face or had done something wrong. He left the table for the chair by the window, wishing he had stayed on the boat where the galley was always a cheerful place. He listened to the terse conversation in the kitchen, instinctively knowing the subject was himself.

"He's upset," Nicole said.

"I know he is," Beck replied. "He's been that way for a week."

"God, Nate. This is crazy. You're playing with his life."

"I'm giving him a life."

"How are you going to explain that to him?" Nicole wanted to know.

Beck checked his handheld radio in the charging stand on the kitchen counter. After he hung the leather holster for it over a chair, he waved Hernán to the table. Nicole leaned against the sink with her hands tucked under her arms.

"Your mother gave me a job to do," Beck began in Spanish. "Just like the little boats help the big ones on the river, I need you to help me. Understand?"

"*Entiendo*," Hernán answered.

"Your father died in a coal mine," Beck continued.

"*Yo sé*. My mother told me."

"Then I must tell you, Hernán, that I am not your father, but now you are my son. This is the job your mother gave me. When we're finished, we'll go back to see her."

"*Entiendo*," Hernán repeated, understanding that his real father was dead, that Captain Beck was going to fill that role, and Saint Michael was watching over them as evidenced by the medal around his new stepfather's neck.

"Do you love his mother?" Nicole asked.

Beck straightened up. "I don't love you if that's what you're asking."

These words were unclear to Hernán, but it was the last time he saw Nicole. She took her purse and found her way out, leaving nothing but the sound of her heels echoing up the crooked stairway. Fifteen years later, as he guided *Tenacious* through the

Atlantic, he considered that Ramirez remained married, Tony had been twice divorced and still dated, Syd never strayed from the lady who had been his high-school prom date, and Captain Beck had never found another woman.

LIKE CHIEF CALENDA, Luz made her rounds every day. They typically began at eleven in the morning with a stop at Minchi's. She inspected the bar, going through the motions of checking all the toilets, coolers, air conditioners, and the billiard table. By the time she finished these mundane tasks, a delivery-man was knocking on the door, ready to unload cases of beer and liquor to replenish the bar's stock. Teo promptly arrived to help. Within half an hour, Luz signed a receipt, scanned the shelves, and climbed the stairs to the second floor.

This routine was the easy part of operating a bar in San Nicolaas. Broken refrigerators, blocked toilets, and warped pool cues required nothing more than a few reliable hands like Teo and his pals to keep things in working order. Handling the girls was something else. Personality clashes and petty jealousy, if not carefully managed, could escalate beyond shouting matches into violent confrontations. Several years ago, two girls fought with broken bottles behind Baranca Bar. More recently, a girl at the Tropicana threw another girl's clothes into the dumpster minutes before the trash truck collected it.

Having come to San Nicolaas the same way these girls did, Luz understood how desperation brewed anger. The easiest thing to do was blame the girl in the next room. The challenge was to anticipate and diffuse the problems. In this area, Luz had a fine teacher in Carlotta.

"Give them a reason to live and rules to survive," Carlotta said soon after Luz bought Minchi's.

Climbing the stairs above the bar, Luz thought of Carlotta's rules, which had been posted inside the door of every chica's closet. Among the two most important were not to ask for the money first and never promise anything in the bar that you wouldn't do upstairs. Any Colombiana who followed them did as well as she could in San Nicolaas.

The common area between the girls' rooms contained a hot plate, microwave, refrigerator, sink, and a table with four chairs. Here the girls took their meals, sharing tales of the previous night's clients. The smart ones, which rarely populated this part of town, backed away from gossip, never loaned money, and left nothing worth eating in the fridge longer than a few hours. Luz spoke of these issues on a rotating basis, and it was the day for a reminder about cleanliness. Maria, Julia, and Angela sat around the table. Luz remained standing.

"How many of you take a shower between clients?"

Maria and Angela acknowledged rinsing off.

"I wipe myself with a wash cloth," Julia said with a smirk.

"It's your body," Luz said. "Don't you want to be clean?"

"I shower at the end of the night."

"None of your clients notice?"

Julia giggled. "They're too drunk to care. Some of them can't even finish." She added a drooping finger to make the point.

The other girls chuckled; Luz was annoyed. "You want to be cautious around the drunk ones," she warned.

"If I don't go upstairs with the drunk ones," Julia blurted, "I won't go up at all."

After waiting a few seconds for the laughter to subside, Luz said dismissively, "Take the man into the shower with you. That way you'll both be clean."

Agitated, Julia started to rise off her chair. Then she thought better of it, sat down, and glared at her boss.

Next came a visit to the rooms. Under Luz's direction, the rooms and baths had been renovated in order to provide a comfortable place for the girls to work and live as well as to make an impression on the men. Each had a television and CD player, a queen-size bed, two chairs, bureau, closet, and plenty of mirrors. The electronics were attached to the walls because trust went so far and steel bolts finished the job.

During the few minutes in the room with its occupant, Luz discussed any problems that may have come up. She asked pointed questions about arguments with other girls, both at Minchi's and from other bars. She did her best with marginal success to quell any trouble before it festered. And if the room was dirty, clothes lying about, or the bathroom smelly, she levied an instant fine. For this reason, she rarely found anything amiss. Today was no exception.

Once or twice a week, as Carlotta had taught her, Luz extended a small kindness to the girls if they stuck to the rules. She would present bottles of hair products or small makeup kits or a voucher for a free smoothie at the corner stand. These little gifts demonstrated generosity in an otherwise stingy climate. They also proved her fairness when she had to impose discipline.

Today, Luz gave each of them a tube of body moisturizer. It was made on the island and contained native aloe. Angela squeezed a dot onto the back of her hand, rubbed it in, and urged the other two to give it a try.

Satisfied things were in order, Luz headed to the post office. Her mailbox frequently contained letters, small packages, and once in a while, larger parcels. Most of these came from past clients. They sent notes inquiring about her well-being, photos of themselves, and gifts of jewelry and trinkets. The sentimental streak in these men amused her, and she was careful to keep the items in case one day they asked about them.

More important, every summer she received a heavy envelope filled with photos of her son and a long letter describing where he had been. The stilted Spanish of the letters made her smile as much as the photos made her cry. It wasn't her son who sent these, but Captain Beck, the man to whom Luz entrusted the boy's life fifteen years ago. A better man she had not met, not in her life in Colombia, nor during her first two stints in Aruba.

Captain Beck had never been a client, not officially. He did give her money and share her life, but the relationship remained platonic. What impressed Luz most was how he arranged for Hernán to join her in Aruba. There had been interminable delays until Beck confronted those not honoring their part of the bargain, which was a condition of her marriage to Andrés. From the day Hernán arrived at the airport, Beck treated him like a son while making no demands of Luz. They lived this way long enough for Luz to understand that Hernán's future lie with Beck.

As for her own prospects, she gambled that Beck would raise Hernán to be a man who would ultimately understand his mother's sacrifice. She declined Beck's offer to join them, fearing the weight of her presence might someday be too much. If ever he rid himself of her, Hernán would have to go as well. She placed an incredible burden on Beck, the responsibility of raising her son, but she didn't increase it by adding herself. Her experience in San Nicolaas taught her the boundaries of generosity and the depth of promises. She remained in Aruba, supporting herself and her family back in Colombia, which she felt was her duty.

Judging by the contents of those annual updates, Beck exceeded her greatest hopes. The last one came unexpectedly in January, and it was tucked under her bed in a box with fourteen others. The letter within mentioned that he and Hernán were to return to Aruba at the end of September.

Luz scrambled to tidy up her life, seeking to sell the bar and prepare herself for whatever was to come. Mortgage payments forced her to continue operating. Similarly, she needed cash flow to support her aging mother and sister in Colombia. There was also the house in Barranquilla, which, thanks to Carlotta, was only half the cost it might have been. For these reasons, she kept her regular clients or else she would have worked as nothing more than a waitress at the nearby Restaurante Pueblito Paisa. Fortunately, Herr Diedrik had a buyer for Minchi's, and she would be out of the business in less than a week.

Inserting a key to unlock her mailbox, she said a silent prayer that there would be a letter inside. From Captain Beck and other men who worked at sea, she learned their schedules were unreliable and changed frequently through no fault of their own. Still, she longed for confirmation that Beck and Hernán were en route to Aruba.

The box was empty. Disappointed once more, she told herself no news was good news. It might be coming from the other side of the world. In the past, Beck's correspondence originated as far away as Norway, Australia, and Spain.

She disguised her sadness behind a muted smile, tucked away her key, and turned for the door.

"¡Señorita!" the postman behind the counter called.

He was the only one who called her that anymore. Everyone else referred to Luz as señora because she had been married and was a woman of some means. Still, she liked the term when used affectionately, and the doddering postman didn't have a sarcastic thought in his head. She returned to his counter where he handed her a letter.

"Lo siento," he said, smiling beneath his droopy mustache. "I am alone today to sort the letters and didn't put this out for you."

"Gracias," Luz told him.

"That's come a long way," commented the postman, pointing at the envelope now in her hands.

In the left corner was a single word in all capitals: TENACIOUS. Her own address occupied the center of the field. The stamp and the postmark over it indicated Malta was the nation of origin.

"Malta," Luz mouthed.

"The center of the Mediterranean," the postman replied. "Another pin I can put on my map."

Squeezing the envelope, she felt something solid between the folds of paper.

"Are you going to open it?"

Normally she would have waited until she was alone. This

time she didn't hesitate. Her fingernail lanced the top of the envelope in a single sweep. Spreading the edges, she saw a piece of gold. She removed an oval object, holding it up to the light by its chain, which was made of sturdy links of the type a man would wear.

"A medallion," said the postman. "Looks like a saint."

He was correct, Luz learned, upon reading the short note inside.

"The Feast of Saint Michael is the 29th of September. We'll be there. Capt. Beck."

Her legs folded beneath her so that Luz slumped against the wall.

"*¡Por Dios!* Are you okay?"

"Help me up," Luz breathed. She smoothed her skirt, took a couple of deep breaths, and apologized to the postman. Somehow, he ended up with the medallion.

"Let me assist you," he said, working the chain's clasp. She pulled her hair away from her neck, and the postman secured the necklace with a deft snap of his fingers.

"Saint Michael," Luz told him with her hand fingering the piece.

"The protector and patron saint of mariners," replied the postman.

After thanking him and apologizing again for her collapse, Luz tucked the letter into her purse and made for the door.

Minutes later, she was home, digging under her bed for the box containing the envelopes from Captain Beck. She set it on her bureau and gently removed the lid. The envelopes were in chronological order from newest to oldest. She removed them one at a time, taking the oldest into her hands and carrying it to the kitchen.

After wiping her hand across the table to make sure it was dry, she emptied the envelope. The pages of Captain Beck's note she set aside along with a few other items. It was the photos she wanted. There were several, including one of Beck with Hernán having a meal at a tiny table. She tilted the photo back and forth to gain a better perspective. It was difficult to see clearly, but she thought the medallion that now hung around her neck was in the gap of Beck's shirt.

The saint was something he must have acquired in the first year after he left Aruba, because she'd never seen him wear it while on the island. She didn't know Beck to be a particularly religious man either. He hadn't gone to church with her, nor did he pray before meals. Had he made a conversion in those early days with Hernán? He hadn't mentioned it in any of his letters.

Shifting her eyes, Luz gazed at Hernán. In the photo he was barely older than the boy she'd taken to the park in Bogotá. She thought of his father, the man who dismissed her from his life after impregnating her, something Hernán would never know. Strangely, she felt a sense of satisfaction at having told Hernán that he'd died in a coal mine. It prevented her son from knowing his real father hadn't wanted him. He was free to accept Captain Beck. The other photos showed that he had done just that.

Her cell phone chirped, interrupting her reverie with the demands of a client. They were supposed to have lunch and then an hour in her room at Minchi's. The guy didn't know it, but this was the last time he would be in her private company. Her other clients she'd let go one by one, which was an arduous task because a woman like her was not supposed to turn down a regular paying customer. Most eventually took the hint, finding another girl to meet their needs.

She rushed out of the house, leaving the photos on the table. On Main Street, the guard at the bank waved. Luz enthusiastically returned the gesture to him as well as to one of the women working at the pharmacy across the street. A block later, she was in front of Jaime's salon. Instinctively she touched her hair, although he had cut it for her barely two weeks ago. She would wait until the 28th for him to shape it again. He was the best stylist on the island, one the tourists were starting to know about.

At that moment, Luis stepped out of Charlie's Bar. He faced her with his arms out. "Just what I've been looking for," he said brightly, "someone to dance."

She fell into his arms but only twirled around twice before pushing away.

"Was it something I said?" Luis asked.

With a friendly smile and a dismissive wave she hurried down the street.

This was the course of her life, from the arms of one man to another but never the one she wanted most. No matter, he was on his way. She had less than two weeks to wait.

WITHIN THE ZONE OF TOLERANCE, one day was the same as another. Any random Tuesday could be as festive as Friday or Saturday in other parts of the island. Likewise, a weekend could be as dull as a Monday. San Nicolaas was where people, locals and visitors alike, came to live the wild life or just sit and nurse a drink, depending on the circumstances and events. It happened spontaneously, which was part of the appeal, a little like waiting for the lottery numbers.

Whatever their intentions, San Nicolaas regulars knew Minchi's closed at midnight on Saturday because the owner honored the Sabbath. Luz attended the first mass on Sunday morning, arriving at least twenty minutes early to secure her regular seat near the west entrance to the church. The service was well-attended, filling most of the pews, but rarely did anyone sit next to her. This morning, however, she had company.

"¡Señora!"

She recognized the voice and paused at the door.

"May I sit with you?"

"Claro, Angela."

They entered the church, taking their seats under the gaze of the other parishioners. Unnerved by their looks, Angela shifted closer to her boss, who seemed unfazed. In fact, before the service began, Luz gently kneeled, folded her hands, and whispered a prayer.

Straining her right ear, Angela caught a few of the words.

"... thank you for my health, the comforts of my life ..."

Angela caught glimpses of those comforts, including her boss' expensive dresses and the sedan in which she rode with Teo at the wheel. She hoped to have the same for herself someday.

"... watch over my sister and mother ..."

Though an only child, Angela wanted the best for her parents, too. They didn't know what she was doing in Aruba or even that she was on the island. She told them she'd gone to work as a dancer on a cruise ship, a lie easily believed because she'd been a good dancer, winning a few local awards while still in school. But her desires exceeded cheap trophies and the jealous looks of girls in her class. She wanted to own a small business of some kind, a place where she could work for herself. She'd told Turner that she wanted to own a bar like Minchi's, but it was only to provoke him. Truth be told, she preferred to have a little shop, perhaps a clothing store.

"... and, please, bring my son back to me ..."

A son? Angela squelched a cough. One of her friends made the mistake of getting pregnant, only to be abandoned by the boyfriend who promised her too much. She couldn't imagine the same thing happening to Luz. Maybe her husband had been killed by *narcotrafficantes* who still plagued parts of Colombia. And if he had, what was she doing here in Aruba? She had the brains to do anything. Angela had been in San Nicolaas only two weeks, long enough to catch a few rumors about the town and the people in it, but scarcely enough time to decode them.

Her boss finished the prayer by making the sign of the cross, returned to Angela's side, and waited for the service to begin.

Nearly an hour later, Father Dario stood by the door, greeting each of his parishioners. Some of them skated out the side, no doubt in a hurry to begin their Sunday BBQ festivities as was the custom in Aruba. Others took their time, greeting friends and neighbors until it was their turn for a personal moment with the priest. He knew their names and foibles, laments and exaltations. Regular people they were, most of them.

Near the end of the line was his favorite. Dario knew her profession was the oldest, that her sins were many, and her family fragmented. Despite these realities, or perhaps in light of them, he admired her faith. He could hardly remember a Sunday without her in the congregation. She contributed liberally to the offering plate and to separate causes as well. While she never confessed, he frequently saw her praying, perhaps acknowledging her shortcomings directly to God.

Whatever the case, he was happy to shake her hand before she left. Dario believed his job was to steer people down the path of redemption. To that end, it was only appropriate that he recognize those with the most potential, even if it occasionally perturbed the rest of the flock.

"Luz," he said with an open hand extended to Angela, "you've brought a friend."

"This is Angela," Luz replied.

"Welcome," Dario said. "Thank you for coming. You're in

good hands."

Whether he meant his or Luz's or God's, Angela wasn't sure. She drew strength from Luz, who seemed not the least bit nervous to be this close to a man of the cloth.

"Peace be with you," Dario finished and looked to the next person in line.

On the street, Angela asked, "He knows you?"

"I rarely miss a Sunday," Luz answered.

This Angela heard from the other two girls working at Minchi's, which is how she knew where to find the boss this morning. They said other things about her, too, not all of them flattering, but nothing truly hurtful or outrageous. Most of it centered on how much money she made, a talent Angela hoped to learn. For this reason, she studied her every move.

"Were you out late with a client last night?" Luz inquired.

"Yes," Angela replied. "He dropped me off around the corner from the church."

"Hmm. Well, for your own good, don't work late every Saturday. Make time to rest."

"If I'm upstairs sleeping, I'll lose clients."

"Men don't like to see you haggard or run down. They'll pass over you for another. If you're bright and fresh, you'll have a better chance with men willing to pay more. Understand?"

"I do."

"One other thing. Don't wear perfume unless it is the same brand as your client's wife."

"*Sí, señora.*"

"Take care, Angela. I'll see you tonight."

It pained her to dismiss Angela because Luz knew the girl had dozens of questions. Luz herself had been in that position, a young woman away from home with no friends, doing a vulgar job that was supposed to pay enough to solve all her problems. During her first stay in Aruba, Luz earned the all-important money thanks to good luck and the help of Carlotta, Charlie, and one or two less honorable characters. They were gone now, most of them, but she remained, as did the flow of cash.

Lately, she had been neglecting the educational sessions she held with the girls who came to Minchi's, replacing them with a single crash course in how to protect themselves from the worst of the business while earning the most money for their time. In the past, she took them to a restaurant for a drill in proper table manners. Once in a while she accompanied them to the hair salon or a clothing boutique, demonstrating how a subtle change could enhance their appeal. Some learned; others didn't want to.

These efforts she discontinued because the bar would soon be sold. She decided to sell it the moment she learned her son was returning to Aruba. The last thing she wanted was for him to see her as the owner of a brothel. As for her working there, she might drop dead if he discovered that.

Eight months should have been enough time to arrange a sale for one of the most popular bars in town. Like too many things in Aruba, though, the process moved slowly and frequently stopped. Now it was the middle of September, and if the pending deal did not close, she would cease operating and spend her savings on the mortgage. She had an image to protect.

Then again, drastic measures might not be necessary, especially if her regular Sunday client, Herr Diedrik, had good news for her. She enlisted his help to effect the sale, and he finally found a buyer, albeit a difficult one Luz suspected bargained more out of sport than a desire to arrive at a fair price.

Neither Luz nor Herr Diedrik spoke as he drove out of town. They held hands across the center console of his BMW like teenagers. The ride from San Nicolaas to his villa passed through familiar territory. There were the new houses built at the edge of town, then a stretch of open highway to Savaneta, where Luis maintained his uncle's beachfront bungalows. After that, a winding climb took them through Frenchman's Pass, Jamanota, and finally to an area known as San Fuego. Here, Herr Diedrik built his idea of a dream home in the form of a Mediterranean-style mansion complete with swimming pool, guesthouse, multi-car garage, and maid's quarters.

The compound was an incredible extravagance for a man who was not married, had no children, and rarely hosted friends. Visitors never slept in the guest rooms. Diedrik ate in his kitchen, ignored the dining room, and often dozed in the salon among towering shelves of books. On rare occasions, his sister, her husband, and their three children used the swimming pool. His sister nagged him about marrying a local woman, usually one of her friends, but Herr Diedrik refused so much as a dinner date. She also held him in contempt for being seen with Luz, a dalliance she thought would one day ruin his career.

Of the many things Herr Diedrik worried about, his career was not among them. He shepherded international investors through the maze of regulations that governed financial transactions on the island. He assisted them with selecting the right partners for offshore ventures. His reputation as a considerate mediator often brought people at odds to his office in search of a wise judgment that would keep them out of court. No one, aside of his sister, had the nerve to criticize his social life, not when they could trust him with their fortunes. Naturally, his keen advice found its way to Luz as well.

They went directly to the swimming pool, which was secluded in a central courtyard. They swam naked for an hour before sitting on loungers, sipping champagne, and letting the breeze dry their skin. Thoroughly relaxed, they made their way to his bedroom. Herr Diedrik was a romantic lover who relished every part of the act as if it might be the last time.

Afterward, they leaned against the balcony railing outside his bedroom. In the distance, a row of wind turbines danced in the stiff breeze that buffeted the eastern edge of the island.

"They work day and night," Diedrik commented. "I remember the day you called me about the project. What was that man's name?"

"Jeffrey," Luz answered. She also remembered the day. She was at the Westin Hotel with Jeffrey, and he had bored her with the details of his proposal. It might have gone nowhere had Luz not put him in touch with Herr Diedrik, who knew the right politicians and bureaucrats to get the venture moving.

It was her turn to make a deal, one that would release her from any permanent obligation on the island. Only Minchi's tethered her to it. She rented her house, would happily give the car to Teo, and the people she loved most had either left or died.

Regarding the sale of Minchi's, Diedrik had news bad and good. "Maybe you should rethink this offer," he began.

Knowing better than to react immediately, Luz patiently waited for the rest.

"There is something going on in San Nicolaas. Things are being said about the refinery."

No bigger topic fueled the rumor mills than this one. Most of it was nonsense: comments about a new operator, calls for strikes by the union, or stories about a complete shutdown. Whatever the case, if Diedrik was advising caution, she paid close attention, especially because Turner said the turnaround was on hold.

"Quiet inquiries are being made about what real estate may be for sale. As you know, property values rise and fall with the fortunes on the other side of the wall. No one would be in the mood to buy if the situation was going to get worse."

His statement contradicted her earlier analysis. If the refinery was not spending money, and Turner confirmed that it was not, how could the situation be anything but worse?

"There is particular interest in Main Street," Diedrik said. "Possibly even that pile of concrete at the end." The unfinished hotel to which Diedrik referred had been an eyesore for so long no one noticed anymore.

"The bars, too?" Luz asked, fearing that Montoya had sold China Clipper for a good price and that's why he was suddenly being generous.

He answered vaguely. "Whatever is available."

"What does this mean for me?" Luz wanted to know.

"Minchi's may soon be worth more than the contract price," Diedrik explained, adding quickly, "It's my fault. I shouldn't have let you reduce the price, but I think I can find a way to renegotiate ..."

Touching his arm, Luz said, "The current price is acceptable."

"You may be letting it go cheap. Give me a week to work on this, to find out exactly what's going on."

"I thought we were scheduled to sign the agreement of sale at the notary's office."

Diedrik acknowledged the appointment by rocking his head. "I wouldn't be a good lawyer if I couldn't find a loophole to squeeze some more money out of this guy. Besides, he hasn't been easy to deal with."

Diedrik was a cautious man who took few risks yet seemed ready to chance the whole thing falling apart only days before it was supposed to be final. No matter, Luz had a more important reason than money to finish the transaction. "I'd like to sign the agreement on Thursday and finish next week," she said without telling him why.

After a long moment, her host said, "You're the client."

In this specific case she was, but in every other way, their roles were reversed. Of course, that didn't mean the balance of power favored him. She circled her arms around his shoulders, focused her eyes on his, and lightly kissed him on the lips.

"I want to sell," she said, "before I'm too old to do something else."

Diedrik blinked and drew a short breath. He gently squeezed her arms as he struggled with the right words to express his confused emotions.

Her years with men taught Luz that a moment like this was dangerous. If she didn't provide a quick distraction, Herr Diedrik would say something not so ridiculous as it was incredible. He would offer her marriage, money, a life of her dreams. It had happened before with men of more and less means than Diedrik. Some believed their declarations. Others said them to fulfill fantasies of their own. It wasn't that she didn't appreciate such drama; it was that she understood the impossibility of it.

"*Venga*," she said softly, "*a la cama*." She turned for the bedroom and tugged his hand. There, in the comfort of his bed, she was safe. She knew the best and worst of what happened in that space. None of it affected her the way a broken promise would.

Frankie was the only choller to have free rein in San Nicolaas. While he was unwelcome in some places, there were none forbidden. In the course of his days and nights he meandered through the streets and alleys, lurked behind the trash bins and parked cars, and loitered in the shadows, abandoned corners, and vacant doorways. Although he was the most informed citizen in town, he didn't know everything, but not for lack of trying.

In pursuit of small change and more, Frankie discovered the goings-on of the populace. Among the monotonous activities that occupied his powers of observation there had been several significant events. Having overheard a radio call through the open window of an ambulance, he was the first to know Charlie had died. Listening to two lawyers chatting beside their cars, he heard that Andrés Cortés had sold Minchi's Bar to raise money for his artistic career. He saw the plans for the third set of windmills spread over the hood of a pickup truck long before the blades arrived on the island.

While these incidents brought sadness, joy, and curiosity, none caused him to worry. After all, Charlie's nephew, Luis, and his barman, Herr Koch, knew how to operate the World Famous Charlie's Bar. And Luz, well, she deserved to own

Minchi's; she'd been managing the place and had once been in an arranged marriage with Andrés. As for the windmills, Frankie lived mostly outside or in abandoned buildings, neither of which had electrical service, so what did he care if the island got another 20 percent of its power from the breeze? Therefore, he cataloged these events in his vast memory with no more than a casual scratch of his balding skull.

However, this Sunday, something happened that worried him more than his rotten teeth, aching stomach, and thin soles. Frankie had passed through a crevice in the refinery wall blocked by an ancient Divi tree. This was his private entrance to an otherwise secure facility. He skulked down to the farthest pier where he liked to drop a line in the water with the idea that he might catch a fish. No sooner had he rigged his pole than a motor launch glided in from the sea. It nudged up to the dock where several men stepped ashore. They walked back and forth along the wharf, pointing in various directions both on land and out over the water.

Aside of trespassing, Frankie should have had nothing to fear. Still, he was petrified. It was the logos that frightened him. One man's shirt bore the image of a famous cruise ship line. Another sported the name of a fancy hotel chain. Finally, there was Hans Dorlan, whose chest featured the letters ATC, which stood for Aruba Tourism Commission. The president of ATC smiled and shook hands like a proud father with everyone present. How could these men be so happy while standing in the shadow of the refinery and not a single bottle of beer among them?

Frankie knew the answer. He nearly yelled it out loud, but that would have revealed his position and brought him a fair amount of trouble from Chief Calenda. Instead, he waited for them to roar away in their boat until they passed through the channel in the reef and turned north for Oranjestaad. Then he was on his feet, back through the wall, and into town in search of a worthy ear.

But who to tell? This was the middle of Sunday morning when the good citizens of San Nicolaas swept their patios, washed their cars, and barbecued slabs of meat the scents of which made his mouth water. None of these people had any interest in what Frankie had to say even if his news would profoundly affect their lives. They wouldn't believe him, not because he was the boy who cried wolf, but because he looked every bit the choller and not the slightest part town crier. Although self-appointed to both roles, he took each as seriously as if Queen Beatrix of the Netherlands had knighted him.

Popping out of the wall, he hustled past a funeral home, then the fire station, and finally police headquarters. Casting a nervous glance over his shoulder, he stepped off the curb only to be missed by a speeding car that angled toward Main Street. Frankie charged after the vehicle, keeping a keen eye out for a notable citizen to whom he could pronounce his revelation.

Normally, Luis remained ecclesiastically in sync by maintaining Sunday as a day of rest. Besides, it was a changeover day, when one group of tourists surrendered their timeshares to the next. Initially, they were less likely to venture beyond the boundaries of a manicured complex in search of something different. Midweek, when they grew bored with what had become the regular thing, Charlie's Bar did a fair trade.

Nonetheless, like an old boat or a new baby, a famous bar

required an inordinate amount of care and love. Luis and Herr Koch spent half a Sunday now and then doing things they couldn't do when people were lined up three deep for drinks.

This time it was the replacement of a cooler. They hauled it out of its spot behind the bar, then dragged it to the side door for the junkman. Next came the tricky part, setting the new one in the same place. They nudged it, but it wouldn't go the last inch.

"I have a pry bar upstairs," Luis said. "I'll be right back."

Frankie stopped at the corner of Main and Caya Charlie Brouns, Sr. From here, he glanced up at the balcony above Charlie's Bar in search of a familiar face. No one was there, not even Screwball.

He considered his options, the consequences of each, and finally decided to risk it all. After a look down the sidewalk, he crawled through the open window into Charlie's, where he was promptly greeted by a stern voice.

"Get the hell out!" ordered Herr Koch.

"I have a revelation," Frankie declared with both hands raised like Moses just down from the mountain.

Having catered to tourists, drunks, sailors, and regular folks for more than thirty years, Herr Koch tolerated a fair amount of nonsense with no small measure of patience. Just the same, Frankie was stinking up the bar with body odor and tooth rot. It was enough to chase away the stench of ammonia, which he used to mop the floor behind the old cooler.

"Whatever it is, Frankie, be quick about it," Herr Koch warned.

"The refinery is finished," the choller said. "We're on the

chopping block, doomed, done for, wiped out."

With that he stepped to the door, flipped the lock, and exited to the street.

Hearing harsh words exchanged below, Luis rushed down the back stairs and entered the bar from the storeroom.

"What was that all about?" he asked.

"Did Charlie ever mention losing a crystal ball?" Herr Koch replied.

"Not that I can remember," Luis answered, surveying the thousands of items hanging about the bar. "It might be somewhere among all this junk. Why?"

"I think Frankie has it."

The day unfolded exactly as Luz expected, including the drive from Diedrik's villa to San Nicolaas. They took the long way, enjoying the scenery before rejoining the main road. Rolling past the airport, Luz thought it seemed big for such a small island. It was to this airport that she'd come as a woman too eager to solve her problems and too young to know better of the methods.

Soon after getting a blue stamp smacked onto a page in her passport, she'd been squeezed into a minibus with six other girls. Their luggage was stuffed in the back, blocking out the window. The driver discharged them on Rembrandtstraat, the alley behind the bars where they would soon be working if they passed their medical exams. The process remained the same to this day. After three months working in San Nicolaas, the girls returned to the airport and then to wherever it was from which they came.

For Luz that meant Bogotá, Colombia. She made the return

trip twice after working in Aruba. Then things became more complicated. She ended up married to Andrés when he was working in an auto-body shop, and stayed on, returning to Colombia only to visit her family, not to live the normal life she thought would be hers. She survived her errors, prospered, and ultimately became a fixture in San Nicolaas. In doing so, she replaced Carlotta as the longest-working woman in town. As much as she admired Carlotta's achievements, Luz had no desire to follow the same route. She prayed for better things than a life dependent upon the proclivities of men, no matter how generous they might be in the process. Nor did she want to spend four decades working this way.

Like everything in her life, her days in San Nicolaas began as a temporary measure, a way to earn money to keep her family together. However, it had the opposite effect. Her brother disappeared after being caught stealing from his boss. Her mother and sister accepted her financial help but gave her no love in return. They treated her like a distant cousin, albeit a rich one who supported them in a comfortable way. Monthly phone calls contained all the sincerity of laundry lists as their requests and updates droned through the line. For all the disdain she sometimes felt for them, Luz did her best to maintain the relationship with the only blood relatives she knew.

Which left her in San Nicolaas, a place where she was respected as the doyen of Main Street. The short and narrow thoroughfare angled through a proportionately small town of low buildings on the edge of a petite island that might have otherwise been overlooked by civilization had not a bunch of oilmen got the idea to build a refinery just beyond the reach of unruly South American politicians. And now the refinery, the source of so many of her clients, was slowly shrinking like the vanquished monster in a fairy tale. It worried her as much as her mother's failing health, especially when powerful people made public statements about selling off the land to build more hotels, condominiums, villas, and another cruise ship terminal.

While other bar owners reveled in the illusion of a glorious future bought by tourist money, Luz had her doubts. No bank offered cash for promises. Why should she accept them at face value? Crude oil and the products made from it were international commodities, tangible items of considerable worth. Wars were fought for less. Trinkets, T-shirts, and hats, gold necklaces, fancy watches, and diamond rings, these were available on every island in the Caribbean. This fact she gleaned from clients, men like Diedrik who took her to shops on the other side of the island where sometimes five cruise ships a day discharged thousands of passengers.

"I saw this in St. Maarten for ten dollars less," she heard a woman say.

"You're right," her companion agreed.

"Let's see if it's cheaper in St. Lucia."

It was a competitive world, Luz knew, having learned the hard way how fickle customers could be.

Oil money, on the other hand, flowed in the millions of gallons. As big as the cruise ships were, the tankers were bigger. As fancy as the jewelry shops were, the clerks earned a pittance compared to experienced welders, technicians, and engineers at an industrial facility. Those people, the men at least, but occasionally a woman or two, sought the services provided by the brothels of San Nicolaas. They were very reliable, especially when treated as well as they were at Minchi's, the bar Luz purchased from her former husband, the one she married to secure citizenship in Aruba for herself and her son.

This was her perspective, one built over the course of her tenure in a town that some couldn't wait to sweep clean of such demonstrable prosperity. Fortunately for her, these brilliant ideas had yet to bloom. If they were about to, she could only wish everyone the best of luck. She counted the days until her son returned, knowing that when he did, her life would once again change in ways she could not predict but for which she would be ready by freeing herself from any obligation on the island.

"I think I'll take the road by the sea," Diedrik said, interrupting her thoughts.

"*Está bien*," Luz replied. She squinted out at the ocean in an attempt to distract herself from a question that haunted her for years.

Where will you go if someday the refinery disappears? Among the many answers, she had the option of living with Diedrik. Maybe not him specifically, but several of his type had made the offer. Today, this life was still hers for the asking, the way it had been several times in the past. The most memorable proposition came from Sam, the man known as Samito and affectionately called the Crown Prince of San Nicolaas. He'd been a good friend of Charlie and a boy at heart. She almost accepted his proposal, which included a soon-to-be built house by the sea very close to where she and Diedrik drove at this very minute. Sadly, Sam passed away suddenly, not that she would have been his bride had he lived.

Reflexively, Luz sat up and craned her neck to pick out the location of Sam's property. She still visited the place, arranging a few rocks atop the ones he put there to mark the corners of his imaginary home. It was a pristine location, one Charlie inherited from Sam and preserved in trust so that it would remain untouched forever.

"Are you okay?" Diedrik asked.

"*Todo bien,*" Luz answered, though she was definitely unsettled. Like always, she hid her worries well. Men didn't pay to hear her problems, not that Diedrik was a typical example of her regular clients.

Her resistance to these proposals seemed foolish. After all, a man with Diedrik's means could provide her with things she dreamed of as a girl. The material goods she had of her own volition: a well-furnished home, closets overflowing with clothes, and a car usually driven by Teo, who looked after her like a big brother. These are the things some women long for, and Luz was grateful for each and every one. But while they brought her comfort, they could not deliver peace. There was only one man who could give her that, and he was en route to the island.

She waited, not always patiently, for notice of his return. It came in January and was confirmed yesterday. No longer would she worry about the waxing and waning of the refinery the way the fisherman did of the moon.

"A beautiful afternoon," Diedrik commented as he turned onto the main road to San Nicolaas.

"Hmmm," Luz replied, leaning her head against the seat. Most days in Aruba were beautiful. It was the reason so many tourists invaded the island: plenty of sunshine during the day, walks on the beach under a million stars at night, a cooling breeze most of the time. Strong attractions, yet none with enough power to erase her cares.

They rounded the traffic circle at the beginning of town. Ahead, the flares of the refinery cast a yellow-gray trail to the west. For another day at least, the refinery functioned as usual.

Diedrik escorted Luz all the way to her door. There, he returned to the subject of Minchi's.

"I'll speak with the notary tomorrow morning," he said. "However, I think a brief delay would be wise."

Rarely did Luz use the word "no." She learned dozens of ways to achieve the same effect because a short, powerful word had the potential to offend more easily than a languid phrase with the same meaning. Still, she resisted the urge to scream, "NO!"

At last she said, "A favor, please?"

"Luz, of course, anything," Diedrik replied, and without knowing it, fell into her trap by agreeing to fulfill her wishes.

"Tell the notary we will arrive on time," she said.

Realizing he lost to an expert, Diedrik grinned and vowed to do as instructed. In its current form, the deal would net her a decent profit.

"Will you allow me to accompany you to the gala for Andrés?" he asked using her technique as a foil against the potential for rejection.

"Won't your sister be angry?"

"If her opinion is the only thing that matters, I'll make sure my tuxedo is pressed and my shoes are shined."

"The blue dress you bought me matches your eyes," Luz added.

"Unless you want to shop for another one?"

"*Bon dia, mi amor*," she said, leaving him for the quiet of her house.

Inside, Luz quickly laid out the clothes she would be wearing later that evening. Then she stretched out onto her bed for several hours' sleep. She would awake to start another day inside of the one that had not yet ended. Hence, she lived two for each one marked on the calendar, which meant she'd spent thirty years in San Nicolaas, not fifteen.

THE STORM WHISPERED ITSELF into existence, drawing outer bands of clouds over the horizon, obscuring the stars and making the night that much darker. According to Fleet Weather, the system was not supposed to gain hurricane strength, but it had enough power to ruin regular cruise line schedules. It would also delay *Tenacious* more than the three days her captain and first mate predicted.

Hernán sat in the wheelhouse, alternately glancing at the radar, the chart plotter, and what little he could see outside.

"The night is nothing to fear in deep water," Captain Beck had told him.

This was one of the earliest lessons he'd learned. They were aboard *Marlena*, leaving the Delaware Bay on a trip to New York. It had been a starless night like this, the only difference being Cape May Lighthouse's beacon flashed at them. Hernán had watched nervously as they passed into the ocean. Ahead was nothing but black wool. He tried to concentrate on his English book but found himself growing increasingly agitated that the boat was headed toward the end of the earth.

"The planet is round, more or less," Beck said. "If we go too far, we'll only end up back here again."

Hernán looked at him dubiously.

"One way or another," his mentor added.

True to those words, Hernán, Beck, and *Marlena* returned to Philadelphia time and time again during that first year. More English words stuck in Hernán's head, the most important one being "school." He heard this term repeated over the telephone, in Beck's conversations with Syd and Ramirez, and occasionally in the presence of serious-looking men and women whose positions weren't clear.

Eventually, school became a brick building, four stories tall, with wide windows and concrete steps leading to doors with handles that he had to reach up to grasp. Beck took him to this place on a hot August afternoon. They waited half an hour until a stern woman wearing a jacket led them into an office. Questions were asked, forms completed, and Beck presented a green rectangular piece of paper that made her smile. The same woman loomed over those concrete stairs a week later when Hernán and a hundred other children attended their first day of class. Beck, Syd, and Ramirez joined him on the sidewalk. He noticed that most of the other boys were there with their mothers. He missed his mother terribly but didn't want to show it in front of the men that were smiling and encouraging him to do well.

Beck leaned down, keeping one hand on the radio hanging from his hip. "Make us proud," he said with a nod to Syd and Ramirez.

Hernán trudged up the stairs more than a little worried that everyone on the boat would see his grades. He didn't understand why he couldn't continue his studies in the galley, the wheelhouse, and his bunkroom. Why did he have to join a bunch of strangers on land when he already had a floating classroom?

He asked the same question several weeks later when he passed his first round of tests with straight A's. The exams were almost boring, given that the men on the boat tutored him during the previous year. His teachers praised his efforts and gave him extra work.

Once in a while someone poked fun at his accent, but there were other boys with the same color skin and yet a different lilt to their English than his. Their parents came from places like India and the Philippines, and their names were longer than the space provided at the top of their lesson books.

When school ended the next summer, Hernán wrote a note in Spanish to his mother. Those words and several photographs went into a heavy envelope that was dispatched from the massive post office in Philadelphia. "Your mother will be happy about your grades," Beck told him as they handed the envelope to the clerk on the other side of the counter.

Hernán wanted to tell her in person about what he learned. "Can we go to her soon?" he asked as they exited the building.

Beck answered with a question. "Remember those days at sea after we left your mother?"

The boy nodded.

"There are many more like that ahead of us, Hernán."

"How many?"

"I don't know exactly."

"More than when my mother left Bogotá the second time? My grandmother told me she was gone for a year."

"More than that," Beck affirmed.

"Why?"

"It's what your mother wants," Beck said.

Hernán didn't know what to make of this statement. He believed his mother loved him. She told him so. He remembered the look on her face when she met him at the airport in Aruba. The same look had been on her face when she sent him with Captain Beck. If she loved him, why could he not see her? This question he didn't ask. He was a boy, a good boy, one who did as he was told. For his obedience he was rewarded with the affection and honest praise of Captain Beck. As a bonus, the crew of *Marlena* welcomed him into their fold. They taught him their language, their skills, and their ethic of teamwork and mutual support. The boat was their home and place of work. Aboard it they were a family of sorts, a group of half brothers who knew their places at the galley table.

In the manner of Captain Beck, Hernán learned to pack his seabag. He lugged it up and down the uneven stairs at the narrow brick house every time they shipped out. It went with him during that first summer when they took a long voyage south, along the east coast of the United States. They towed a barge from Philadelphia to Jacksonville, Florida. There, they picked up another barge, which they delivered to Houston, Texas, before heading to New Orleans. In that city they cast lines upon their final tow, a brand-new deck barge bound for a contractor in Philadelphia.

Throughout the journey, Hernán stood the midnight watch with Beck, who insisted they read books together. Each morning as they handed the boat over to Captain Wilkie, *Marlena*'s aging first mate, their position was logged. Hernán asked why they did this when the computerized chart plotter displayed their exact position every second of the day.

"Never rely on a single aid to navigation," Beck warned.

"Here," Wilkie said, pointing at *Marlena's* chart table. "Let me show you how we used to do it."

Wilkie read aloud the coordinates from the plotter. Then, holding Hernán's finger in his hand, he traced a line from the latitude scale on the side of the chart. He placed the parallel rulers beneath the boy's finger and scribed a faint pencil line over that spot. He repeated the procedure for the longitude.

"X marks the spot," Wilkie said. "Now, let's say that fancy computer over there goes kablooey. No worries, you see, because we know where we were at a certain time. We know how fast we're going, and the general direction thanks to the compass. If we had to, we could work out about where we are."

Hernán stared at the X a few moments, then shifted his eyes along the whole series of them that led up the coast.

"You'll be doing plenty of this soon enough," Wilkie finished.

The lesson over, Hernán excused himself and stole into the cabin he shared with Beck. The flat drawers beneath Beck's bunk contained old logbooks, tide tables, and port directories. He leafed through them until he located the charts used aboard *Kathryn*. He found what he was looking for, the one that showed the island of Aruba in the Caribbean Sea. A series of X's, connected by a pencil line, led from the island all the way to the edge of the paper. He stared at the line for several minutes before carefully returning the chart to its rightful place. If he had to, he could find his way to Aruba and his mother.

That chart became part of his boyhood treasure, things he kept with him as links in a journey that already spanned two continents. He stared at it once again as *Tenacious* plowed waves somewhere north of Bermuda. Over his shoulder, he heard a door open.

"You want something to eat, Captain?" Syd asked from the companionway.

"Whatever's on the stove," Hernán called back. The windup clock on the pillar between the windows chimed half past five. He gently folded the old chart and slipped it into a worn envelope. Taking note of his current position, he followed the procedure Captain Wilkie had showed him all those years ago by marking it on the new chart that spanned the table in the back corner of the wheelhouse. He also logged their speed, miles covered during his watch, and the sea conditions. They were riding ten-foot swells that would soon become breaking waves, none of which would menace *Tenacious*. He felt sorry for lesser vessels that might find themselves out there.

"Sorry bastards," was the phrase Captain Wilkie had liked to use. Sometimes it was "poor, sorry bastards," or "stupid bastards" or "foolish bastards." The common term was bastards, a word Hernán hadn't studied in any of his primers.

It wasn't long before he learned exactly what Wilkie meant when he said it. Captain Beck arrived at his school on a Friday afternoon. The first question he asked was, "Do you have everything you need to do your homework?" Hernán nodded that he did. Beck patted him on the shoulder and smiled. "Good. We've got a salvage job and have to get underway as soon as possible."

They drove directly to the pier where *Marlena* hung by only her bow line. Beck and Hernán weren't aboard a full minute before Tony stowed that line and they were off. An hour later, they were pushing a massive floating crane down the Delaware River.

"Get your homework finished if you want to be on the job

with us," Syd told Hernán. "Call me if you need some help."

Hernán needed no help. He found school to be not so easy as it was methodical. Knowing that Captain Beck would keep him cooped up in his bunkroom until his lessons were complete, he set to work. Every once in a while, he glanced through the porthole at the crane outside. Men milled about the deck, staging equipment and stretching out cables.

By the time he finished his homework, the sun had gone down. He ate supper with the crew, all of whom talked about the upcoming job.

"When are we going to be there?" Hernán asked.

"About midnight," Wilkie told him.

During the school year, Hernán went to bed early, unlike the summer when his schedule was altered to stay up through the earliest hours of the morning with Beck.

"Get some rest," Wilkie advised. "We'll come for you when we need you."

At first, he couldn't sleep because of all the excitement, but once he drifted off, he was out until the next morning. True to his word, Captain Wilkie shook his shoulder, telling him, "Come on, young man. All hands to the foredeck."

He yanked on his pants and work boots and scrambled down the companionway to the main deck. Swinging open the door to the outside, he saw an amazing scene. The cables from the floating crane hung in the water. Five divers bobbed not far from where the cables disappeared. The water itself stank of oil, and a floating yellow dam penned in a shiny slick.

Hernán had no sooner stepped on deck than he heard the crane's engine groan. He noticed the operator was pulling one of the levers. Movement in the water redirected his attention as bubbles and eddies churned the surface. Then a steel pipe poked up. It grew longer and longer until Hernán realized it wasn't a pipe, but a mast just like the one atop *Marlena*. The action stopped as the divers repositioned themselves. A few moments later, the entire wheelhouse of a tugboat rose above the surface.

In search of an explanation, Hernán moved to *Marlena's* bow, where Wilkie, Tony, and Syd leaned on the forward bit.

"Poor bastards," Wilkie was saying. "Every last one of them dead."

"Dead?" Hernán queried.

"Dead," Wilkie repeated. "Tripped their boat going into the canal. Had all the doors open. Sank like a stone."

The only thing that made sense was that some people had died. He would learn later what it meant to trip a tugboat. Presently, he absorbed the serious nature of Wilkie's countenance. Poor bastards implied death and destruction.

In school several weeks after that first salvage job, Hernán met with another definition of the word bastard. He and some other boys were playing at recess. A tall kid named Jimmy fell and smacked his head on the asphalt.

"Poor bastard," Hernán commented as Jimmy was helped to the nurse's office by the playground supervisor.

"What do you mean?" his pal Mark asked, adding, "Jimmy has a mom and a dad."

"What do his parents have to do with him hitting his head?" Hernán replied.

"You called him a bastard. A bastard is a kid without a dad."

This was news to Hernán, who didn't question Mark, one of the smartest kids in class. Instead, he shrugged, muttering he didn't mean anything bad by it. Just the same, Hernán did not like being wrong. He pulled a big dictionary off the shelf and looked up the word the way Captain Beck had taught him. The definition contained a lot of bigger words that were not entirely clear. *Illegitimate, misbegotten,* and *spurious* made no sense. The phrases "born to parents who are not married to each other," and "a son of unknown parentage," were easier to grasp.

Upon closing the dictionary his first thought was of his own father. He'd never known the man. His mother had told him, "Your father died in a coal mine." Still, this didn't make him a bastard. He may be unable to remember his father, but his mother assured him that he had one. It was simply that he died, like those poor bastards in the sunken boat. Would Captain Wilkie have called his father a poor bastard? It didn't matter, Hernán decided, because he had a father and a mother. In fact, he had two fathers, the other one being Captain Beck.

LUZ HURRIED THROUGH HER PREPARATIONS
for the night. She'd overslept, leaving her with less than an hour
to get ready for the evening's trade. It was a miracle that she put
herself together in record time. Still, Teo came to the door to
collect her instead of waiting in the car.

"*Un minuto*," Luz told him.

Teo was the son of the bar's former bouncer and took over
his father's responsibilities at Minchi's with the added task of
being Luz's driver. He spent six years in the Dutch Marines and
had an excellent driving record, perfect training for his current
position.

The first order of business was to collect for the casa. Each
girl paid a nightly rate of 150 florins for the use of her room. A
girl might also be in debt to the bar for her permit fees. In this
case, it was her responsibility to pay this obligation as soon as
possible. Finally, there was a record of the number of glasses
of vino sold. At the end of her tour of duty, she would be rewarded with a florin for each vino, unless there were any out-
standing costs, in which case she would receive the balance if

any remained.

A simple ledger was sufficient to monitor the system. At thirty rows per page, a girl's name was written atop four pages: three to keep track of her casa payments, vinos sold, and incidentals; the fourth page to summarize the totals and make any notes. Luz learned this system from her predecessor, Marcela, who had been a wicked tyrant at Minchi's but knew how to count money. In case there was a question from the taxman or immigration, Luz retained all the ledgers in boxes beneath her bed. To date, no one cared.

Arriving at the bar, Luz hoped there had been plenty of men in Rembrandtstraat spending money with Angela and the others. It was unlikely given that it was a Sunday, the day many of them spent gathering with family.

At the start of her tour, every girl received a serious lecture about the rules under which they worked. Luz delivered this in a tone that was stern but with a measure of empathy. She didn't want to be vicious the way Marcela had been. Nor did she want to be a pushover. The things she told the girls Luz had learned through experience. If they followed her prescriptions, their time in Aruba would pass in the best way possible: quickly, safely, and profitably.

There were girls who thought they knew better. They missed their doctor appointments. They fought over clients. They promised a man one thing in the bar, then refused to do it in their room. All of this caused easily avoidable trouble. Like an honest judge, Luz forgave them the first time, chastised them the second, and if it went beyond that, reminded them that their ticket posted with the office of immigration would take them home as easily as it had brought them here.

Passing through the side door, she thought of the girls' names: Angela, Julia, and Maria. *An angel, a jewel, and the divine,* Luz mused, thinking of the mothers who optimistically named their daughters. She named her son after his grandfather who bore the moniker of a conquistador. Religion, myth, and legend were powerful forces in Colombia. She said her prayers with true conviction that the Almighty heard them, that He would provide for her according to His will.

She entered Minchi's and immediately sensed that God had left her to sort things out on her own this night. Angela stood near the jukebox, instead of at the bar with the other girls and Pablo. For the moment, Luz ignored the separation. Angela was the odd one out because the other two saw her as a silly neophyte who stole their clients. Naturally, this was a contradiction. Angela was going through her first foray into the world of prostitution, but she was not silly, a characteristic that was more liability than lure. The theory of relativity drove clients to Angela because she was relatively younger and more attractive than the other two. This was no one's fault. Maria and Julia would better use their time on makeup, clothes, and hairstyles than plotting against Angela.

Normally, Luz would have addressed the situation with a creative solution, such as a trip to Jaime's Salon for all of them. The regulars at Minchi's noticed changes like that, and the three girls would see the benefit of improving themselves instead of attacking each other. It worked in the past. Presently, Luz lacked the desire to engage this crew the way she would have in years gone by. She felt guilty for not doing her best, but with the sale of the bar only days away, she refused to invest the energy.

"*Buenas noches,*" Luz began in a polite tone. She accepted

their casa payments one at a time and marked the ledger accordingly. She correlated Pablo's count of the vinos and logged them, too. Feeling their discomfort that Angela had yet to join them, Luz decided to give a refresher course in the rules of Minchi's and ways of San Nicolaas in general.

"The refinery is a little slow," Luz said after handing the ledger to Teo. "If your time here has been difficult so far, be prepared for it to get worse if you don't do something to make it better."

Upon hearing this, Angela made her way across the room.

"There are some cruise ships coming this week. The crewmen often come here with a few male passengers. Stick to the passengers. They're the ones with the money." She waved her arm to encompass the Zone of Tolerance. "This is a real treat for them. Just remember, you deserve to get paid for your time. Don't do it for less when the bar is closed than when it is open. Don't do it for more without a condom; you're only risking your life. Don't leave the bar with anyone unless someone else knows whom you are with and where you are going. Never ask for the money up front, especially from an American. They'll be insulted and tell all their friends you can't satisfy them. Are you listening?"

"*Sí, señora,*" they replied almost in unison.

"They're paying for a fantasy. Make it real for them, and they'll pay you more than you can ever imagine."

Julia stepped forward and asked, "How much do they pay you, señora?"

Luz paused a moment to appraise this chica. Her shape drew catcalls in the street; her clothes might have been featured in a third-rate fashion magazine. She smelled like a slumming princess, too. Not surprisingly, she spoke like a fool, taunting her boss when she should have been learning something.

"I'm twice your age," Luz replied, "which means they pay me half what you're worth."

This caught them all by surprise. They had peeked into her room, noted her choice of jewelry, saw the shoes she wore. How could she, Luz, the boss, make less than them? So it was that their young minds were distracted and could not solve the equation. It was they who sold themselves cheap, not grasping the full value of the pleasure they provided.

"Then how will I ever pay my debts?" Julia asked.

"Focus on improving yourself," Luz answered and motioned for Teo to unlock the door. Minchi's was open for business.

Among his regular duties of keeping the peace, Chief Calenda fielded requests by the refinery to escort trucks bearing oversized cargo. The job required nothing more than a car ahead of and behind the truck itself. Aruba's roads were among the best in the Caribbean, but they were still narrow at places, and it was sound practice to warn less competent drivers that maneuvering space was about to be limited.

The current request came from headquarters in Oranjestaad, which was a surprise because that district dealt more with car crashes and the odd tourist fracas than oversized machinery. This time they wanted him to arrange an armed escort. Specifically, six men in two vehicles were to be on hand for the transfer of important cargo to the Marina Hotel and Casino.

"An invading army steals the women first," Calenda said to himself. "Then they go for the art."

Of course, Aruba had not been invaded since the Spanish

arrived in 1499. Subsequent handovers had been mostly peaceful. There had been a few spectacular robberies, including a daring raid on a casino during which bandits landed on the beach, helped themselves to several hundred thousand dollars, and sped away in fast boats. That had been before his time and not in his district, where stealing was limited to household items and personal property.

A firm believer in prevention is better than cure, Calenda phoned his counterpart in Oranjestaad, informing him his men would be there. It was no secret what type of cargo was coming. Famous the world over, the paintings of Andrés Cortés would soon be on display in the largest ballroom at the Marina Hotel. Any thief interested in stealing them would need an operation more sophisticated than a couple of speedboats and a bunch of bold men. The paintings were huge, some measuring ten feet tall by twenty in width.

As he considered which of his men he would assign to the escort, he decided to go himself out of curiosity. Moving delicate objects like that had to be a tricky undertaking and certainly out of the regular routine. It would be a treat to get out of San Nicolaas for a few hours. He might even indulge in a lunch at a beachside restaurant when the job was complete.

His thoughts shifted to the gala itself, which was slated to be the biggest event of the year. Normally, he wouldn't attend such a haughty event, but he was pleased to see a native Aruban rise to such heights as Andrés had. Calenda recalled a few nights on Charlie's veranda when the bar owner commented on his understudy's talent.

"He's wasting his time with me," Charlie had said. "If he gets the chance, he'll be as famous as Rembrandt."

Calenda himself played a part in seeing that Andrés had the opportunity to demonstrate his talent. Therefore, the chief was keen on seeing the paintings, raising a glass of champagne to toast the artist, and maybe having a dance or two. After all, the Arends Family Orchestra would be on stage. They rarely played in Aruba anymore, having made a name for themselves across South America.

Of course the chief would wear his dress uniform, which needed to be cleaned. He would take care of that tomorrow. At present, it was almost nine o'clock, the hour when the bars opened and the time when he made his first walk through town.

With Unit Two shut down and no decision from headquarters about repairing it, Turner had less work than usual. He made the mistake of taking an afternoon nap, which left him grumpy and restless. He missed the sunset, a chance to run errands, and another call from Bill Fenner. It was too early for Black & White, too late for supper, and only the right time to do nothing.

Before settling into a funk, Turner resolved to get out of the house where the television was the only enticement. Halfway through the refinery, he got the idea to stop in Charlie's Bar. Luis was surely there, listening to his music, and the Balashi was as cold as anywhere else.

Frankie loitered just outside the gate. He leaned against the wall, striking a Zippo lighter with his thumb, then snapping it closed as soon as the wick caught.

"You want to sell that lighter?" Turner asked the choller.

Looking up, Frankie said, "Not for all the sand on Palm Beach."

"For a Zippo?"

"For a priceless relic once belonging to the Crown Prince of San Nicolaas," explained Frankie.

"I didn't know Aruba had royalty."

"Beatrix is our queen!" Frankie cried. "There's more than that you don't know."

"Like the lottery numbers," joked Turner.

"Like the day this beast goes cold," Frankie lamented with a finger pointed at the refinery. "It's coming soon. Then you'll be on the street with me."

"We're on the street now," Turner retorted.

"You with a full belly and me with holes in my shoes."

"But you have a priceless relic."

Frankie put the lighter deep in his pocket and muttered, "I can't eat it."

To avoid Frankie's contagious melancholy, Turner headed for Charlie's with all due haste. There, he found Luis swabbing the bar to a mellow salsa beat. His first Balashi had barely dampened the coaster when several men surged through the door. One of them was Montoya.

The gang occupied five stools with Turner seated only one vacant spot from Montoya, who reached out for the bell that hung over the bar, ringing it for several seconds.

"A round of tequila shots!" he ordered, adding, "For everyone, even the *macamba.*"

His pals chuckled over Montoya's clownish glare at Turner.

Luis knew the sight of five drunks in search of trouble. The problem was deciding whether to aggravate them by denying their order or serve a round and send them on their way. The bottle of tequila was more than half empty, which gave him the answer. He set up the glasses and made a point of showing the bottle as nearly finished.

"What's the matter?" Montoya asked Turner. "You don't like tequila?"

Turner slid the glass down the bar, saying, "As a matter of fact, I don't. You can have it."

Gulping the drink, Montoya let a few drops spill onto his shirt. "Tell me where you're from, gringo."

"Bungalow 58," replied Turner.

The guys snickered at that, inspiring Montoya to the next level. "I thought you lived at Minchi's," he said, "with the puta queen."

This remark stunned Luis. Montoya had never shown any disrespect to Luz. They were competitors, each on their side of Main Street, but never in a vicious way. He raised her rent a few times but didn't kick her out of the house he leased to her, which made sense because a reliable tenant who took good care of a property was hard to find.

Having dealt with fools his entire career, Turner didn't rise to Montoya's insult. He kept his mouth shut, wondering how long it would be until Luis threw him out.

Montoya wiped the corners of his mouth, rolled the shot glass around in his hand, then set it on the bar. "Remember what I told you about a rich man and poor man?"

"What about it?" Turner replied.

"If you're a poor man and a rich man takes your wife, what do you do?" Montoya continued.

"Let him have her."

"But what if later on you become a rich man yourself? Would you go find her and take her back?"

"I'd find another wife."

"Good answer, but what if you suffered like a poor man and now you're a rich man and could do whatever you wanted? Wouldn't you want a little revenge?"

"It wouldn't be worth it."

After a mocking snigger, Montoya pressed on. "You must be a poor man," he said. "How much do they pay you to work over there?"

"Just enough," Turner told him.

"If I pay you a few florins more, would you work for me? You could trim the Divi tree by my house, scrub the toilet, wash my car."

"If you have the money."

Bristling, Montoya moved closer to say, "I have the money to pay the refinery your salary, send you and your puta bride back to wherever you both came from, and still buy a round of tequila for my friends."

"Let's see it," Turner said, finally aggravated enough to get off his stool.

"Gentlemen!" Luis hollered smacking his palm on the bar top. The crack caught their attention, momentarily distracting them from their pending quarrel. "We're friends here, one and all. If not, get out."

"But I just got here," Chief Calenda said walking through the door.

Teo drove Luz to Garufa, a cigar and cocktail lounge located a few blocks from the new Marina Hotel in the middle of Oranjestaad.

"Need me to pick you up?" he asked as Luz exited the car.

"Keep an eye on the bar. I'll taxi home." She worried more about something going wrong at Minchi's than on her last date with Jerry Frazer, an American technology consultant. He worked for the casinos, maintaining the computers that guaranteed a steady take for the house.

Patrons of El Gaucho, a steakhouse across the street, crowded the bar. These people were either waiting for a table or finished with dinner and having a drink. Most of the men smoked cigars, a few of the women, too. Every form of cocktail was available, including the most expensive brandies. Garufa rented private lockers to its customers who wanted to have their own bottles and cigars. Possessing a sterling silver key, Frazer was a member of that club.

"*¡Hola, Luz!*" Frazer called over the noise of the crowd. In one hand he held a cigar worthy of Winston Churchill and in the other a snifter swirling with golden liquid. He appeared foolish with these props. He was only twenty-eight but looked like he was hardly out of his teens. Because he paid cash for both, not to mention Luz's time, no one poked fun at him.

For his sake, Luz accepted a glass of brandy.

"That stuff cost $500 a bottle," he informed her. "I had them put three bottles in the vault, you know, in case I get thirsty."

While he laughed, Luz took a sip. It tasted like fire, and she nearly gagged.

"Want a cigar?" Frazer asked. "I have some tiny ones, perfect for ladies."

"*No, gracias.*" Her life didn't need the addition of another health hazard.

A combo took to the little stage at the front of the room. Frazer puffed away, drank his booze, and once in a while patted

Luz's knee. At the end of the first set, he left several hundred-dollar bills on the table and ushered Luz to his car.

"That was great," he said.

She understood his hurry. He wanted to get to the main attraction, which was sex with her at his condominium on Eagle Beach. They were there in record time, standing on the balcony, his cigar still burning. Luz considered that it was quite an accomplishment for a man in his twenties to own a place in another country, one he used for business and pleasure only a few months a year. *He must be a wizard with those mysterious boxes called computers,* she thought.

For all his capabilities, Frazer was a hapless romantic. He got half the details right. His cigar went into an ashtray. The lights were dimmed. He donned a robe. All the while, he left Luz alone on the balcony without giving her the opportunity to prepare. No matter, she was used to being thought of last. When he approached from behind, she reached around to be sure he'd properly sheathed himself with a condom. Then she allowed him to raise her skirt.

Full of energy and brandy, Frazer thrust frantically, the way a teenager would, as if Luz might run away like a frightened rabbit. At times he lost track of what he was doing, randomly groping her breasts and thighs. She was about to laugh when he took hold of her hips and began to pound in earnest. His climax came with a throttled grunt.

"That was great," he said, panting.

An hour later, after using his shower and redressing, they sat on his couch in the climate-controlled living room, where it was almost cold enough to snow.

"I leave for Miami soon, then I'll be back in early October.

Why don't we plan a whole night? How about October 6th?"

A year ago, Luz would have readily agreed. Used to acquiescing to her clients' demands, it was difficult to tell him no. Tonight, however, she had the resources and the justification for denying his request. As she struggled with the words, she realized it didn't take a computer genius to change her phone number.

"Call me," she said, reaching for her purse.

"Sure. Great. Hey, thanks. You don't mind going downstairs by yourself, do you? I'm wiped out. That brandy, and what you do for me, I'm exhausted."

"*Buena fortuna,*" Luz waved from the door.

10

ANXIOUS ABOUT SELLING MINCHI'S, Luz conducted a surprise visit the next morning. The building and business were valuable assets she didn't want diminished in any way prior to the sale. To that end, Maria, Julia, and Angela would see that without warning the boss might appear. Luz didn't expect any of them to be awake at half past nine, but after completing her walk-through on the ground floor, she found the girls seated around the table upstairs.

"*Buenos días,*" Luz greeted them.

"*Buenos días, señora.*"

Using the ledger downstairs, Luz calculated the previous night's profit. Each girl sold no less than fifteen vinos and serviced several men. They would have no trouble paying the casa or their daily expenses. Luz made a point of thanking them for keeping the common area clean and not hanging their laundry where it could be seen from the street.

"Don't forget, tomorrow you are due at the doctor for your weekly checkup. If anyone is having any problems, please tell him. Don't be embarrassed; he's a professional."

"Is he the doctor you trust?" Julia asked.

Luz fingered her keys for a moment. "If you find him inadequate, I'll be happy to give you the number of my own. Would you like it now?"

Grinning at some minor victory known only to herself, Julia said, "What is his fee?"

"One hundred dollars for a checkup," Luz stated. "More if there is an issue requiring more care."

"No special rate for the girls at Minchi's?"

If Julia was thinking of trading sex for a consultation with the doctor, she would be severely disheartened. In the first place, her physician was a married man with no interest in a paramour either for a fling or the long term. More important, barter ruined both professions. It was better to exchange money for each service in the proper setting the way Luz did with Herr Diedrik. Julia, for all her experience, hadn't learned that but she would if she approached the doctor with such a proposal. She thought of her body as a cash machine, which, in a way, it was, but without fixed prices, the value inevitably decreased to the point where she would be committing the most disgusting acts for a greasy lunch or a cheap pair of shoes.

Standards, Luz knew, had to be set and maintained. She said, "Please don't embarrass me."

"I would never—" Julia tried to say with her hand pressed to her chest in a cute way.

"But you already did," Luz interrupted, leaving no doubt that another offense would land Julia on the next plane to Colombia.

Perturbed, Luz stepped into her room to cool down. In a few hours she would be at the notary, signing the agreement of sale, and afterward, enjoying a pleasant lunch with Herr Diedrik. She wanted to be relaxed and confident, not aggravated by the stupidity of a chica.

There was a soft knock on the door, and before answering, Luz whispered a quick prayer for tolerance.

Angela came in, her eyes wide, her voice cracking. "Señora, it's not the best time, but …"

"Don't be afraid," Luz said evenly. "Tell me what you need."

"Can we talk about money?"

"Close the door."

Her clients paid well judging by the $2,000 Angela said she had earned so far. The amount left Luz wondering if the girl was doing risky things for premium prices. If so, she would know before the week was out. San Nicolaas novices tended to spread secrets like headlines.

"I'm sure you make more," Angela was saying, "but I've never had this much money in my life."

"It'll be gone if you don't put it away."

"That's what I wanted to ask you. Where can I hide it?"

During her first trip to Aruba, Luz hid money in various places around her room and among her clothing. Her biggest fear was the bar burning to the ground, taking all her cash with it.

"You can wire it to your mother," Luz suggested.

"She thinks I'm on a cruise ship. How would I explain the amount?"

Disappointed in herself, Luz said, "Come on. I'll show you how to wire it to yourself."

They were on the way down the back stairs when Angela asked another question. "Are you going to the gala for the artist everyone is talking about?"

"Yes."

"I'd like to go with Luis."

There it was, what Angela really wanted to talk about. Luz continued down the stairs, shaking her head at Angela's cleverness to enlist her help in both matters.

"Why Luis?" she asked.

"I don't know."

This was a lie, one Luz let go for the innocence it protected. What had Charlie always said to his friends? "Don't fall in love."

Rarely did Frankie stray from his regular theatre of operations, which consisted of the few blocks surrounding Main Street. But he was on the hunt for a pair of shoes, an item that sometimes showed up on trash day. Naturally, it was better to search where people actually lived as opposed to where they worked. Frankie was that smart. His need for decent tread was pressing because if the refinery closed, he would have to temporarily relocate to Oranjestaad until something new was built in San Nicolaas. It was a long walk to Oranjestaad.

He worked his way through a few barrels before a rental pickup turned the corner down the block. After ducking behind a wall, he peeked out to see where the truck was going. Only new refinery contractors used rental pickups. For a moment, Frankie considered that he'd issued a false prophecy on Sunday. If there were new contractors in town, the refinery was safe. Then again, what were they doing in this part of town? He decided to find out.

The truck turned left, then right, and stopped in the middle of the third block. The two guys who got out had no idea Frankie shadowed them by dodging through backyards and behind parked cars. They stood for a long moment in front of the house, the driver scratching his chin, his passenger tapping a pencil against a notebook. At last they passed through the gate in the wall.

Burglars! Frankie thought. *Giving me a bad name! But why would they be there in the middle of the day when anyone passing by could see them?* He remained in his position, observing their every move.

The driver took out a tape measure, and with the help of the other guy, proceeded to take careful measurements of the house. They were particularly interested in two walls. When they finished with the structure itself, they moved into the street, exchanging gestures as if they were backing in a concrete truck.

As they pulled away from the curb, Frankie memorized their license number. He no longer feared their intentions. Most likely they were repairmen. Why else would they be there in the middle of the day, measuring things, planning on how they were going to get their trucks in? Whatever the case, he had the license number, which he could hand off to Chief Calenda if something bad happened.

With no one else in sight, Frankie proceeded to dig into the next trash barrel, hoping there was a teenager who had recently outgrown a pair of sneakers.

For more than fifty years, the offices of Eman and Eman conducted real estate transactions in Aruba. As a notary, the firm researched a property's history, checked for any liens or tax obligations, and held payments in escrow until the final signatures dried. The process began with an agreement of sale between the two parties, and for this purpose, Bert Eman sat at his desk with the buyer and seller of Minchi's Bar.

Months ago, at the request of Attorney Diedrik, Eman did his homework in anticipation of a sale in the very near future. This was an easy task given that the firm handled the previous transfer between Luz, who currently sat on his right, and her former husband, Andrés Cortés, who at the time had been living in Holland. This had been a curious turn of events, but stranger things had happened in Aruba. Eman found nothing untoward about the sale then, just as he found everything in order now. He looked across at Luz, then shifted his gaze to the new buyer, a fellow named Kiko Sanchez, and began to read the terms aloud so there would be no confusion.

Luz hardly paid attention to Eman's voice. She fingered the medallion that hung from her neck, patiently waiting for the moment to sign her name. Thanks to Herr Diedrik's foresight, the usual 3-month process had been compressed to a week. After today, all that remained was for Sanchez to wire the money to Eman and Eman's escrow account. Then they would meet again for one more minor ceremony in order to sign the final transfer document and exchange the keys.

The day couldn't come soon enough. It wasn't exactly the nick of time, but a week to spare left her little room for anything to go wrong.

"Luz?" Diedrik said softly.

She blinked out of her trance and took the pen he offered. In careful, deliberate script, she inscribed her name. The buyer took his turn next. Copies were made, given to each party, and a round of handshakes concluded the official business.

Sanchez had one last request. "Will you reconsider my offer to stay on as manager?"

"*Claro*," Luz lied. She understood his desire for continuity at the bar. There were regular customers, such as Garrett Turner, and many more like him who knew what to expect in terms of drinks, music, and the limits of what would be tolerated. Changing the guard was notice to seek new allegiances. People would know the place had changed hands, but if they saw the regular bartender and bouncer, the perception would be that nothing much had changed.

Only Teo knew of the pending sale, and he informed Luz he would work for Sanchez or anyone else who paid his salary. He would gladly continue as her driver, too, if she preferred to keep things as they were. She wanted it exactly that way because there was no substitute for the deterrence of brute force.

With these pieces in place, Luz was ready to conclude her business in San Nicolaas. For the first time in years, her life would be unbound. She could ignore the calls from clients, go to bed at a reasonable hour, and dress comfortably. The joy it would be to wear flats and blue jeans, casual blouses and plain skirts! Then again, there were men who propositioned women no matter how they dressed. Still, she could act like the tourists at Charlie's Bar, who were oblivious to much of what went on around them, which was no fault of their own. They were on vacation, basking in the sunshine with fruity drinks in hand. It was an experience she'd rarely had without the pressure of satisfying a client at some point during the excursion.

There was no reason why she couldn't enjoy a part of life that was available to every visitor to Aruba. She would take a seat at Charlie's, order a Baileys from Herr Koch, and let men come and go without evaluating them as potential customers. If a man offered her a drink or tried a clever line, she would politely decline. "I'm waiting for someone," she would say, which was the truth. Was there a better place to expect a sailor to show up than Charlie's? Not anywhere on the island.

"I must be paying too much," Sanchez said.

Catching herself with a foolish grin, Luz told him, "I'm happy for you." She meant it, too.

A folder in Chief Calenda's hand contained the kind of irrelevant minutiae that gave him a headache. His colleagues in Oranjestaad provided a heavy document detailing every aspect of the transfer of "precious works of art" from the port to the Marina Hotel. There were only two essential pieces: a route map and a timetable. The size of the trucks, the straps used to secure the paintings, the size of the doors leading to the ballroom, all these were ancillary and beyond a policeman's purview. He and his men would stand on the lookout for nefarious actors until dismissed by the Oranjestaad team. The worst thing he imagined happening was a sudden rain shower.

Just as he finished noting the assignments, his secretary came in. "There's a lady here to see you," she informed him.

"Send her in," Calenda said. Seeing Luz walk through the door, he rose from his seat and extended his hand. In a glance he noted her generally upbeat manner, which put him at ease. She was present to discuss a matter for the police, but it couldn't be too serious.

"Is there a way to find out when a ship arrives in San Nicolaas?" Luz began.

"The port captain has a schedule. Are you interested in a particular one?"

From her purse she removed a photo and placed it on Calenda's desk. He studied the image for a few seconds. It wasn't a ship she was inquiring about but a salvage tug, a big one. They showed up in Aruba, usually to tow a tanker with engine trouble or to get fuel. Painted across the bow of this one was the name *TENACIOUS*, and she looked every bit worthy of the term. Standing before the wheelhouse were two figures. While they were too small to make out faces, Calenda knew who they were, especially the one on the right whose shirt was crossed by a leather strap connected to the radio holstered on his belt.

"When are they due?" Calenda asked.

"The 29th of September," Luz answered.

Calenda dialed the port captain's number, gave him the name and date, and received a quick briefing. "*Danki,*" he said, hanging up the phone, then focused on Luz. "It's not on his list at the present time, but the schedule is updated every day. Apparently boats are not as reliable as our visitors' airplanes."

"May I call the port captain myself? Perhaps in a couple of days?"

"Absolutely." Calenda gave her the number on a slip of paper. "He'll be happy to take your call. Is there anything else I can do for you today?"

"*No, gracias,*" Luz replied, rising from her seat. She carefully returned the photo to her purse, inquiring about Calenda's family as she did.

"They're all well," he told her. "Yours?"

"*Muy bien, gracias a Dios,*" Luz said. She thanked him one

more time for his assistance, then excused herself.

Andrés Cortés having a premier gala at the Marina Hotel, the return of Captain Beck, and all the usual island mayhem. *Incredible,* Calenda thought.

"I only wish Charlie had lived to see this," he heard himself say.

Bungalow 58 featured a covered patio large enough to host a wedding. Beyond the tiled floor stretched a lawn that ended with a low wall that could have been a picture frame for the view beyond. On the other end of the island, hotel guests paid extra for a room facing the ocean. With it came two chairs on a narrow balcony, which was an exact copy of the others above, below, and on both sides. Then again, they didn't have an oil refinery snarling over their shoulder.

Garrett Turner didn't mind the refinery. He did appreciate the rest of the panorama and took most of his suppers either on the patio or on the lawn near the wall. As a rule, he cooked meals on the grill then propped his feet up with a plate on his lap. The sunset provided a show more evenings than not, and this one was looking fairly spectacular until it was interrupted by his cell phone.

"Turner," he said into the handset.

"Bill Fenner here," came the reply.

"Sure, Bill, go ahead," Turner prodded, knowing what was coming next. Fenner was the most persistent of the professional recruiters that nagged him, trying to place him with other oil or chemical companies that always seemed to be in need of professional management.

"How are things in Aruba?" Fenner continued.

The small talk annoyed Turner much more than the pitch. He'd met Fenner only once so why would he be interested in chatting? It wasn't like he shared a bed with the man the way he did with Luz. Then they'd have a reason to discuss life's minor events. This, on the other hand, was business, so there was no need to delay the important parts.

"You're interrupting a fantastic sunset, Bill," Turner warned. "What have you got?"

"Let's talk about Chemica del Sur in Argentina."

"We already did."

"That's true, but have you had time to think about steak every night and tango dancing with beautiful women?"

His first thought was about Luz, who was a fine dancer as opposed to himself who could barely clap to the beat. Thus, the tango dancing was a weak incentive.

"Relocation expenses, signing bonus. Are you with me, Garrett?"

"I'm with you."

"Good. You want to hear the revised salary?"

"Not really," Turner wanted say, but let Fenner give it to him anyway.

"You can't tell me the number doesn't raise your eyebrows."

It raised his eyebrows but not his ass off the seat. Money alone was no good reason to leave Aruba. No, he wasn't a millionaire, but then again, he owed nothing to anyone. He had no wife, no children, nor any high-priced toys. His biggest expense was his tab at Minchi's, and that hardly dented his bank balance.

If he had to swear under oath to Chief Calenda, he would admit Luz had more to do with him liking Aruba than anything else. Sure, there was the beach and the sunset and the restaurants on the other side of the island. His evenings joking with José were fun, too. But Luz was the one who grounded him here. It wasn't love, rather a type of friendship that was previously unknown to him. He had girlfriends before, the kind who pushed for marriage or manipulated for extravagant gifts. Luz, on the other hand, asked for nothing. Yes, she charged a fee the way every girl working in San Nicolaas did, and that's where it ended. Or, he thought, maybe that's where it began because, free of any further expectation, it was much easier to settle down as friends than if something more loomed over the relationship.

"You want me to FedEx you more details and a proposed contract?" Fenner was asking.

"I don't know, Bill. I'm sitting here with a full stomach, watching the sun go down, and thinking about a lady."

"You sound like you're in love," Fenner said.

"Almost, but not quite," Turner said.

"To pass on an offer like this it can't be anything else."

"Yes it can," Turner explained. "I'm comfortable and not ready to change horses just yet."

"The horses may get changed by someone else," continued Fenner. "I don't hear good things about your facility. Another unit was shut down last week, wasn't it?"

"That's right."

"Any word from the boss about when they're going to bring it back on line?"

"A survey crew is visiting soon."

"So you're running at less than half capacity with no plans on the board. I hate to preach, Garrett, but you might want to get off the ship before the rats start scrambling."

Everything Fenner said made sense. Still, Turner stood fast that he was content the way things were.

"I'll call you next week," Fenner finished.

Rather than telling Fenner not to bother, he rang off and went inside to complete the paperwork concerning Unit Two's shutdown. He could take his time; José didn't open until nine, and Luz was usually occupied until midnight. With any luck, Montoya had drowned himself in tequila.

Because the port captain couldn't give her solid information about *Tenacious'* arrival, Luz decided not to mention Captain Beck's note to Carlotta. She feared something might go wrong or there would be a delay. Better to make the news a joyous surprise than a disappointing explanation. Still, Luz was eager to hear about progress on their house, and she dialed the number in Barranquilla.

"The dust settles," Carlotta announced. "No more demolition, and I've taken the liberty of selecting some beautiful appliances for the kitchen. It's about time I learn to cook."

Luz wouldn't mind learning some culinary skills herself. Too many of her meals came in Styrofoam boxes or from the expensive restaurants near Palm Beach.

"The curious neighbors have come to see what I've been doing," Carlotta was saying. "They can't wait to meet you."

"Me?" Luz questioned.

"*Hija*, you're the mother of a sea captain, a man with his own ship who sails the world. These uppity folks are happy to have you on their street."

"Captain Beck is the owner," Luz clarified.

Carlotta dismissed this fact. "Your son wears the white shirt, too. I know what that means. Anyway, they can explain it when they get here."

Luz appreciated Carlotta's confidence in the future even as she worried about her exaggerations. Then again, it didn't matter. Outside of San Nicolaas, she was free to be whoever she wanted to be.

HERNÁN WAS ENTITLED TO the captain's suite aboard *Tenacious*. Nonetheless, he lay down in what had been his bunk in the first mate's cabin for the past several years. No one questioned his decision. Upon Captain Beck's death, he inherited *Tenacious* and was free to do as he wished with her. The crew mumbled about what was to come, albeit in a speculative way. No one doubted their young master's abilities. He proved himself in circumstances that would have left the average young man delirious. Of course, he'd had a good teacher in Captain Beck, a man who wasn't so much fearless as he was committed to overcoming whatever obstacle lay ahead. If his stepson wanted to honor the man by letting his bunk remain empty for a while, well, that was okay with them.

Unlike Beck, Hernán didn't actually sleep on his life preserver. He hung it within arm's reach, on a peg beside his bunk. Of the few times he thought he might be killed, it wasn't the sea that was the danger. It was people and the stupid things they did. However, as he closed his eyes, none of their faces came to mind. Instead, he conjured up images of his first boyhood friends.

Phil and Sandeep were new the way Hernán had been the previous year. They replaced Mark and Jimmy who moved away. Having been initiated into the school a year before, they saw him as a veteran in the know. It was the beginning of fourth grade, and on the first day, the teacher asked everyone to say a few words about their summer. Hernán told the class he'd traveled aboard a tugboat all the way to Houston, Texas. Upon hearing this tale, the teacher looked over his glasses at the boy excitedly making this claim. The students at this exclusive institution were the sons and daughters of investment bankers, real estate brokers, and college professors. They might enjoy a few weeks in Europe with their parents or even a ski trip to the southern hemisphere. However, they did not traipse about in tugboats.

"A tugboat?" the teacher asked.

"Her name's *Marlena*," Hernán replied. "She has two big engines. My dad is the captain. I mean my stepdad."

The teacher digested these facts, made a note in his lesson planner, and said skeptically, "That's very interesting, Hernán."

At recess, Phil and Sandeep granted Hernán celebrity status. They wanted all the details. Did Hernán see a mermaid? No. Any sea monsters? No. Did his stepdad let him steer the boat? All the time.

"All the time!" Phil exclaimed.

"At night mostly," Hernán added.

"At night, too?"

"That's his watch, midnight to six in the morning."

"He lets you stay up past midnight?"

His stories about dead men in a sunken boat, giant oil tankers, and engines taller than any of them captivated his fellow students. He knew guys with tattoos, guys missing their front teeth, and guys who could lasso a bit with a 6-inch rope from thirty feet away. What were the other kids going to say? That their father had an office with a view of the city? Hernán saw the whole ocean from the wheelhouse. That a half-dozen vice presidents reported to their dad? Captain Beck had that mixed bunch of a crew, none of whom wore a jacket or a tie. That their dad let them hang out in his office on weekends? Not when Hernán steered the boat in the middle of the night.

"Not by myself," Hernán clarified. "Unless my stepdad has to go to the head."

"What's the head?" Sandeep wanted to know.

"You know, the bathroom."

Wow! These boat guys had their own language, too, one they spoke among themselves like a code. They called the bathroom the head. The kitchen was the galley. The bedrooms were bunks. Port and starboard were left and right. Not miles per hour, knots.

Hernán and his buddies formed a clique that traded these words in the halls and on the playground. He never had so many friends, not in Bogotá, not during his short stay in Aruba. Everyone begged for a ride on *Marlena*. Each Monday, they wanted to hear where he'd been over the weekend. They were in awe when Captain Beck himself waited for Hernán at the gate. Although he didn't wear a uniform, he exuded ten times the authority of their teachers. And there was that radio on his hip, a device that linked him over secret channels to his crew.

All that year, they acted out scenes from Hernán's travels. They didn't have ropes or a boat but pretended they did. Hernán called out orders from an imaginary wheelhouse. Phil scrambled to start the engine; Sandeep tossed make-believe lines to a make-believe barge. They towed it around the playground before docking it alongside the door. Then they were off to the swing set where a ship awaited to be helped away from a pier.

"Why do a lot of boats have girl names?" Phil asked Hernán one day at recess.

As much as he'd learned about boats, Hernán didn't know anything about girls. He wasn't sure if they had anything in common to justify the same names. He was aware of a drawing of his mother that Captain Beck looked at once in a while. Syd and Ramirez had photos of their wives hanging near their bunks, too. Surely one of them would know.

"I'll have to ask," Hernán replied. The following weekend he put the question to Syd.

The engineer's answer was vague. "When you have one, you'll understand," he said.

"A boat or a girl?"

"Both."

Perplexed, Hernán relayed this to Sandeep and Phil. The trio agreed it was one more thing they wouldn't get until they grew up. He wrote about his best friends and their antics in a letter to his mother. A photo of them went into the package with his report card. He also sent a few pieces from his trove of bric-a-brac: a rough copy of a chart he made, an old coin he found, and the cuff of his worn-out gloves on which Syd had written his name in capital letters.

"Why doesn't she write back?" he asked after the trip to the post office.

"Because she's always with us," Beck replied.

Again, Hernán thought of the drawing his stepfather slipped from the back of the logbook every once in a while. Did Beck think of the picture the way Ramirez told him to remember Saint Michael was looking after them? Is that what he meant? Hernán said his prayers before going to sleep and at the galley table, but it was a one-way conversation. Saint Michael didn't say anything back.

Aboard *Tenacious*, the lights flickered and Hernán caught himself wondering if Saint Michael was finally sending him a message. No, it was Syd switching generators down in the engine room. Just in case, he reached up and touched his life jacket.

12

THE ENVELOPE OF MONEY in Teo's pocket felt like a brick. It wasn't as heavy nor as big, but it was strange to have it there when it should have been in the hands of someone else. Each month Luz gave him a business-size envelope that contained 12 one-hundred florin notes and an index card with the date on it. On his way to the gym, Teo stopped to see Montoya, presenting him with the money, receiving a signature on the index card as confirmation the rent had been paid. Luz took the card when they met later at the bar. This had been the process since his father performed the task, which was as long ago as Teo could remember.

The problem was Montoya didn't want the money. He stopped Teo at the door and gave him the same line. "This month is free," he said. He seemed sober, too, which left Teo wondering what got into the man. Montoya was known to be as generous as a hungry jackal. Maybe he won the Mini Mega, the local lottery.

Whatever the case, it left Teo unnerved to carry the cash back to Luz, especially when she had important things to do.

He was to pick her up at five, and then they were going to the airport, specifically the General Aviation Terminal on the west side of the field. Andrés was flying in aboard a corporate jet. This also perplexed Teo because if the artist had the money to fly privately, why did he need Luz to provide a car?

Although distracted by these events, Teo pulled to a stop at Luz's door a few minutes early. He let the car idle with the air conditioner on maximum as he trotted up the walkway. She must have been waiting because he barely made it halfway when she stepped out.

"*Buenas tardes,*" he greeted his boss. Noticing she was a bit out of sorts, he decided to deal with the rent issue later.

"I hope this goes well," Luz replied, following Teo away from the house. Andrés' request for a car was not a large favor, but it was a surprise because she hadn't spoken with him in years. His request came through Herr Diedrik. Andrés told the lawyer an unknown vehicle would fool the reporters, which sounded like a slim ruse. A couple dozen people worked in the terminal. One of them surely had the phone number for the newspapers or TV station. On that note, she wasn't famous like Andrés, but people knew who she was. The Arubans, aside of Herr Diedrik's sister, didn't give her profession a second thought. Andrés' critics, on the other hand, or members of his current social circle might see her differently.

Teo and Luz entered the terminal building where a desk agent informed them the plane was only minutes from landing. *So much for secrets,* Luz thought, scanning the lobby for press people. She saw none.

"You've been requested to meet them on the ramp," the agent said. "This way."

They followed him through a cursory checkpoint, then outside to the tarmac where the breeze and heat attacked Luz's hair and makeup. She prayed the plane was truly about to arrive or she would be a mess.

Not two minutes later, a gleaming white jet rolled into a vacant space beside a line of others. A door in the side of the plane folded down, revealing a set of built-in stairs. One of the plane's crew descended the steps and waited for his passengers. If only a red carpet and the prime minister had been there, the moment would have been complete. Even without them, Luz was impressed. She knew Andrés as an 18-year-old who drove a jalopy and worked at an auto body shop. Their other transactions took place remotely, with a local lawyer representing him.

The man who exited the plane resembled the teenager she had married. He was the same height and build, but a smart suit with a flashy tie replaced his tattered jeans and T-shirt. There was confidence in his movements, too. This wasn't the first time he was greeted at an airport.

"Luz!" he called. "Do you want to get married again?"

She joined in the joke, replying, "Only if you'll paint my portrait."

Putting his arms around her, he said, "I already have, but that's not my only surprise."

Men, Luz thought, *showing off or complaining too much of the time.* Here he was gloating about another trip down the aisle when she had been fretting about his career.

"Let me introduce you to my friend and patron, Mr. Kim," Andrés said next, turning back to the plane.

An Asian man appeared in the doorway. He was at least sixty but could have been ninety. Luz couldn't be sure. Like

Andrés, Mr. Kim was well-dressed and cheerful.

"Mr. Kim," Andrés said. "This is Luz."

Not knowing exactly how to greet the man, Luz simultaneously mimicked his slight bow and stuck out her hand.

"Colombian women," Mr. Kim said, "so beautiful."

"You should know," Andrés put in.

At that moment everyone turned their attention to the top of the stairs where the last passenger appeared.

"Luz!" she shrieked. "It's me, Inez!"

Luz sooner expected Charlie back from the grave than Inez to show up in Aruba. The things they had done together during their first time on the island were still talked about among San Nicolaas regulars. What no one discussed was how Inez had been expelled, along with Marcela, Minchi's previous operator, after working illegally outside the Zone of Tolerance. Luz had been there on the fateful night when Chief Calenda had taken them away. Inez had appealed to her for help, but there was nothing she could or wanted to do.

After a flurry of smothering kisses, Inez pulled away for a thorough look at her former co-worker.

"You always were a bit conservative," she commented. "Except for the sequined dress I bought you. Remember that?"

With half a smile, Luz said she did.

"Tell me," Inez went on, "what do you think of Mr. Kim? When I left here all those years ago, I traveled quite a bit, but then I went to Macau. We met, and it was love at first sight. We've been married ever since."

Upon hearing this news, Luz raised her eyebrows.

"I know, it's a shock," Inez was saying. "He's a wonderful man who gives me everything I want so long as I give him what he needs." She let out a laugh. "What a pleasure it is to speak Spanish, Luz. You have no idea. Mr. Kim sent me to language school to learn Chinese, but it's so strange. I ended up with more English than Chinese."

"*Tan bueno,*" Luz managed to squeak.

"I have so much to tell you," crowed Inez. "About six months ago, Mr. Kim took a liking to Andrés' paintings, and I told him I knew this man and you. It was Mr. Kim's idea to bring us all back to Aruba. Isn't that great?"

"It is," Luz agreed.

"Kind of like old times, no? And Luz, look at this plane. This is the way to travel. Your own schedule, your friends. So much nicer than the way you and I had to do it when we were poor."

Although she'd made remarkable economic progress, Luz didn't consider herself rich. When she flew to Colombia to visit her sister and mother or Carlotta, she sat in coach, not first class.

"You know," Inez rambled on, "I was thinking about asking Mr. Kim to take us to Colombia. I haven't been back in a couple of years. What do you say? No, don't answer. Let's get to the hotel. We can talk there. I need a drink."

Mr. Kim, Inez, and Andrés sat in the back while Teo drove and Luz rode in the front passenger seat. It was impossible to get a word in as Inez pointed out things she remembered to Mr. Kim. Thankfully, traffic was light, and they arrived at the Hyatt in less than ten minutes. Luz told Teo she would meet him at the bar later.

"Take care of the rooms," Inez said with a kiss to Mr. Kim's cheek. "We'll be at the bar." Locking her arm in Luz's, she launched toward the bar, which was only a few yards from the beach.

After a round of Baileys had been placed before them, Inez sat back and let out a long sigh. "Imagine us being here again," she said. "Incredible. I often think without Aruba I would have been a poor Colombian girl forever instead of married to a lovely tycoon."

Luz sipped her drink to avoid saying anything.

"You have to stay with us. I mean, not in the same room. No, nothing like we used to do. We'll reserve a suite for you here at the hotel."

"Thank you, Inez, but I can't—"

Inez cut her off, "I insist. Forget about San Nicolaas for a week. You're not actually working are you?"

"No," Luz lied.

"It's good to hear you took my advice and realized we're better than that type of thing. I was terribly worried about you back then. You were young and cute and didn't know a thing about that life. Well, you had me there, and it turned out okay. You look great, by the way."

"*Gracias,*" Luz said, thinking that Inez might have just described Angela.

"So tell me," Inez continued, "whatever happened to the man who washed up on the beach? He was in love with you, wasn't he?"

The answer to that question Luz did not know. By the packages he sent every year, she knew that he cared for her son the way a father should. As for his feelings toward her, to this day they remained mysterious.

"No secrets," pressed Inez.

"He sends me letters," Luz said.

"Oh, old school, stoic. I like that, but I'll bet he's not the only one. Listen, let's make plans to fly out the morning after the gala. That's the 29th. What do you say?"

Nothing would keep Luz from being in Aruba on the 29th, least of all a jaunt to Colombia aboard Mr. Kim's jet with a woman who had once been a nemesis of sorts. No, she would be at the refinery gate looking for that big tugboat her son was on.

From behind a casual wave, Inez said, "We can work out the details later."

Only one customer sat in Charlie's Bar. Angela took the little table just inside the door, sipping a Coca-Cola and watching the street. This week, during her regular visit to the doctor, she heard that tourists came to Charlie's Bar, some of them men who wouldn't enter the other bars in town. They sought a woman's company but needed the cover of a less incriminating location.

What no one mentioned at the doctor's office was that Saturday night was typically slow at Charlie's. Regular visitors, the ones who owned timeshare weeks, some of whom might be the men mentioned, were enjoying a nice meal with the rest of the tourists. It was a ritual, one that marked their last evening in paradise. This wasn't to say the odd man out would not appear. Sadly, she was presently out of luck in terms of finding a client.

In a way, she was relieved because Luis took over when Herr Koch ended his shift. Luis tidied up the bar, picked songs on his computerized jukebox, and added ice to her glass when it melted away. As much as she wanted to land a rich American client, she was content to steal glances at him. Unlike Teo, who was physically massive, Luis was a compact specimen who moved with a smoothness that implied hidden sensuality. After servicing the men in her room, a session with him would be a vacation. She heard he was an incredible dancer, too, which was a strong indication of sexual prowess.

For his part, Luis didn't charge Angela for the Coca-Cola. The scenery she provided was worth the cost of the soda. If there was a lonely man on the street he wouldn't be able to pass a pretty young woman like her without at least contemplating a drink.

"There's no better advertising than a great set of legs," Charlie once said.

This time, despite the quality of the imagery, it did no good. Luis completed his work, tapped a glass of ice water, and sat down opposite his only customer.

"*Saludos*, Angela," he said raising his glass.

She met it with her own, then glanced out at the street.

"A lull before the storm," Luis told her. "They'll be plenty of men on the street later."

"I thought there would be a few here this evening," Angela complained.

"There's me," Luis offered. He felt her leg against his and realized he might have stuck his hand into the jaws of the tigress.

With a bit of an edge in her voice, Angela asked, "Are you going to the gala?"

All the girls were talking about it. A few claimed to have dates with access to the event. She believed none of them but had a suspicion her boss would be there, if not with Garrett Turner, with someone else.

"I've been invited," Luis answered. This reply left not only his commitment to attend but also his desire for a companion impossible to determine.

Frustrated, Angela opened her purse only to have Luis put his hand over hers.

"Give me a dance instead," he said.

Consolation prizes did not interest Angela. It was first or nothing. However, it never hurt to stay close to the judges.

"Okay," she said, placing her purse on the bar.

They moved outside where they had the sidewalk to themselves. Luis augmented the faint music from the bar with a quiet hum. The vibration from his lips tickled her neck, causing Angela to giggle. She suddenly felt lighter, happier, less worried about how much money she would make and whether she attended the gala. Out of the blue she was reminded of her grandfather who had lost his mind and sang little songs to himself all day long. She missed him and her whole family.

When they finished, Luis retrieved her purse and handed it over with a gentlemanly kiss.

"It would be a shame to be alone at the gala," Angela said. She then cupped the back of his head with her free hand and pressed her lips against his for a long moment. Having surprised him with this stunt, she chuckled a second, then headed for Minchi's.

Heart pounding, Luis retreated into the bar. He was young enough to be thrilled by a passionate kiss, yet on guard because he was thoroughly versed in the art of female deception.

"The eye of the needle," Charlie had said. "A fat, blind man will find his way through if there's a woman on the other side calling him."

Ah, it didn't matter, Luis told himself. He'd done his good

deed for the day by pulling her out of a funk. She went down the street grinning, didn't she? That fact gave him as much satisfaction as a minor romance. Plus it enhanced his karma. Who could have too much of that? Not him, which is why when he was about to close the door and Frankie coughed loudly from the edge of the sidewalk he spared a moment to listen to the choller's plea.

"Ahem," Frankie began. "If I had a good pair of shoes, there would be a line of girls waiting to dance with me."

"I doubt that," Luis returned.

"Hah! You're afraid of the competition."

With a laugh, Luis stepped inside, locking the door behind him. A few minutes later, he greeted Screwball on the veranda with a fresh bowl of water. The cat didn't budge on the parapet from where he looked down at the street. Following the cat's gaze, Luis saw Frankie performing like a confused ballerina. He tiptoed across the street with his arms circled overhead, then bounded back with them flapping like a scared chicken.

"Not a candidate for the Bolshoi," Luis remarked to Screwball.

For his part, Screwball had seen enough. He eased down to the floor, sipped from his bowl, and curled up in the corner.

"A pair of shoes!" Frankie hollered. "My kingdom for a pair of shoes!"

"What do you think?" Luis asked his uncle's favorite cat. Getting nothing more than a slow blink in reply, he went inside to his bedroom closet, dug out an old pair of sneakers, and returned to the veranda. Taking careful aim, he launched the sneakers at Frankie one at a time.

"Manna from heaven!" cried the choller. "Proof that God

loves me!"

His karma fully fueled, Luis took a seat on his recliner, put his head back, and dreamed of dancing with a beautiful woman.

Luz arrived home a few minutes past midnight. Had she been with half a dozen clients it would have been an easier day. She expected to meet Andrés at the airport, take him to a hotel, perhaps have supper, and then get back to her normal routine. She wanted to keep a close eye on the bar, making sure nothing happened to jeopardize the pending sale. She trusted Teo to do his job, and she was sure he would. At the same time, she preferred to be there herself.

Inez refused to let her leave the Hyatt until they relived some of their more comic and tragic moments. During the early weeks of their first trip to Aruba, a client left Inez for Luz. Like Angela, Luz had not yet understood the nuances of the business. She hadn't deliberately stolen the client. It was Marcela, Minchi's manager, who introduced him to her, thereby denying Inez the rewards of his company, which included a suite at the Hyatt, breakfast in bed, hours lounging by the pool, and gifts from expensive shops. Still, Inez blamed her and went on to conquer Samito, Luz's best client, out of revenge. What Luz's rival didn't know was that Samito had plans that didn't include her no matter what she did for him. As frequently happens in San Nicolaas, Inez and Luz eventually struck a truce in the spirit of economic cooperation. Two men came into Minchi's looking for a lesbian show. It became the stuff of legend until other girls mimicked their act, lowered the price, and the demand faded.

Surprisingly, Inez casually glossed over their previous rivalry. From her tone, Luz sensed the woman felt guilty that she jetted about the globe while Luz remained in San Nicolaas. There was a measure of loneliness in there, too. Luz appreciated the condition, having spent too much time with men she didn't love and precious little with men she did.

"We're going to catch up in a hurry," Inez declared. "We're two Colombianas away from home. We should stick together."

Luz raised her glass in agreement, thinking how easy it was to forget the past when your husband had the money to buy a new future.

Thankfully, Inez didn't push for them to spend Sunday together. "Go to Mass," she said, "but Monday, we're going shopping. A nice breakfast first, then we'll spend the day going from store to store."

What did Luz need to buy? Nothing. However, after finally convincing Inez to forget about the suite at the Hyatt, she had to give in on the retail excursion.

"And don't bring any money," Inez scolded her. "I owe you, Luz. Without you, I never would have met Mr. Kim."

While she knew Inez didn't mean this as an insult, it still chafed. Woman to woman, they both knew the truth about Luz's life in Aruba. Who could have worked in San Nicolaas and not grasp the reality that anyone still there did more than pour drinks? To her credit, Inez never pressed the issue. Just the same, all night Luz heard about how good life was with Mr. Kim, aside from the food, which Inez despised but forced herself to eat out of respect for his culture.

"We'll have lunch at Casa Vieja," Luz said as they parted on the steps of the Hyatt. "Real Colombian food."

"I can't wait."

Nor could Luz, but for the day when Hernán and Captain Beck sailed into San Nicolaas.

13

TO AVOID THE WORST of the storm, *Tenacious* detoured east and pulled into Bermuda, where she lingered for several days. Although her destination hadn't changed, the date of arrival was pushed back further and further by the tropical depression that stalled along the Atlantic Seaboard. Another storm forming near the Virgin Islands was forecast to track north, effectively hemming the vessel in port. Her crew was anxious to move on, but everyone agreed that unless someone needed assistance there was no reason to go looking for trouble.

The midnight watch took their supper at eleven. Six men sat down to eat. Two were missing. No one expected the head of the table to be occupied. Captain Beck sat there for meals, and the only one authorized to take his chair was Hernán. He was absent, too.

While routine and discipline ruled their lives, the galley of any ship sits men close enough to whisper about their fears, and this night the sound of forks and knives mingled with concerned words for their new master. It had nothing to do with managing the boat or the weather. Rather, it was the coming reunion with his mother that worried them.

"The captain must have explained the situation to him," Syd said.

Ramirez pushed his fork across his plate but temporarily kept his thoughts to himself.

"Between Suez and Malta, they were talking in the wheel-house," the chief engineer went on. "I overheard some things about Aruba."

Looking up, Ramirez asked, "Do you think he told him everything?"

"He wasn't a man to hold back," Tony put in. While his comment was generally accurate, it didn't answer the question specifically.

"Someone young as him would have taken that news hard," Ramirez speculated. "We would have noticed."

"Considering how he's handling what happened, I'd say he's mature enough to put it in perspective."

"What if it was your mother?" Ramirez asked.

The trio focused on their plates. At last Syd said, "What if he was your father?"

Again, no one at that end of the table managed a reply.

A stickler about time and the condition of the ropes he used on deck, Tony said, "It's already quarter after. I'm going to get him." He filled a clean mug with fresh coffee and made his way forward. Light spilled into the hallway, indicating Hernán's door was open, surely a good sign.

"You want some coffee, Captain?" Tony asked, extending the steaming cup into the room ahead of him.

Looking up from a book, Hernán replied, "Thanks, Tony." He took the coffee and pointed at the ragged scar on the deckhand's forearm. "That ever give you any trouble?" he asked.

Rubbing his arm, Tony said, "Nah. A little ache here and there. Nothing worse."

The deckhand nearly lost his arm in an incident that taught Hernán how dangerous working aboard a tugboat could be. They were in the final stages of putting a barge to the dock. Beck was at the helm, and Tony on deck with 11-year-old Hernán close by.

Ten feet separated the top of the empty scow from *Marlena's* bulwarks. Tony lassoed a cleat with the bow line, made it fast, and scrambled up to the barge with another rope over his shoulder for the stern. As he reached to pull his body over the edge, Tony lost his grip. He pitched over backward and plunged to *Marlena's* deck. His good luck followed him down, landing him atop the pile of rope that he intended to become the stern line, which was only two feet from Hernán. However, his right arm struck the gunwale, causing a compound fracture that exposed several inches of bone.

Mesmerized by what happened, Hernán never heard the general alarm sounded by Beck. He stared at Tony's arm, vaguely aware of the man groaning. Then Ramirez appeared, followed by Syd.

"Give me your shirt!" Ramirez demanded. When Hernán didn't respond, he shouted in Spanish, "*¡Tu camisa, dámelo!*"

Coming around, Hernán stripped off his shirt. Ramirez snatched it, tore it down the middle, and wrapped Tony's wound.

"Syd! Stand by where you are," commanded Beck. "I'll bring her to the dock and hold her there. Ramirez, get the ladder. Hernán, swing Tony's feet around so he's out of the way."

The other men ran to their tasks as Hernán took hold of Tony's feet. No sooner had he moved them a few inches than Tony wailed in pain.

"Get his legs around!" shouted Beck. "He has to be out of the way."

With Tony screaming, Syd staring down from the barge, and Ramirez positioning the ladder, Hernán followed orders. When he had Tony alongside the gunwale he caught sight of the blood that soaked through his torn shirt and pooled on deck.

The barge landed against the pier with a jarring bump that almost sent Hernán tumbling atop Tony. He saw Ramirez holding the ladder and Syd looking down from the barge. He glanced back at Tony, thinking that he should do something to help him. His rudimentary first aid training had not prepared him for an injury like this.

"Hernán!" Beck called. "Come here now!"

The boy leapt to the upper deck, rushed to the wheelhouse, and entered nearly out of breath.

"Hold her straight ahead," Beck instructed. "Use the rudder to keep the bow right where it is. Let the throttle at idle."

He'd done this before but never alone, and when Beck ran out the starboard door, Hernán suddenly found himself with no one looking over him. From where he stood, he watched the captain gather Tony into his arms, then hoist the deckhand over his shoulder. Ramirez held the ladder as Beck ascended to the barge. There, Syd helped him to the other side.

"Steady!" Ramirez shouted.

Hernán bumped the rudder so the nose of the boat remained in position. In the manner of Captain Beck, he glanced at the engine instruments then out the side windows for the possibility of other traffic, and finally at the bow again.

The sight of exposed bone and the sound of a man shrieking in pain never left Hernán. Unfortunately, he would experience both again and more than a few times. At the moment, there was nothing more dangerous than the possibility of striking his head against his bunk in the first mate's cabin of *Tenacious*.

"You going to eat with us?" Tony was asking.

"Not hungry," Hernán replied.

"Sausage and peppers," Tony tempted him.

"Thanks, but I'll be in the wheelhouse."

A few minutes later, after he relieved Andy, Hernán took the helm. He remembered how he'd been alone for what felt like an hour at *Marlena*'s controls. It turned out to be closer to ten minutes until Captain Beck returned with blood on his shirt, face, and hands.

"Good job," he said, taking his regular place. "Give Ramirez a hand with the ladder, then bring me a bucket of soapy water."

Tony wasn't back to work for six months, and then on light duty for another six after the doctor removed several titanium screws and plates. For much of that year, Hernán was stuck in school. He spent less time on *Marlena* and more hours with Sandeep and Phil, occasionally sleeping over at their houses.

One weekend, his pals organized a video game tournament. Phil's console had the latest games displayed on a four-foot, wall-mounted screen in front of a sectional couch that formed a miniature coliseum. Half a dozen kids from their class were invited, and Phil's mom continuously refilled a buffet of hotdogs, hamburgers, potato chips, and salads.

Hernán was quickly eliminated from play. He didn't like

the scenarios, most of which involved shooting people, stealing cars, or flying spaceships through fictional worlds while blasting everything in sight. What bothered him most was the gore. The other kids reveled in the bullet wounds and sword slashes. Not Hernán. He'd seen Tony's arm, the bone protruding through the skin, the blood smeared on the deck and Captain Beck's hands. The screams weren't those of an actor, recorded for playback when electrons struck a make-believe character. The man suffered terribly until he blacked out. There was no reset button either, which surely Tony would have preferred to the year of recovery. The same could be said for those poor bastards who went down with their boat.

As Hernán learned during that salvage job and on deck the day Tony fell, there was no way to pause the action for a Coke or a hotdog while you figured out a strategy to defeat the enemy. You had to deal with the emergency on your own with what you had at hand. Sometimes it was too late, and there was nothing you could do. No one had a reset button, not even Captain Beck.

THE PREVIOUS SUNDAY, Angela watched Luz pray before Mass began. This week, she arrived early, went to the same pew, and made an appeal to the Almighty. It was an awkward effort because she hadn't been to church since her confirmation. She did her best, ending with a request for God's wisdom to steer her toward a prosperous future.

Other people entered the church, some of whom knelt for a second before taking a seat. They noticed Angela sitting alone near the west door. Nervously glancing around the sanctuary, she wished she'd waited outside for Luz. The night before, Teo assured her the boss rarely missed a Sunday. He also said an old friend of hers had come to the island, which is why he collected for the casa. Had the old friend disrupted her schedule? Apparently not, because at that moment Angela saw Luz pause in the doorway to take off her sunglasses.

Luz followed her routine of a pre-Mass prayer, then settled next to Angela. She was gratified to see the girl refreshed and animated. It meant her recent advice hadn't been wasted.

From the elevated pulpit, Father Dario preached a sermon

about mercy. He quoted the Gospel of Matthew, the passage from the beatitudes. "Blessed are the merciful for they shall obtain mercy." His message evolved into a reminder about the need to forgive one another. Luz thought of Inez, how she made a point of saying she didn't hold a grudge. At Father Dario's urging, she resisted the cynical temptation to chalk it up to Inez's fantastic life.

After the service, Angela and Luz filed out with the rest of the congregation.

"That's new," Father Dario said, referring to the medallion hanging around Luz's neck. He knew it was important by the way she flushed at his comment. "By the way, Señora Flores lives near you, right?"

"Two blocks down the street," Luz acknowledged.

"I'll be visiting her tomorrow. Perhaps we could have a cold soda afterward."

"My friend from Colombia is here with her husband," Luz said. "I'm sorry."

"Another time," Dario said, adding, "Good to see you again, Angela."

Outside, the look on Angela's face revealed her shock at the scandalous possibility of Father Dario meeting with Luz.

"You can trust Father Dario," Luz said, sensing her companion's dismay. "He helps wherever he can, including the chollers and the girls."

"Wouldn't people talk if he came to your house?"

"He's been here a long time, and I don't think he cares what people say. For his sake, I would sit with him outside where anyone could see."

Impressed by her boss' insight, Angela nodded, opened her

mouth to ask another question, but clamped it shut when a group of parishioners passed by them. Anxiously she looked toward Main Street, then at the people leaving the church. Sensing Angela's desire to spend more time with her, Luz decided to change her own plans. Normally she would have spent the day with Herr Diedrik, but he was busy with his sister. Looking at Angela she remembered what it was like to grind days off the calendar without leaving San Nicolaas. There were few men in town who paid the *molta* and took girls to the hotels or even down to Baby Beach for the afternoon. A day with Angela might give her a chance to help the girl.

"Do you have any clients today?"

Angela shook her head.

"Come with me," Luz said, putting her palm on the small of Angela's back, steering her away from Main Street.

"This is amazing!" Angela declared upon entering the living room. "You were married to Andrés when he painted them?"

"I was," Luz said.

"That means you actually saw him do it."

This time Luz raised her shoulders. She wasn't about to tell Angela that she had been working constantly, sometimes with as many as eight clients per day. She returned home to find more and more of it complete but had never watched Andrés maneuver his brush.

Luz invited Angela to her bedroom closet where she told her to pick out a bathing suit, a sundress, and a pair of sandals.

"Are you serious?"

"Don't waste time," Luz implored her employee. "We have places to go."

Less than an hour later, they were splashing about Herr Diedrik's pool. Luz called to ask permission to use his villa in San Fuego. Of course he granted it, telling her where to find a hidden key. He moaned that he was stuck at his sister's place but might be able to escape for supper. They would be gone by then, Luz said, before reminding him about the notary on Tuesday.

"This is the life," Angela noted as she paddled her raft closer to Luz, who sat waist deep in the water at the shallow end. "With a client like this, why do you bother with the others?"

Luz wondered if Angela was cognizant of how astute her question was. She might have asked for the obvious reason that if the lap of luxury was available it made no sense to sit anywhere else. On the other hand, she may have perceived other considerations.

"Did you have boyfriends in school?" Luz asked.

"A couple," Angela replied.

"Do you have one now?"

"Sort of."

"Is he one of the boys you knew in school?"

"No. I met him after."

It took barely a second for the message to sink in. Still, Angela protested. "The longest I had a boyfriend was a year and a half. You said you've known Herr Diedrik for fifteen years."

"Tomorrow he may meet another girl, one who is younger, prettier, who for whatever reason charms him. Then where will I be?"

"But—"

"It's not that he's angry with me or unsatisfied. He's simply distracted. When a man becomes distracted, he forgets."

After digesting this statement, Angela said, "My mother and father have been married twenty-five years."

"They live in the real world."

With refinery flares burning day and night, tankers calling at the piers, and a smattering of industrial shops scattered about, San Nicolaas seemed more real than the center of Bogotá with its fashionably dressed businesspeople ducking into office towers between lunches at swanky cafés. Or so Angela thought.

Seeing the consternation on the girl's face, Luz continued her explanation. "The Zone of Tolerance is a fantasyland. If this is your life, you have to accept flexible rules."

"What if you leave? If Herr Diedrik took you to Holland?"

This opportunity had been presented to Luz more than once. She turned it down, and presently she considered how she would react if again Captain Beck invited her to go with him.

At last she said, "He knows me from here, from what I've done in this town."

"He—"

"Let me finish. Not only does he know me from San Nicolaas, I know him."

"You could never trust him?" Angela put in.

"Put yourself in his shoes," returned Luz. "Would you trust me?"

The question perplexed Angela for its boldness. She assumed her boss would change roles for a good life with a decent man, even if it were temporary. Now she considered that Luz might be sustaining herself by simultaneously using multiple men, some of whom may come and go. If that's what she did, she'd been successful. She enjoyed all the trappings of a luxurious life, with few of the commitments. The evidence hung in her closet, parked in her driveway, and made her cell phone chirp.

"You didn't answer my question."

Should she answer the question was Angela's worry. Then again, this woman prayed on her knees and therein she found the correct reply.

"I would trust you."

Behind her sunglasses, Luz's eyes welled up. Plenty had been said about things she did upstairs. Never had the conversation extended to her loyalty.

"Let's make something to eat," she said rising from the pool.

"I used to work in a grocery store," Luz said, handing Angela a handful of vegetables from Diedrik's refrigerator.

"Sounds boring."

"Not really. The customers came and went all day long. There were plenty of nice people. I met a guy on the bus one day."

"Good looking?" Angela wanted to know.

"Nothing special."

"You're teasing me."

"Okay. He was cute," Luz continued with a grin. "We stared at each other across the aisle for weeks before he asked me out, but it wasn't meant to be."

"What happened?"

"There were problems in my family. We needed money. I came back here. I married Andrés."

Money was Angela's reason for being in San Nicolaas, too. She earned five times more on the island than she would have in Colombia. With Luz's guidance, she was positioned to do even better.

"I think about him sometimes," Luz was saying. "And the manager at the store."

"The manager?"

"Yes. He was looking for a girlfriend, maybe more. I don't know; he might have married me."

Her experience in San Nicolaas showed Angela some disgusting men, but there had been a few decent ones. They enjoyed themselves with her body, but they weren't filthy or violent about it. Already she was getting used to the less pleasant aspects. Nonetheless, given the opportunity to live with one as opposed to servicing a couple of dozen per week, she would surely pick the best of the herd. Yet, no man seemed good enough for Luz. Thoroughly confused, Angela carefully sliced a pepper.

"What did you tell your family about Aruba?" Luz asked next.

"Nothing," Angela whispered.

"The first time, I told my mother and sister that I was working at the hotels as a maid."

Concerned that her parents might discover her lie, Angela asked, "Did they believe you?"

"Probably. The second time, I left in a huff."

"My mom helped me pack. She thinks I'm on a cruise ship, part of a dance troupe."

A common story, Luz knew, from listening to girls she worked with or managed. As for packing, she did that on her own, before her mother could sell the dresses she bought during her first trip. From then on, she hadn't needed to shuttle her clothing.

"What are you going to do with the money you make here?" Luz asked from the table as she set plates out for their salads.

"I'd like to have a little shop," Angela said, "a place where I could work for myself."

The entrepreneurial spirit ran strong in Colombians. Luz herself maintained Minchi's as one of the most successful bars in San Nicolaas. Some girls who worked for her went on to own taxis, restaurants, modest sewing operations, and even small apartment buildings. Others were less fortunate. She paused to appraise Angela's skills, noting the girl sought good advice and was willing to learn. She was a bit too earnest but that could be attributed to her age. A few years would polish her edges, leaving a slippery character with the benefit of rough experience. That is, if she didn't become obsessed with the present at the expense of the future.

"Your mother loves you," Luz said suddenly. "Don't let her down."

"I won't," Angela was quick to say.

After taking a few moments to tidy Herr Diedrik's kitchen and patio, Luz and Angela departed San Fuego. They drove north, taking the inland highway through the towns of Santa Cruz, Paradera, and finally Noord. At the risk of being seen by Inez, Luz turned toward the hotels. The row of towers blocked the beach but their glamorous façades were impressive in their own right. She parked in the lot between the Acqua Condominiums and the Holiday Inn.

"Is this like Miami?" Angela asked as they walked toward the water.

"I don't know," Luz replied.

"One of the girls from Buchi's Bar says it is. I'd like to go there some day. New York, too."

They stopped at the Hadicurari Restaurant. A waiter sat them at a table on the upper level, where they drank frozen margaritas. The Marriott complex sprawled to the northwest. To the south, beyond the Holiday Inn, stretched the rest of Palm Beach's famous hotels: Playa Linda, Hyatt, Occidental, Radisson, Riu, and Westin. Angela commented on their size and beauty, then asked if Luz came here with clients.

"Not anymore." Last night was her final outing as hired company to this part of the island. Luz did not count her pending attendance at the gala because Herr Diedrik would not be paying her. Her presence was courtesy of a personal invitation from Andrés.

"Is it illegal?"

"Only if they pay you here," Luz clarified. "If a man wants to take you to a hotel, be sure you have your passport and permiso in your purse. No matter what, don't accept a single florin from him unless you are in San Nicolaas."

Angela made a face.

"It's the law," Luz said. "It doesn't have to make sense."

On the beach below, couples walked hand in hand, teenagers romped in the water, and people stretched across loungers with books in their hands.

"I heard there are going to be places like this in San Nicolaas soon," remarked Angela.

"From the same girl who thinks this is like Miami?" queried Luz.

"No, the purchasing agent at the refinery. He says the refinery needs so many repairs that it's dangerous to work there.

He's worried about losing his job. He's my favorite client so far."

Your job is dependent on his job, Luz wanted to say, but kept the thought to herself. It would only fuel the rumor machine and cause Angela unnecessary stress.

"Did you ever watch the sunset from here?"

Luz smiled at her empty drink. "I know a better place."

On television and in magazines, Angela had seen images of idyllic Caribbean scenes. Few of them compared to the spot in Savaneta where Luz took her. They parked on the side of the road near a small complex consisting of an outdoor bar, a pavilion, and several bungalows. Twenty yards away, a small pier reached into the water.

"Charlie called this his country estate," Luz explained. "He had dozens of friends, maybe hundreds. They all came for his birthday and at other times of the year. No one ever left hungry or sober. Sometimes there was live music. People danced and played dominoes late into the night."

"Oh, I heard about this place. It's where you found a dead man on the beach."

"Who told you that?"

After hesitating a few seconds, Angela said quietly, "A girl on Rembrandtstraat."

"It's true," acknowledged Luz, "but he was alive."

"Really? What happened?"

Not knowing how much Angela had heard, Luz gave only the facts. "Charlie and Sam took him to the hospital where he made a full recovery."

Hoping for a juicier story, Angela said, "That's it?"

No, there was much more, but Luz didn't want to reveal

everything. Instead, she started up the beach, walking to a place just beyond a patch of mangroves. White sand slipped under the water, turning deep blue until it merged with the sky at the horizon. No one was there. No kids playing in the sand. No waiters delivering trays of drinks to patrons under palapa huts. No one windsurfing or parasailing across the water.

Having picked up a few stones near the road, Luz now placed them atop the piles set back from the beach. She issued a silent prayer for Samito and another for Charlie. Far in the distance, beyond the reef and no doubt several miles out to sea, steamed a supertanker. From the white froth at the bow, she knew it was moving at full speed. Its course pointed north, away from the island. She remembered sitting here, watching them appear over the horizon, angling toward San Nicolaas. This one had no reason to slow down, much less stop where many more had previously called. Maybe that purchasing agent was right.

Angela sensed this site was as sacred to her hostess as the church was to Father Dario. She wasn't sure if she should place a rock or two the way Luz had. In the end, she observed in silence, thinking that success in prostitution came with more than the usual amount of serious rituals.

The line between sky and sea seemed to rise toward the sun. Gradually, orange and purple erupted from the surrounding blue. An iridescent pink dabbled the few clouds skirting the scene as if Andrés Cortés tapped his brush gently against an otherwise finished canvas.

"Let's go," Luz said, her eyes still fixed on the darkening sea.

15

ARUBAN HOUSES ARE typically constructed using concrete blocks. A foundation slab is poured first, then the blocks are laid in a running course of mortared joints to the height of the roof, at which point a ring beam is poured to tie the walls together. Montoya built such a house in San Nicolaas and lived in it until he moved to more spacious accommodations belonging to his wife, Marcela, who inherited them from a previous husband, the father of Andrés Cortés and the owner of Minchi's Bar. Even after Marcela was deported from the island, Montoya continued to live in that house due to some vagaries in the law and Andrés' lack of money to pay a lawyer to pursue the matter. The artist was satisfied to gain title to his father's bar, the same one he sold to Luz to buy his own studio in Amsterdam. For her part, Luz rented Montoya's original house because she invested her profits into the bar rather than her personal accommodations. So it is that building a house in Aruba is much simpler than understanding the pedigree of its owners or inhabitants.

Although he possessed more knowledge than most on these

subjects, Frankie lacked the initiative to record them anywhere aside of his own memory, which functioned automatically and inexpensively. He happened to be exploring trash cans in Luz's neighborhood, enjoying the comfortable walk in the sneakers Luis gave him last week. On shoes of this quality he moved as sure-footed as a roaming panther in search of game.

Rich people gave up the most but San Nicolaas had too few of them. Poorer people who lived closest to the refinery wall tossed out the least. There were businesses in that area, but he'd already been through their dumpsters, finding a ripped T-shirt, a battered wallet, and nothing else. Therefore, Frankie sought out the middle class, whose teenage children could be remarkably wasteful.

He wasn't fifteen minutes into his mission when he came upon a series of trucks blocking the street. Men milled about, arranging tools, stretching power cords, and taking orders from one of the guys Frankie spied last week. He suddenly realized all this work was taking place at Luz's house.

The neighbors were out, too, which ruined Frankie's chances of picking their trash. He stuck to the far corner with his eyes fixed on the men moving between the trucks and the house. If they dropped a sandwich or a bottle of Coca-Cola, he would pounce. He might even be lucky enough to catch a ten florin note that fell from someone's pocket. It happened before when a crew repaired the refinery wall last year.

This gang worked diligently. The man in charge allowed no slacking. His partner wore a silly white hard hat and what looked like surgeon's gloves. Frankie released a gap-toothed smile at him, but no one cared what a choller loitering in the shade of an old Divi tree did. They stuck to their tasks, not so much as stopping for a drink from the cooler on the back of the largest truck.

About an hour into the operation, Montoya showed up. He shook hands with the man in charge, then went in the house. Coming out a few minutes later, they moved to the back of a truck where the guy with the gloves unrolled a set of plans. There was a lot of finger-pointing at the drawings, but everyone seemed to be happy, especially Montoya.

"Do what you have to do," Frankie heard him say. "I don't care if you knock the whole house down."

Of the three languages Frankie spoke, Dutch was his least favorite. Still, he understood what he heard and knew what it meant for Luz's dwelling. This was no remodeling job. Something else was going on, and in the process, Luz would end up like him, without a roof over her head. As if he needed more confirmation, one of the workers poked the wall with a jackhammer. The concrete fractured and fell away in fist-sized bits.

The best person to tell was Chief Calenda. However, as he approached Helfrichstraat, Frankie considered that police headquarters was a fair distance as opposed to a telephone. He charged only one more block to Pueblito Paisa, the restaurant where he most often ate leftovers. The cook didn't want to hear his plea for help. She waved him off, telling him to come back after midnight when she closed.

He gave up on her, crossed the two short blocks to Main Street, and turned west. He banged on the glass at the Western Union office, only to be met with an angry fist from the guard inside. He didn't so much as attempt to enter the clothing stores. Then he saw Herr Koch exiting the bank across the street from Charlie's Bar.

"I need to use the phone!" he called.

So far away was he that Koch didn't know Frankie was trying to talk to him.

"The phone! I have a guilder. I need to use the phone," Frankie hollered. He was running so fast that he nearly hit the bartender like an errant bowling ball.

"Use the pay phone at the refinery gate," an aggravated Koch told him.

"They're tearing down Luz's house," Frankie puffed. "I have to call the chief before it's too late."

Koch had heard some tales from Frankie over the years, even listened to the choller sing Christmas carols to a group of drunken revelers one night, but he'd never heard a story this preposterous.

"Montoya. Jackhammers. Saws cutting into the walls."

"Jackhammers?" questioned Koch.

"I'll show you," Frankie pleaded.

"I don't have time for your nonsense, Frankie. The tourists are on their way."

"Ahh, then let me use the phone." Frankie took out the one guilder coin that lurked in the depths of his pocket and dangled it in front of Koch.

"Wait outside."

He was just about to sprint off to the police station when Luis came out and said, "Let's go," with a wave toward the back of his pickup.

At first Frankie hesitated. Then, at Luis' urging, he leapt in and kept his head down.

In the short time that Frankie had been gone, the workers made astounding progress. Four of them assembled a steel framework, while two other teams continued cutting through the walls. Neighbors kept their distance as they chatted among themselves.

"You weren't lying," Luis said to Frankie as they approached the site. "Did you see Luz?"

"The car is gone."

In its place sat a crane with it outriggers digging into the asphalt driveway.

"This is my fault," Frankie suddenly cried.

"Your fault?" Luis countered. "We don't even know what's happening."

"Last week I saw those two measuring the walls. I thought they worked for Luz."

"Maybe they do," Luis put in.

"You're crazier than I am hungry."

Just then, Montoya returned in a Mercedes sedan. Luis jogged across the street to speak with him.

"A private art collector wants the murals," Montoya explained.

Through the open door, Luis noticed the furniture inside was coated with concrete dust.

"Andrés painted them before he went off to Holland," said Montoya. "I'm getting paid this afternoon when they're certified as genuine."

"Where's Luz?"

"Who cares," Montoya shot back. "She can live in this rubble rent free for the rest of her life if she wants to. Frankie can keep her company."

"It looks like her stuff is still in there."

The next person to arrive was Father Dario. He spotted Luis and Montoya arguing near the front gate. Stepping over the cables, hoses, and tools of the workmen, he strolled up to the scene, inquiring what was wrong.

"He's tearing out the walls," Luis informed the priest. "He didn't give Luz a chance to get her things out, either."

"It's my house," Montoya growled. "She can get her stuff later."

Having heard about the paintings, Father Dario ignored the argument and walked straight in the front door. He found the living-room wall covered in heavy plastic. A pile of furniture huddled in the far corner. Bits of concrete rained onto the floor as the blade of a diamond saw cut into the structure.

"You're going to get hurt!"

It was Montoya's voice, and Dario disregarded it. He went into the master bedroom where nothing was happening. From the bureau he gathered up a small jewelry box, framed photos, and containers of makeup. When his arms were full, he made for the door.

"What are you doing?" Montoya shouted.

Pausing in the middle of the living room, Dario said, "I'm removing her things for safekeeping."

"They'll have to stop everything. We can't do that."

"Then let God strike me dead."

Incredibly, the transportation of Andrés' paintings from the container port to the Marina Hotel was ahead of schedule. There were only three trucks, two of them normal size, the third a few feet taller to accommodate a particularly large painting. Chief Calenda yawned as he waited in his car for the convoy to pass by. When they were clear, he followed close behind, keeping a sharp eye out for anyone looking to disrupt the move.

No one bothered aside of a few shopkeepers who paused a moment before unlocking their doors. By the time he arrived at the hotel's back entrance, the regular morning rush hour began as the workers who lived inland proceeded toward the tourist area. The Marina Hotel covered the site of the former parliament building. A progressive government sold the structure, which brought a commanding price thanks to its proximity to the airport, the marina across the street, and a stretch of beach a hundred yards on. As for the seat of government, it had been moved to a large parcel in Balashi with plenty of parking and room to grow.

More out of a desire to avoid the traffic than a genuine interest in the process, Calenda left his car to watch the movers in action. What made the job easy was the specialized equipment. From electrified dollies to miniature cranes, these guys had it all. Nothing moved quickly, but it did move safely. Through the oversized doors went the paintings, one at a time, until the last and biggest of them all was staged on the loading dock.

He was about to walk inside for a look at the installation when his cell phone rang. After listening for a few seconds, he repeated, "Tearing out the walls?" He maintained the connection as he darted for his car.

Traffic be damned, Calenda switched on his sirens and lights. In a few minutes, he was clear of Oranjestaad, hurtling past the airport, and climbing the grade past Parkietenbos. He believed what Luis told him, knowing that old wounds, when reopened, bled the most. He imagined the situation unfolding in San Nicolaas: Montoya shouting, Father Dario clearing out the house, Luis improvising as best he could. This wasn't about the paintings; it was about revenge. Calenda's biggest fear was the start of a cycle that could spiral out of control. Push comes to shove comes to fists, madness, and misery. It was his job to get in the middle, to stop it in a way that everyone understood and respected.

Arriving at the scene, he quickly saw he was too late. It looked like a target on the artillery range. Holes punctured the house. Rubble mounds dotted the yard. A pair of pickups loaded with clothing and small pieces of furniture blocked the street. Worst of all, Montoya was pointing and yelling near the front door.

"Let's step over here," Calenda said as he moved around the debris.

"This is my property," insisted Montoya. "I don't have to get permission from you to do anything."

In an even tone, Calenda replied, "All I'm asking for is a few minutes of your time."

It took a long moment, but Montoya finally walked around the corner with Chief Calenda at his side. Out of earshot of the others their conversation continued.

"Are the paintings going to be part of the gala Saturday night?" asked Calenda.

"I don't know, and it doesn't matter."

"Calm down. I'm trying to get a sense of how we can work things out."

"Work things out?" complained Montoya. "I have to pay that crew to remove the walls and deliver the paintings. They're all sitting around afraid the priest is going to curse them. Who's going to pay for that?"

"You could have avoided all this trouble by giving Luz time to move out."

After spitting a disgusting lump into the gutter, Montoya said, "I gave her the same amount of time you gave Marcela."

There it was, the pathetic logic of a bitter man who held a grudge against someone with no culpability. It wasn't Luz who operated a prostitution ring outside the Zone of Tolerance and recruited girls for this purpose. Montoya's wife, Marcela, did that and more, earning a seat on the next departing flight to Colombia. Luz had nothing to do with it. Andrés pushed the issue with the help of Samito. Naturally, Montoya didn't unleash his anger on Andrés because that would have negated the value of the paintings. In a better world, Calenda thought, something that happened fifteen years ago would have been long forgotten. Sadly, it was as memorable as yesterday, brought to the surface by an opportunity to profit on a couple of paintings that sat in the shadows for a decade and a half.

"I understand your position," Calenda said at last and turned back toward the house.

Father Dario, Luis, and the neighbors managed to get Luz's personal belongings into the pickups. The larger furniture they stacked in the bedroom, covered it with plastic, and left it to good luck. When Chief Calenda entered the house the crew was already back at work. He shepherded the others outside, giving them the bad news that there was nothing he could do.

"Any of you know where Teo might be?" he asked.

"At the gym," Luis replied, recognizing the wisdom of the chief's rapid departure.

Father Dario looked over the pickup. "Any ideas where we can put this stuff?"

"Hotel Astoria," Luis told him.

Compared to the previous day with Angela, Luz's retail excursion was a like a military operation. No one Luz knew shopped like Inez. Not an impulsive or ignorant buyer, Inez sought exactly what she wanted. When she didn't find it, she moved on. They barnstormed through shops, boutiques, and malls like a pair of wolves, slowing only to try on a dress, coordinate some jewelry, or test a pair of shoes.

Luz expected her to be more wasteful, but it seemed Mr. Kim's money taught her thrift. She checked prices and asked for discounts, rejected poor quality and refused unworthy compliments. Her only extravagance was what she bought for Luz, and in this area she spared nothing.

"A full closet makes a happy woman," Inez said when they entered the first store.

"Only if the dresses fit," Luz reminded her.

With a burst of laughter, Inez drew Luz into a hug. "I love you, a sensible woman with class," she said. "Let's do ourselves a favor. Turn off the cell phones. It's only us today. No Mr. Kim. No Andrés. Nobody bothering you from San Nicolaas, okay?"

"Okay," Luz agreed. While she expected a few recently terminated clients to harass her, it was only Herr Diedrik she worried about. Then again, if he couldn't contact her he would be less likely to delay closing the deal for Minchi's. She switched off her phone, slipped it deep into her purse, and smiled for Inez.

Inez embraced her once more, saying, "I'm so happy to be with a real Colombiana."

This was a sincere remark Luz found out as the day progressed. There were the bags of things bought, but there was also the talk of Colombia, of life in Asia, of Inez wishing she had children. They shared a platter at Casa Vieja, Luz's favorite restaurant. Inez shed tears for the flavor of home-cooked Colombian food.

Their shopping adventure complete, they returned to the Hyatt for several hours in the pool. Both dozed off in the shade beneath umbrellas, not waking until Mr. Kim himself arrived. "Will you join us for supper?" he asked Luz in weirdly accented Spanish.

"Tonight I have an obligation," Luz replied, gathering her things into a beach bag.

"As it must be," he said with the formality of a major domo and his customary bow.

"Tomorrow night you can't escape me," Inez said as they walked to the portico. "Andrés needs a good woman to keep him out of trouble, especially here on his own island. You should think about marrying him again. You know, a famous artist, his first wife from years ago. It would be very romantic."

It would be something, Luz thought, *something perfect for Aruba where anything could and frequently did happen. Romantic?* She wasn't sure. Either way, she drove toward San Nicolaas with fewer than two hours to spare before Minchi's opened, thinking that she had two more nights as the bar's proprietor. After signing the papers, she would gather Angela, Julia, and Maria into the common area between their rooms to inform them that someone else would be in charge. Julia and Maria would think nothing of it. They were veterans of the trade. For them nothing changed but who collected for the casa. Angela might be more sensitive, and Luz considered how she could make the transition easier.

Then there were her clients, men like Garrett Turner and Herr Diedrik. They might want to spend their time with Angela. A better pair of clients the girl couldn't find, not in the present climate. Neither complained about the price nor dallied with other girls. They were generally kind and clean, polite and honorable. If Angela wanted, Luz would make the introduction.

Stopping for a traffic light, she harkened back to her first trip to Aruba. Inez prompted her into acts that earned hundreds of dollars per half hour. Marcela arranged and profited from her marriage to Andrés. And Carlotta counseled her more effectively than Herr Diedrik. Where did it land her? In a permanent spot on the same street where girls came for only ninety days.

The light turned green, and Luz suddenly flushed with shame, not that this had been her life but that she might beckon Angela into similar circumstances. It was one thing if a girl chose it for herself, making each decision as it arose. However, it was a dubious responsibility to plot her course deep into the world of prostitution.

Negotiating the traffic circle at Pos Chiquito she thought of Abel, the young man she met on the bus when going back and forth to work at the grocery store in Bogotá. What if she had made a life with him instead of running off to Aruba the second time? Or Mr. Garcia, the manager of the grocery, if she had explored his desires a bit further, she might have been his wife. Again, she had already made these decisions, and it was far too late to fret over them for her own sake. However, Angela had not encountered these situations. She mentioned a boyfriend, her family, and a life that may be poor but was not yet sordid. What a girl in her position needed most was a profitable stay in Aruba and a lost passport to prevent a hurried return.

It wasn't until she was two blocks past her house that Luz realized she'd gone too far. Thoughts of Angela distracted her as well as scenery that didn't fit with what she'd left early in the morning. She stopped in front of Mrs. Flores' house, where Father Dario said he was going to be paying a visit. Yes, she had passed her own house, which gave her a chuckle. *A first time for everything,* she thought as she went around the block. Then she stopped in front of her driveway, gaping at the wreck that greeted her.

She walked to the door without so much as her purse. With the side wall missing there was no sense using the keys. Peering into the hole she saw through the vacant living room to the second breach in the rear.

"Who goes there?"

Before Luz could answer, Frankie stepped into view.

"It's my fault," he said.

16

A COLD FRONT SWEEPING OFF the continental United States dismissed the storm closest to shore and denied the other one a route toward land. *Tenacious* finally took in her lines, swung away from the dock, and continued on a slow bell for the open sea. In a couple of days, she would be in the Mona Passage, which separated Hispaniola from Puerto Rico.

There was nothing to be done on deck, which gave Tony an opportunity to linger in the wheelhouse. "Remember the girl you took on the fireworks run?" he asked Hernán. "What was her name?"

"Kelly," Hernán replied.

"Yeah, that's it. That was the summer after my arm healed up."

"And the year of my big American history test."

"Right," Tony said.

The deckhand had been on light duty for several months and was helping Hernán with history lessons. The regular school year had ended, but Captain Beck insisted the coursework go on. Naturally, Hernán knew the importance of the Fourth of

July, but he had yet to experienced the outdoor concerts and fireworks that made Philadelphia a destination for people from around the area. Each summer, *Marlena* and her crew took a long tow that left them at sea when the holiday occurred. This year was going to be different. While Tony and Hernán reviewed the American Revolution, several men rigged a nearby barge with fireworks launching equipment. In a couple days, *Marlena* would push the barge to Penn's Landing, where, not long after dark, the fireworks would shoot into the sky.

Not as stern a schoolmaster as Syd or Ramirez, Tony said, "Let's check on those guys."

They exited the galley, walked up to the bow, and propped themselves against the forward bit.

"They put sand down on the deck to support the mortar tubes," Tony explained with a finger pointed toward the barge. "You see all those wires? They connect back to the guy who sets off the rockets."

Hernán followed Tony's finger but not until after his eyes fixed on his scarred arm.

"When I was your age," Tony continued, "I took my first girlfriend to see fireworks just like these."

Of Hernán's friends, Sandeep was the only one to have a girlfriend. He didn't like her but said she was someone his mom and dad wanted him to marry when he was old enough. There was a girl that Hernán liked, and Tony's comments had given him an idea.

That evening, when he and Captain Beck were at home, Hernán asked about the Fourth of July.

"May I take a friend to see the fireworks?"

"Sure," Beck replied. "There's plenty of room. Why not

bring Phil and Sandeep and some others, too? We'll cook some snacks in the galley. Make a picnic of it."

"I don't know."

"Give them a call," Beck suggested.

"I mean I don't know if my friend can go or not."

Beck was at the kitchen table. Beneath his hands sprawled the plans for a massive tugboat, one nearly three times the size of *Marlena*. He put down his pencil and pulled out a chair for his stepson.

"Does this friend have a name?" Beck wanted to know.

"Kelly."

Marlena had a new captain for the fireworks job. He wore a smart white shirt, his best jeans, and a shiny pair of shoes that he'd spent hours polishing. His left hand rested on the throttles, his right on the rudder. He wanted to put his arm around the waist of the girl next to him, but they were in the middle of the Delaware River with lots of other boats around. His was the biggest in sight, which meant he had the right of way. This fact didn't exempt him from being careful. He hoped there weren't any poor bastards out there who might get in his way.

Taking the microphone in his hand, he squeezed the transmit button and said, "Security, security, security. Tug *Marlena* with a barge on the nose approaching the Walt Whitman Bridge. Any concerned traffic, *Marlena* standing by."

"You let him talk on the radio, too?" a woman's voice said from behind him. What she didn't know was that he'd rehearsed all his radio calls earlier in the day.

"Why not?" Captain Beck replied to Mrs. Fisher, who, with her husband, sat on the bench at the rear of the wheelhouse.

Beck leaned against the starboard windowsill. Ahead of them stood Hernán and their daughter, Kelly.

"Thanks for having us along," Mr. Fisher said.

"My pleasure," Beck told him.

"Looks like your boy is going to be a good captain."

At that moment Hernán bumped the rudder control. The barge turned a few degrees to the left. A motorboat sped past, the people aboard waving up at him. Kelly returned the gesture.

"Toy boat," Hernán told her, a hint of contempt in his voice. After all, he was two full stories above them in a craft built of steel as opposed to fiberglass. *Marlena* wasn't fast, but if you knew what you were doing she would dance. Captain Beck was teaching him how to turn her in her own length, walk her sideways to a barge, and back over her own rudder.

To watch the show, Tony had placed two folding chairs on the apron ahead of the wheelhouse. In these sat Hernán and Kelly, cold sodas in opposite hands, which was necessary because their others were clasped together. Just before the show began and at Captain Beck's request, Tony snapped a photo of them.

Hours later, when the fireworks were over, Captain Beck guided the barge to the pier. Hernán and Kelly remained in their chairs. The breeze off the river gave her a chill, and she leaned against the boy who she would later tell her friends almost kissed her. It was on his mind, too, all the way down the river, to the point where he heard the galley door open. Tony was getting his lines ready, and for a second, Hernán contemplated if he could put his lips against Kelly's without being seen. He should have done it sooner, right after the fireworks ended, when the barge was hardly visible for all the smoke. It would have been a scene for a movie. He could have told Sandeep and

Phil what it was like to kiss Kelly Fisher. But what did they care? They preferred video games to girls.

"Good luck with your new boat," Mr. Fisher said to Captain Beck as they shook hands at the end of the night.

The new boat was the one in the plans that had been on the kitchen table. Hernán overheard Beck discussing it with everyone from Syd and Ramirez to strangers who came to see him at home or aboard *Marlena*.

"What are you going to name her?" Mr. Fisher asked.

Hernán almost blurted, "KELLY!" But he knew better than to talk when the captain was speaking, so he remained quiet. To this point, a name had not been mentioned. Like everyone, he anxiously waited the official announcement.

"I don't know," Beck answered much to everyone's disappointment.

The name would come later, two years later, and soon after it did, that boat would separate Hernán from his first and only girlfriend in Philadelphia.

17

"I FORGIVE YOU," Luz said to Frankie on the street outside Hotel Astoria. He told her Luis, Father Dario, and a few neighbors moved her things there. She thanked him for the info, but the choller refused to leave.

"It's not your fault," she admonished him. No one believed what Frankie said, even though he was correct more often than not. Out of patience, she entered the building, a place he wouldn't dare go.

Astoria had no formal lobby but a covered patio with a bar that also served as guest reception. A tall Dutchman named René served drinks, handed out keys, and sometimes served meals cooked by his pal, Harold. This evening they huddled around bottles of beer, keeping an eye on Teo who sat a few feet away with his cell phone open. They all looked up when Luz came through the door.

René was the first to speak, taking a businesslike approach. "Let me show you to your room," he said. The others watched him go, relieved to avoid the awkwardness of the moment.

"It's our finest suite," he joked, ushering Luz through the door.

The wardrobe overflowed with her clothes. Boxes of shoes filled a corner. Her makeup and jewelry sat on a table by the window. A gritty film of concrete dust touched everything. Her first thought was to the bags of new purchases in the trunk of the car. Where was she going to put them?

René asked, "Would you like something to eat?"

"A glass of Baileys," Luz replied.

"Right away."

She sat down on the bed, marveling at the worldly goods stacked about the room. How many pairs of shoes were there? Two dozen? Three? Flats, stilettos, chunky heels, sleek Brazilian pumps, sandals, and slippers. Dresses? Another pile in every configuration: long, short, above the knee, below. Lingerie, too, lace so fine it was like wearing mist. That Father Dario had seen it all was an embarrassment. While he never looked down at her, he'd never been aware of her success, which in any other enterprise would have been laudable. Now he'd seen firsthand the profits of sin.

The box of packages from Captain Beck sat atop the others containing Minchi's ledgers. She pulled one out, opened the flap, and removed a photo. Hernán and a girl sat beneath a row of small windows she recognized as the kind in tugboats. They smiled for the camera, two happy kids on some kind of excursion. She placed the photo on the nightstand and reached into the envelope again. This time, a heavy sheet of paper came out. It bore an embossed crest and a long signature at the bottom. The words were English, which Charlie had translated for her.

"Congratulations!" he said after reading it. "Your son will be educated at a fine school in Pennsylvania."

Overjoyed that Hernán would have a proper education,

she kissed Charlie twice.

Teo tapped the door and entered with her drink. She accepted it, took a sip, and looked at her feet.

"I'd have taken care of Montoya, but Chief Calenda warned me not to do anything."

"Please, don't," Luz said quietly.

The bouncer placed an envelope on the bed beside Luz. She recognized it as the money that normally would have been in Montoya's pocket.

"Open Minchi's on time," instructed Luz. "I'll be there later."

"You sure?"

"Yes."

He suddenly remembered she had fewer than two days left before the bar belonged to someone else. "What about the things in your room at the bar?" he asked.

"I can carry what's mine," she said, downing the last of the drink. She handed him the empty glass, rose off the bed, and steered him toward the door.

Luis leaned on the edge of the veranda with a strong drink of his own and Screwball at his elbow. Of course he was angry, but what could he do? The house belonged to Montoya, who took the opportunity to settle a score.

"No-holds-barred," Charlie had said, "in love, war, and barroom brawls."

"Catfights, too," Screwball might have added by the look on his face. His fighting days ended with the removal of his testicles, something Luis thought would be a good idea for a certain portion of the human population.

Montoya did a fine job of proving his uncle right. And for

what? To strut around town, flush with cash from selling the paintings and proud to have avenged his deported wife? The man had few friends as it was. If the rumor mills were to be believed, he gained no more. And what if he picked up a new enemy?

At the end of Main Street, Luis noticed a police car parked by the unfinished hotel. Another cruiser peeked its nose into the cross alleys between Rodgerstraat and Helfrichstraat. Chief Calenda was probably marking time until he came out to display the full force of the law.

Luis appreciated the effort but doubted there would be any trouble. It wasn't as if Captain Beck was in town. If this had happened during his tenure, there might have been a cataclysm not seen since the main boiler on Unit Six detonated. That event showered San Nicolaas with enough shrapnel to wipe out a battalion. Luckily, it happened during the early hours of a Monday morning. A few stray dogs were hit and numerous roofs were punctured, but there was no loss of life or limb. When Captain Beck slept at Luz's house, few men sought her services at Minchi's for fear he might take offense. No one would have dared to damage her property.

In this context, Luis saw Montoya's clumsiness as a one-off, a random event that wrinkled the fabric of tranquility yet left things generally undisturbed. There was no one to raise the stakes. In a few weeks the rumor mill would find a new bone to chew.

Proof lay on the street below. Luz got out of her car and walked to Minchi's. Frankie nipped her heels, glancing over his shoulders every couple seconds to find no one but a few guys who thought the set of legs ahead of them were worth a look.

"Back to normal," Luis said to Screwball.

The cat yawned, giving his owner a final reason to relax.

Given that bad news travels at the speed of a Caribbean thunderstorm, everyone in Minchi's was aware of what happened to Luz's house. Some of them had seen the trucks leaving town loaded with the walls, though not the paintings themselves because they were shrouded in heavy plastic. Others might have stayed home, but they possessed a warped sense of curiosity that brought them out. And then there were a few regulars who needed no reason other than a dry throat to enter a decent bar. They all got the story, handing it from one to the other, embellishing it along the way until as it stood at midnight, Luz was suing Montoya for everything he had. Given that her lawyer was Herr Diedrik, she might get it, which would make her the owner of two bars on Main Street. If not, well, she still had this one, which was the gold standard of Caribbean brothels, and that was nothing to complain about.

"Here she comes!" someone called out. It turned out to be a false alarm. The only face visible from the front window was Frankie's.

For her part, Luz went around the block, entering the building from the back where the girls loitered on Rembrandtstraat during the day. She climbed the stairs to the common area. A pornographic soundtrack filtered through their doors: music, grunting, sighs, a giggle. After a quick look around, she descended the front steps, entering the bar with no one but Pablo taking notice. He dropped a bottle of beer, which exploded on the tile floor, sending suds in every direction.

"I'll get the mop," he croaked.

The only sound to interrupt the jukebox was a billiard ball falling into the pocket, that and cheers from the guy who made the shot. His pal nudged him to shut up as the lady of the house wove through the crowd. The conversation slowly cranked up, starting with mumbles of, "told you so," and "you owe me," and moving on to "when are those other chicas coming down?"

Luz stooped to pick up the pieces of broken glass, stacking them carefully in her hand before moving to the trash can. As Pablo cleaned the floor and Teo monitored the room, she scanned the ledger. The girls had been busy: Angela upstairs four times, Maria and Julia three each. Judging by the crowd, there were more clients waiting, and not only for them. Garrett Turner sat near the end of the bar.

Because his beer was full and it was bad form to make herself immediately available, Luz waved with her fingers and kept her distance. Another guy caught her attention, someone whose face she recognized but whose name escaped her. Not long ago she would have appraised him as a potential client, evaluating clues to his temperament, habits, and budget. Tonight she resisted what had become second nature. This man might have a king's ransom in his pocket or barely enough to pay for half an hour. It didn't matter because her room upstairs would not be used tonight. Over the past month she winnowed her stable of clients to two: Herr Diedrik and Garrett Turner. After tonight, there would be none.

With practiced grace she dismissed her new suitor by shrugging beneath a weak smile and pulling Teo aside for a discussion.

"Do you know of a house for rent? Something in town?" she began.

"My cousin has an apartment above his garage behind the gas station in Savaneta."

"That's too far."

Three miles separated San Nicolaas from Savaneta, an easy drive on a busy road. There was also a parish church, a decent grocery, and no Zone of Tolerance. But it was a long way from the main gate, where Luz soon expected to see Hernán and Captain Beck.

"If you hear of anyone with a couple of rooms in town, have them call me," Luz finished.

"I'll ask around."

No one but the guy looking to take her upstairs followed Luz's progress from Teo to Garrett Turner. She put one arm around his shoulder, the other on his leg.

"How was your day?" he dared to ask.

"Hectic," she answered.

"Want to go somewhere quiet?"

"*Perfecto.*"

It was the first time Turner offered to take her to his bungalow, although she'd been there before with another manager who spent two years on the island. The previous occupant always drove her past the refinery complex, into Seroe Colorado, all the way to the front door. Turner, on the other hand, took the shortest route, which was more or less a straight line through the refinery. She assumed it was against the rules to allow a non-employee inside. Perhaps it was, and Turner didn't care. He was, after all, second from the top of the managerial ladder.

Luz had only been inside the complex one other time. Watching through the window of his car, she was amazed by the myriad of pipes, tanks, and towers. Simultaneously, a tingle of fear crept over her as she recalled the explosions and fires that occasionally broke out. Men had been maimed and killed within these walls.

She saw a pier illuminated by a row of street lamps. For an instant she flashed back to the night she sent Hernán with Captain Beck. He stood on the wharf, his tugboat behind him with the crew looking on. Hernán left her side, climbed over the rail and up the stairs to the wheelhouse. The scene repeated in her mind, dampening the corner of her eyes. It had been the most difficult moment of her life. She hoped that it had also been her best.

"You could stay here if you wanted," Turner said as he led her into Bungalow 58. "The rent is cheap."

She appreciated his effort to lift her spirits. However, aside of a touch of sadness over what happened at the pier they had passed, she was remarkably upbeat. In fewer than forty-eight hours she would be free of Minchi's. With any luck, she'd be sitting at Charlie's Bar like any other day-tripper when Hernán and Captain Beck showed up.

"I'll keep that in mind," she said.

The furniture was the same. Glancing around the living room, Luz saw that Turner added no personal effects. There were no framed photos, no knickknacks, not even a couple of books. In the kitchen he helped himself to a beer, asking her if she wanted one.

"No," she said from the sliding door that opened onto the patio. Reflections of the refinery flares played over the sea in the distance.

"Look that way," Turner said pointing toward Rodgers Beach.

For his sake she followed the suggestion. The beach was vacant, the access road, too. A string of little fishing boats pointed their noses into the breeze.

"There's going to be more of that soon," Turner said quietly. After taking a swallow of beer he added, "Nothing but hotels from one end of this rock to the other."

There was one place in Savaneta where that would never happen. Herr Diedrik explained to Luz how Charlie had left Samito's land in perpetual trust, never to be sold, never to be developed. As long as the government honored the agreement an acre of paradise would remain untouched.

"I'm going to get out of here before it's too late," said her host.

What did "too late" mean for him, she wondered. He was an educated man, a high-level manager, an American. He had money to hire her without asking the price. A heart attack was the worst thing that could happen to him, though she doubted that's what he was thinking about. Most likely, it was his career that caused him concern. There was no evidence of a family or friends, which went a long way to explain her presence.

In that vein, she pondered what she was going to do starting Thursday morning, when Minchi's belonged to someone else. Unlike Turner, she had no education other than her experience in San Nicolaas. She did have a Dutch passport in her purse, and her profit from the sale of Minchi's would temporarily sustain her. When that ran out she could tap savings accounts in two different banks. Still, she preferred to work, but in what manner? Open a shop like Angela? Finish school? Train for a technical career, maybe in computers like Frazer?

"Is it true what they said about Montoya tearing down your

house?" asked Turner.

"It's his house," clarified Luz.

"Was his house."

Frankie might find the place livable. Anyone other than him would need to rebuild it.

"I heard there was trouble between his wife and you some years ago."

Of all the subjects he might discuss, this was the one he picked, a miserable tale to share on a starry night with a beautiful view of the ocean. She understood his curiosity. He managed things and probably wanted to know what went wrong so he could fix it.

"There was trouble between her and the law," Luz informed him.

"And he blames it on you."

"No."

Her answer caught Turner off guard. "No?" he repeated. "Then why did he tear down the house?"

"To sell the paintings."

The matter-of-fact tone in which she said this made him grin. Her cleverness impressed him as did her ability to stay cool when she had clearly been wronged in a heinous way no matter what the motive.

"He could have given you a day to move out."

"My rent was only paid through Sunday," she said.

A bit of sarcasm came with that reply, which Turner took to mean she understood exactly how Montoya had screwed her. He suddenly felt a new level of respect for Luz. From the start he liked her, found her interesting, a bit aloof at times, but not snobby. This exchange showed him the caliber of person with whom he'd been sleeping.

Raising his bottle, he said in English, "What comes around goes around."

A past client taught her the meaning of that phrase. She preferred to leave it up to God. "Vengeance is mine. So sayeth the Lord," she whispered in Spanish.

"Better, yet," Turner agreed.

How outside events affected her clients fascinated Luz. One time there had been an explosion in the refinery. Several men were killed. Many of the workers came to the brothels where they spent huge sums on girls and alcohol. At the time she needed the money, was grateful for it, and appreciated the desire for worldly pleasure when death might suddenly cheat the living out of it. There were other things, like the loss of a soccer team or a war on the other side of the planet, neither of which affected a man directly. Yet, he would fly into a rage or whoop with joy, buy a round of drinks for strangers or smash his pal's nose with a pool cue. Why? Because the goalie missed the ball? Because a warplane dropped bombs on an army in a country, the name of which he couldn't even pronounce? Long ago she gave up trying to make sense of it, but that didn't stop her from marveling at the effect.

Garrett Turner revealed himself to be the perfect case study. To this point he'd been a perfunctory lover of unremarkable skill. Luz didn't want to take all the credit, however her misfortune was the only event of any significance that could have inspired him to become a sudden Romeo.

Instead of a brief warm-up, he took an inordinate amount of time with foreplay, running his hands along her shoulders, back, and thighs. Then he eased Luz onto her back, gently probing every sensitive spot before positioning himself between her legs. His lips found her breasts and neck until he entered in a gentle glide.

Luz rose to meet him. In light of the difference in his performance, the physical pleasure was not lost on her. She allowed herself the rare satisfaction of forgetting the act was done for money. Before it was over, she vowed this time was the last.

Screwball was getting ornery in his old age. He liked to spill his water bowl during the predawn hours. Luis wasn't sure if this was a plea for a fresh drink after a long night of randy carousing, an offering to the gods, or a malicious joke to demonstrate who was in charge. On the bright side, the clang that woke him also presented an opportunity to relieve his bladder.

Stepping onto the veranda, he swore one more time to find a twenty-pound bowl that a ten-pound cat couldn't topple. Then he heard a muffled pop, followed by glass shattering. His bleary eyes focused on the street below. The sidewalks were empty and nothing seemed out of order. Still, he definitely heard a smash. Taking up Screwball's empty bowl, he figured it was probably a choller rooting through the trash. Inside, he saw it was just past five. Soon the sky would trade the stars for the sun. Why couldn't Screwball wait until that honest hour to play his tricks?

Coming back with a full bowl cooled by several ice cubes, he saw the cat at the edge of the parapet. "Just the way you like it, señor," he said, placing the water in the corner. He paused a moment, awaiting Screwball's approval. Instead, the cat's ears twitched, which drew Luis close.

Every bar on Main Street was closed, as were the others in the Zone of Tolerance. Five o'clock on a Tuesday morning was about as quiet as it got in San Nicolaas. His eyes now clear, Luis scanned the area from east to west. Finding nothing amiss, he gave the cat a pat on the head and headed for the door.

"You're on duty," he said.

18

ANOTHER CONVERSATION WITH MONTOYA was inevitable, but Chief Calenda did not expect it to occur for at least a week. The bar owner stormed into the police station, yelled at everyone in sight, and barged into Calenda's office with a finger drawn and spit dripping off his lip.

"You better put that puta in protective custody," he demanded.

Of course, the unnamed puta was Luz, but she weighed about 110 pounds, stood 5'3" (maybe a little taller in heels), and couldn't have possibly done anything to Montoya worse than raising her middle finger.

"What's the problem?" Calenda inquired.

"Meet me at China Clipper. I'll show you," Montoya replied and bolted from the station as fast as he'd come in.

The destruction Calenda found was no act of wanton violence, nor the casual vandalism typical of drunks, drug addicts, or chollers. It was systematic, from the shattered bottles to the broken furniture to the untouched cash register. The aforementioned malcontents would have sought the money first, taken the booze second, and left the appliances untouched. The door would have been damaged to the point that any passerby would sound the alarm. Only the lock showed the marks of a pry bar so that a casual glance would miss the evidence.

While he expected some sort of retaliation, the chief presumed it would be personal, such as Teo breaking Montoya's nose. Then again, physical assault was a more serious crime than property damage. The culprit understood the difference and behaved accordingly.

Stepping carefully between the broken bottles, he wasted no time searching for clues. He'd spoken with Teo and knew the bouncer was not responsible. Nor did he need fingerprints, surveillance video, or an eyewitness to confirm the perpetrator. The most difficult part was overcoming the disappointment. He would confirm his suspicion with a personal interview and take immediate, appropriate action.

"Someone's going to pay for this," Montoya huffed.

Yes, someone would, Calenda thought, resisting the urge to remind the man he could have avoided the whole miserable affair with a simple phone call to Luz a week before he pulled the walls out of her house.

"What are you going to do about it?" demanded Montoya.

"Apprehend and punish those responsible," answered Calenda, donning his hat and turning for the door.

"What about this mess?"

Thinking of Luz's furniture jumbled in corners, her clothes heaped in the back of Luis' pickup, and her jewelry on the front seat of Father Dario's car, Calenda faced Montoya and said, "If you don't want to lose business, I suggest you start cleaning it up."

Few people confessed their sins to Father Dario. He maintained regular hours for this purpose though frequently found himself alone in the church. After propping open the doors to let in the breeze, he sat in the first pew for a few minutes of prayer. The sound of heels tapping across the floor alerted him to a parishioner's arrival. Eager to provide spiritual guidance in a place filled with all the hazards of modern life, he rose from his seat, turned, and saw Luz waiting at the end of the aisle.

"How are you?" he greeted her.

"Better," she replied.

"Is there anything I can do to help?"

Already he risked Montoya's wrath, the public's disdain, and maybe his soul by gathering her things from that house. He had assistance from Luis and a few of the neighbors, but she heard it was Dario who boldly led them into the fray. What more could he do?

"I want to thank you for ..." she began, then stopped short. All her life she strived for independence, and just when she should have been protected from most any calamity, she found herself indentured by the benevolence of others. No one, least of all Father Dario, sought payment in kind or some other form. Still, a favor had been done, and thereby a debt created. A woman who worked for the telephone company or a gift shop or any regular job could show her appreciation and balance the account by making a donation to pay for flowers on the altar. The only acceptable currency Luz possessed were good manners because her financial resources came from sin. Opening her purse would be a slap to Father Dario's face.

There was something she could do. While it cost her nothing, she hoped it would be worth more to Dario than a new roof on the church.

"Do you have a moment to talk?" she asked.

"Certainly."

They sat in the last row under a rainbow of colors shining down from the stained glass windows.

"My life in San Nicolaas has changed," Luz began.

Dario folded his hands and nodded for her to continue.

"I should have done it sooner. I could have, but my mother became ill, and my sister has been caring for her ever since. Someone has to pay the bills."

This reality he accepted with a slow blink.

"It's no excuse for living the way I did. There were jobs in Colombia. Not a lot of money but probably enough." She stopped for a deep breath. "At the time, I didn't know that and did what I thought was best by staying here."

Good intentions pave the road to hell, thought Dario.

"My son ... he was only six ..." At this point she dropped her head and shuddered. Her grief came without tears, only a few shallow coughs.

Dario gripped her hand when she looked up, assuring her that he was present to listen.

"He's coming back," Luz said in a suddenly powerful voice.

"Saint Michael," Dario put in with a gesture toward her medallion. "Patron saint of mariners."

"The postman told me that."

"You already knew. You've been praying to him for years."

"I have," Luz admitted. Before organizing her things at the Hotel Astoria, she erected a small shrine with a prayer card, candle, and offertory in the name of Saint Michael.

"Your prayers have been answered," Dario said.

He was much closer to God to make that claim than she was. Luz only managed a nod to acknowledge his declaration.

"Tomorrow … I …" she stuttered. "I'm selling Minchi's. I won't be who I am anymore."

"You've always been who you are," Dario said. "What you do has changed."

At that moment, the priest's face resembled her father's when he came home from work. He would enter the house, put his arm around the first child to greet him, and plant a solid kiss on their cheek. As the youngest of the family, she was frequently the beneficiary of his affection. She did the same thing with Hernán during their time together, before she traded that joy for a stake in the gamble for a secure future.

"See you Sunday," Father Dario said.

A stickler for following proper procedure, Calenda spent the day assembling what he needed to resolve Montoya's case. At the same time, he calculated how many turns remained in this stupid game of tit for tat. Montoya started it, then found himself on the receiving end, which meant he was next to move only because he was too arrogant to understand he invited retaliation in the first place. One way to prevent him from continuing the madness was to have his loss paid, and to that end Calenda worked the hardest. He conceded that financial compensation did little to cool an inflamed ego, but would do his best to bring Montoya to heel under worse threats than he issued to Teo.

One thing the chief liked about being in charge of San Nicolaas as opposed to Oranjestaad was the ability to effect immediate and direct solutions to problems. Whenever possible, he avoided the hassle of coordinating with a prosecutor or haggling with a judge. He preferred to deal with the source of the problem, implementing a custom-designed resolution, that, in the end, was probably the best and least expensive way to close the issue. Thankfully, he worked neither in Holland nor America where police work had become convoluted to the point of near impossibility. He felt sorry for his counterparts in those locations, where he sometimes attended training courses.

By midafternoon, Calenda had a check in his pocket and a patrolman driving him through the east side of town. They slowed at the Essoville Rum Shop to look over an unruly bunch before climbing the hill to Esso Heights. These place names had no relevancy given that Esso was long gone. The company sent their people away, tore down most of the houses where they lived, and left the refinery to the next owners. Several held the reins, none of which came close to Esso's spirit.

Among the homes not torn down were the refinery president's and the string that began at the east gate and ended on the cliffs overlooking Baby Beach. Those houses, with their view of the sea, steady breeze, and sturdy construction were among the most sought after on the island. A few had recently changed hands for prices that startled real estate agents and notaries alike.

There was also Bungalow 58. It was here that Calenda's driver stopped. Together, they walked to the front door and knocked.

"Come on in."

Swinging open the door, Calenda saw through the living room all the way to the patio and lawn in the backyard. Seated on a chair with his feet propped on another was Garrett Turner, smoking a cigar and holding a bottle of beer.

"It appears you're expecting me," Calenda said, stepping through the sliding door.

"No sense running from the best cop I ever met," Turner said.

"You're the most disappointing assistant superintendent I ever knew," returned Calenda.

"I do have my shortcomings."

"This is your severance pay," Calenda continued, showing the envelope containing the check he obtained from Turner's boss earlier in the afternoon. "It's made out to Montoya."

"He earned every penny," Turner reflected, stubbing out his cigar. "Not that guys like him ever learn."

"I could say the same about you."

"Until last night, I would have agreed, Chief, but this lesson is bought and paid for."

"In other words, you're taking it with you," Calenda said.

"All the way to Argentina."

To Calenda's surprise, Turner's packed suitcases waited in the bedroom. He stood by while the man ferried them to the trunk of the cruiser. Then, after a cursory look through the house, Turner pulled the front door closed, and Calenda accepted the keys.

"Would you honor the last request of a condemned man?" Turner asked from the backseat.

"Possibly."

"I'd like to say good-bye to Luz."

"You've overestimated my empathy," Calenda said.

"But not your reputation."

"Big brains, opposable thumbs, and no sense at all," Charlie once commented about the human race when he and Luis shared a glass of rum on the veranda.

For the pure entertainment of the exercise, Luis adopted his uncle's habit of monitoring the lack of thinking on the part of others. People like Montoya, the three chicks from the Playa Linda who insisted Herr Koch pour them a sixth round of Brown Ladies, and now Garrett Turner. The guy was assistant superintendent, in charge of hundreds of men, and well paid to have knowledge between his ears. He was the last person Luis expected to have gone berserk in China Clipper last night. If he'd known it was Turner or so much as had an inkling he might stoop to petty crime, he would have sprinted down the street to rescue the man from himself.

The story of Turner's deed came directly from the refinery superintendent's secretary who told it to the delivery guy from Restaurante Pueblito Paisa when he took a stack of boxed lunches in to the main office. Herr Koch got it from him because news like that spread faster than free fireworks on New Year's Eve.

Had a young guy like Teo done it, well, that would have been expected for reasons of youthful indiscretion and corporate loyalty. He'd worked for Luz and no one else his entire adult life. Or, if Samito — who back in the day fell in love with Luz to the point where she was "the one" as in "the only one" — had expressed his anger in a similar fashion, it would be taken as a matter of honor. Finally, someone like Captain Beck would have done Turner one better by laying Montoya flat in the name of justice, a concept he introduced many years ago to a couple of idiots who made a game of attacking Frankie. But Garrett Turner, a mere steady client and otherwise clear thinker, what got into him?

Luis didn't have an answer, but he did have a swarm of Americans downing Balashi like a victorious World Cup soccer team. He was grateful for the business during what was typically a mediocre month. At the same time, there were strange signs among the natives that might spread to certain impaired visitors. As if that were not enough, Father Dario walked in.

Upon seeing a man of the cloth wearing his collar, the Americans quieted down. Dario wasn't put off in the least. He engaged them in conversation, asking where they were from, if they were enjoying their vacation, and if they'd committed any sins they'd like to confess. It was a tack Charlie would have taken, half joking, half serious, but entirely genuine.

Herr Koch turned to Luis, made the sign of the cross, and folded his hands in mock prayer while looking to the ceiling. Luis did the same, absolutely certain that his uncle's spirit had possessed Father Dario's body.

"*¡Hija!*"

Luz held the phone a few inches from her ear as Carlotta rattled along about progress on their house in Barranquilla.

"I drove these men with a whip and a chair. Wait until you see your bathroom. Tile, floor to ceiling. A shower with a bench big enough to take a nap. And lights! Lights by the mirror for a movie star. *Gracias a Dios.* It's finished."

Just in time, Luz thought. There was only one reason to stay in Aruba, and it wasn't to attend the gala for Andrés or to be Inez's companion.

"In a few days the kitchen will be complete, and I'll schedule the furniture to be delivered. Tell me, how are things with you?"

"Busy," answered Luz, avoiding the subject of her recent dislocation. "Andrés arrived, and the island is getting ready for his party."

"Success and its thousand fathers," Carlotta remarked.

"How about the new girl, Angela?"

"She doesn't have any friends but a few good clients."

"You sound tired," Carlotta said next. "Has someone been stealing your sleep?"

Just as Luz sensed Angela's fatigue, so Carlotta was similarly perceptive. Thankfully, she wasn't as inquisitive because Luz was not in the mood to explain what Montoya had done. There was a moment of silence on the line, the kind of break in the conversation when each side knew there was more to talk about but now was not the time.

"Have yourself a good supper and don't forget you'll have a comfortable bed waiting for you and those two sailors," Carlotta said before disconnecting.

If only her mother were so accommodating, Luz would have bought a place in Bogotá instead of Barranquilla. But the relationship with her mother ossified since she married and subsequently divorced Andrés. Even worse, she'd sent Hernán away. His achievement of becoming a maritime officer counted for nothing. Her mother mostly concerned with great-grandchildren, ignoring that living a comfortable suburban life required significant income.

"God will provide," her mother liked to say. And He did, in the form of opportunities to provide for oneself.

19

A QUIET SUPPER is what Carlotta advised, and Luz got it in Astoria's kitchen. René set up a table, Harold prepared the meal, and by request, no one disturbed her. In bits and pieces, her hosts related Turner's story. He called from the airport several times, but Luz instructed René to tell him she was out. As for her cell phone, she let the battery go dead.

She'd spent the entire afternoon organizing her things. While there wasn't sufficient space to hang, drawer, or stack it all, she did put it in order so that she could function until her situation sorted itself out. Before descending the stairs to eat, she called Herr Diedrik on the house phone to confirm their meeting at the notary tomorrow.

"Half past one," he said, then asked about bringing proceedings against Montoya.

She told him it would be a waste of time, a sentiment with which Diedrik concurred while simultaneously admitting he would file suit for the fun of making Montoya hire his own lawyer. *These boys never outgrow the playground,* Luz thought, and reminded him he had more worthy things to do.

"Dessert?" Harold asked as he cleared away her empty plate.

Full from a big meal, she shook her head.

"Coffee? Glass of wine?"

A glass of wine sounded like just the thing. He brought her a chilled glass of white that she carried out of the kitchen toward the stairs. In the lobby, René stood with someone holding a bouquet of roses too large for anything but a wedding or a funeral.

"Put them there," René said, pointing to a low table.

"They're supposed to go directly—"

The door burst open, and Inez rushed in, her purse flapping at her elbow, giving the impression of a one-winged ostrich.

"*¡Luz! ¡Dios mío!*" she squealed, smothering Luz in a hug that sent the wine splashing on the floor. René took the glass, dismissed the florist, and guided the two women toward the stairs before more damage was done.

"This is … crowded," Inez commented as they entered Luz's room. Her eyes darted from the boxes in the corner to the crooked closet doors to the perfectly made bed.

Luz knew what Inez was thinking: *We worked in rooms like this*. It was true, and she wouldn't have been hurt if Inez asked what she was still doing there. She had an answer ready, the same one she gave Father Dario earlier.

"Mr. Kim is completely distraught," Inez said after a loud sigh. "These Asians, Luz, you have no idea. It's all about saving face. They kill themselves over shameful things we Colombians would laugh off as a silly mistake."

For a second, Luz wondered if Mr. Kim, not Turner, had wrecked China Clipper. Realizing that was impossible, even in

San Nicolaas, her brain put the pieces together. It dawned on her how the walls of her house ended up out from under the roof. She let Inez tell her.

"An art broker contacted Mr. Kim. He had two large paintings by Andrés, ones no one knew about. He sent photos." She took the photos from her purse for Luz to examine.

Upon seeing them, Luz finally felt her anger rise. Montoya had entered without her permission to take those photos. It may have been his house, but it had been her home. By the angle of the sun coming through the window he did it during the morning, which meant a Sunday morning, the only time he could be certain she would be out.

"I can see you're upset," Inez was saying. "Please, Mr. Kim knew nothing. Andrés never told him until they met this afternoon to look at them in a warehouse."

"They're not going to be part of the gala?" Luz queried.

"Mr. Kim forbids it! He thinks it will bring bad luck. Oh, how can I explain how superstitious he is?"

"You don't have to."

"He's sitting at the hotel. He and Andrés are in the room brooding like a couple of little boys who got smacked by a nun."

The image gave Luz a reason to chuckle.

"No, Luz, please, this is serious. Mr. Kim has to make it right or he'll be shamed. Right now, he's burning incense, praying to his ancestors to show you a path to forgive him."

There was no need for her to forgive him for something that wasn't his fault, and Luz told Inez as much. She added, "Tell him to make a donation to the animal shelter if it will make him feel better."

"You have to tell him," Inez insisted. "He won't listen to me."

"You're his wife."

It was Inez who laughed this time.

"Isn't there another way?" Luz moaned.

"Another way?" repeated Inez. "He'll cut his belly open with a sword or whatever it is they do. *Por Dios*, what a mess."

The absurd was becoming the ridiculous. More frustrated than angry, Luz glanced at her watch. Teo would be opening Minchi's in a few minutes. Of all the nights, this was not the one to be away from the bar.

"I'll come to the hotel tomorrow afternoon—"

Inez put up a hand, "That's too late."

"This is Aruba, Inez, a place where none of the clocks but the ones in the bars of San Nicolaas keep accurate time. Too late is something only the Americans talk about."

Suddenly irritated, Inez said, "His blood will be on your hands."

Seeing no way out, Luz snatched her keys off the bureau, stomped toward the door, and ordered, "*¡Vamos!*"

It may have been her last night as proprietor of Minchi's, but Luz treated it as any other. Inez refused to wait in the car and tagged along for the inspection of the rooms, common areas, and ledgers. Teo and Pablo took care of the regulars, but only Angela was seated at the bar. Having heard no sign of them above, Luz asked Teo what happened to Julia and Maria.

"Take away," he said. "Two Englishmen staying at the Marriott. I made them show me room keys to be sure."

"The *molta?*"

"They paid three hundred each for the next several nights. The girls took suitcases."

"Florins or dollars?" Luz questioned.

"Dollars, *señora*, dollars. I figured it complicated things for you tomorrow and the extra money would come in handy." He flashed a wily grin, then said, "Angela's afraid of sleeping here with the other two gone."

Luz crossed the room to Angela. Mindful of Inez's gaze, she said quietly, "I'll be back in a few hours."

In the car, Luz anticipated half an hour of commentary from Inez. Surprisingly, nothing was said until they were past the traffic circle at Pos Chiquito.

"I travel most everywhere with Mr. Kim," Inez said. "He has factories in Taiwan, China, Korea, places whose names are written with funny characters. I watch him talking to the managers. They look at me like I'm the pretty second wife, but I'm really the third. The number doesn't matter to them; they think we're good for entertainment, and we are. But you and I know we wouldn't be where we are without some brains."

Luz accepted this compliment in silence. She remembered Inez as a crafty young woman, and tonight, she showed the same qualities in a more refined form.

"You know how to run a business," Inez finished. "If ever you wanted a factory that stamps out computer parts, tonight is the night to ask."

Considering that Samito had promised her a house by the sea and Herr Diedrik a villa in the hills, a factory on the other side of the world held exotic appeal. What Inez, and Mr. Kim for that matter, didn't know was that what Luz wanted cost mere pennies compared to these things. And yet, it was worth more than all of them combined.

"I'll keep that in mind," Luz said at last.

Tragedy became comedy at the Hyatt. Inez entered the suite alone, leaving Luz standing in the hall like a room service waiter with an empty tray. Before this indignity settled in, Andrés came out.

"I can't wait for this to be over," he whispered. "Who thought he would discover those paintings on your walls? I forgot about them myself. It's why I insisted Mr. Kim take me to see them before he paid, in case they were fakes."

"They're not fakes," Luz assured him.

"No, but they're not my best."

Inez peeked out and waved for them to enter. For Luz, it was like stepping into a movie set. Mr. Kim occupied the center of the room, a sentinel guarding the altar positioned against the far wall. Banners with those strange characters Inez mentioned hung dangerously close to sticks of burning incense that filled the room with a sticky fog.

Luz stopped a few feet from Mr. Kim without an inkling of the proper protocol for such a situation. She held back a cough, looked to Inez for guidance, and getting nothing but a shrug, endured what had to be a full minute of silence. Then, Mr. Kim bowed at the waist, keeping his arms fixed at his side as he lowered his head to the point where he was close to toppling onto the carpet. He remained in that position for another interminable pause before rising.

"It is with the deepest regret that I accept all the blame for this tragedy that has befallen you due to my ignorant behavior. Please allow me to compensate you for the damage tenfold that

I may return to a place of honor in your eyes."

It wasn't exactly what he said — because Mr. Kim spoke a form of Spanish worse than the young American workers at the refinery — but it was what Luz understood him to mean. It would have been flip to answer with a simple, "*De nada.*" Thus, Luz fixed a stern look on her face and played her part. She pressed her hands against her skirt, bowed only half as far as her host, and straightened her spine to issue the most convoluted words of concession she could imagine.

"You are a brave man to accept blame for the acts of others and to correct their mistakes at your expense. Be that as it may, any debt owed me was paid in advance when you brought my friends to this island. Please display the paintings at the gala so the rest of the world may enjoy their beauty."

Luz spoke each word deliberately to give him time to grasp the message completely. At first, she thought her effort was wasted, but then Mr. Kim allowed himself the smallest curl at the edge of his lips. As if snapping out of a trance, his eyes flared, and with a single clap of his hands, ended the ceremony.

"*¡Gracias a Dios!*" exclaimed Inez. "Let's celebrate."

The celebration involved karaoke at the beach bar. They found a table surrounded by vacationers singing their hearts out to American pop music. Mr. Kim took his turn, wailing a version of "Sweet Caroline" that could have been a stand-up comedy routine. Inez held her hands over her ears while Luz and Andrés laughed. Mr. Kim didn't mind. The crowd rewarded him with a standing ovation that he greeted with his arms up like a rock star. Was *this* the same man who nearly killed himself earlier in the evening? No one would have recognized one for the other.

They spent the next two hours drinking and singing. The sunburned and drunk people around them cared only about enjoying their vacation. Surely they had their worries, but they left them elsewhere. It was the kind of genuine fun Luz looked forward to.

The end of karaoke gave Luz a signal to leave. Andrés walked with her to the parking lot. Beside the car, he gave her the kind of kiss that preempted bolder acts.

"Will I see you before the gala?" he asked.

For once, she answered directly. "No."

"That makes me sad. You're my favorite model."

If that was the case, there must be more hidden paintings out there because Luz knew of only one sketch Andrés made of her. Captain Beck had it. Still, it was a kind remark.

"*Bon nochi,*" she said, getting behind the wheel.

Frankie recognized Luz at the top of the block. He leapt into the middle of the street and flagged her into the vacant space near the corner by Black & White.

"Midnight and all's well," he said, holding the door open.

It occurred to Luz that Frankie had the amazing ability to know what time it was without wearing a watch. "How do you know?" she asked.

"Carolina Bar closes at midnight, Chief Calenda took Garrett Turner to the airport this afternoon, and I haven't seen Montoya yet." He rubbed his temples for a second, then finished with, "I think that covers it. No, Screwball is on the balcony."

She almost paid for this report with a smile. Instead, she felt for a five florin coin in her purse and gave it to him.

"The winds of fortune blow strong in San Nicolaas," Frankie

announced, "but not for long. I need some sleep, too."

Right or wrong, his statement meant nothing to Luz. The deadline on her business interests was about to arrive. She pushed into the bar where the regular faces stood at their usual places. These were people she saw every day, week after week, month after month. They spent their money, had their fun, and supported her in the process. Some told her jokes or related their problems. Others played pool and never said a word except, "*Uno más*," to ask for another beer. She felt obligated to say good-bye to each of them, though the notion quickly passed.

Out of habit, she scanned the ledger, finding that Angela had been upstairs three times and was currently in her room with a client. She also sold a dozen vinos, a good number for a relatively slow night.

"When Angela comes down, we're going to close," she instructed Teo, then headed for the second floor to gather a few things from her room.

Another wave of nostalgia passed over her as she opened the corner bureau. Fingering the slips hanging within, she decided to give one to each of the girls currently in the bar. From the top drawer she removed an empty perfume bottle. Unscrewing the top, she drew barely a hint of the scent it once contained. She found it during her first stay at Minchi's and again when she returned for the second. One of the many girls who passed through Minchi's had left it behind, and because no one took it, Luz kept it as a good luck charm. For the last time, she put it in her purse.

The sound of Angela and her client drew Luz out to the common area. The client was a middle-aged man who pecked Angela's cheek and skipped down the stairs.

"Put this in with your things," Luz said.

Angela held the slip up to her shoulders.

"Pack what you need for a few nights and meet me downstairs."

A much-relieved Angela scampered out of sight.

Not wanting to tote the other slips to Astoria, Luz used her master key to enter Maria's room in order to leave one for her. Inside, she found no sign that anyone was using the room. Every chica brought a photo from home or a stuffed animal or a trinket that linked them to Colombia. These weren't items that made the trip to a hotel or a client's house.

On a hunch, Luz opened a drawer. It was empty. A cursory search of the room showed nothing but a bottle of shampoo in the corner of the shower. Julia's room was in the same state.

After locking her own room, Luz propped herself against the door and contemplated what her other two employees might be up to. It wasn't likely the Englishmen proposed marriage. Perhaps the chicas heard about the sale of the bar and made a deal to work somewhere else. She resolved to contact Chief Calenda in the morning.

"Ready," Angela said.

Fifteen minutes later, they were sharing the sink at the Hotel Astoria. As she wiped off her makeup, Luz wondered what it would have been like to have a daughter as opposed to a son. Would she have brought her to Aruba the way she had Hernán? Would Captain Beck have taken a girl on his boat the way he did a boy? Thankfully, she didn't have to find out. Was it all part of God's plan? She believed it was.

"Are these books all from Minchi's?" Angela asked, pointing to the boxes stacked against the wall.

"They are," Luz said, studying Angela's face as the young woman tallied the number of Colombianas they represented. What she didn't know, but possibly figured out, was each of them contained an untitled section, the one for Luz herself. There were only two ledgers bearing her name. As for the rest of them, she remained anonymous.

"If I want to have a business," Angela said, "I'll have to learn some bookkeeping."

"Write everything down," Luz told her without adding, "except the things you wish to forget."

Their routine finished, Angela pulled on the slip Luz had given her. The silk was the finest thing ever to touch her skin. She was about to thank her boss again when it occurred to her there was one bed in the room. This being her third week in San Nicolaas, strange behavior was a definite possibility.

In a tone that reminded Angela of her mother, Luz said, "I've always slept on the right, you can have the left. Please turn off your cell phone. We both need the rest."

"*Ningún problema,*" Angela agreed. What she didn't know was this would be the first time Luz slept with another person in her bed since sharing it with Captain Beck.

It wasn't Screwball's bowl hitting the wall that woke Luis. It was the cat himself. He leapt onto the bed, walked up the length of his owner's body, and growled. Cracking open an eye, Luis saw the gazelle's view of the lion, which was only half as frightening as the smell of smoke. In fact, there was smoke in the room, the sight of which launched him and the cat out of bed.

Initially, Luis thought the bar was on fire, but upon reaching the stairs that led down to the backroom, he discovered less smoke and no heat. He bolted through his second-floor apartment in search of the source, only to end up on the veranda with a view of the real problem.

On the street below, a guy with a small flatbed truck spun his wheels. It was the kind with dual tires and the rubber tore at the asphalt, emitting a stream of oily fumes. The vehicle suddenly raced toward the end of Main Street, slid around the corner, and bolted toward the refinery gate. There, it turned again, this time on two wheels, before slamming down and coming to a screeching halt at the pedestrian alley that separated China Clipper from Bongo Bar. Here, the driver carefully backed the truck into the alley, its bed pointed at Minchi's. After gunning the engine, he released the clutch and the truck hurtled through the passage, across Main Street, and buried itself in the bar, sending a shockwave down the street that set off the alarms at the bank and Western Union.

"Someone needs to switch from tequila to Jack Daniel's," Luis said to Screwball.

20

MOST TUGBOATS have a brass builder's plate, usually affixed to a spot in the bow. On it can be found the shipyard's name and a hull number. *Tenacious* had one fitted in a corner of the wheelhouse, just above the console on the port side. Her name, according to tradition, was first fixed upon the keel, where it might never be seen again.

As he turned a new page in the logbook, Hernán wrote "*TENACIOUS*" in the upper left corner the way Captain Beck had taught him. As he printed the capital letters, he thought back to the day the boat got her name. She'd been built under the supervision of Grover Lawrence, and the man was growing impatient with the lack of a proper moniker.

"Please, Beck, I'm begging you to give this boat a name!" cried Lawrence. "I'm sick and tired of calling her Hull 252."

"That's why I'm here," Beck retorted.

"At last, a number gets a name. Lord have mercy!"

The banter between Grover Lawrence, shipyard manager, and Captain Nathan Beck entertained their workers and crews to no end. Lawrence loved building tugboats, and Beck couldn't wait to have one of his own specification. Hull 252 was the order book designation for the pile of steel taking shape in Lawrence's facility, which was located in what had once been the Philadelphia Naval Shipyard. Not far from where legendary battleships like the *New Jersey* were built, a salvage tug that had once been a stack of oversized pages on the kitchen table was fast becoming reality.

"Are you going to tell me?" Lawrence asked.

"Let's have a look first," Beck insisted.

"Young man," Lawrence said, turning all of his attention to Hernán, "promise me we'll have a name on this boat before you have to shave."

Hernán smiled. No, he didn't need a razor yet, but he was outgrowing his jeans, shirts, and shoes faster than the other kids in his class. His shoulders were a little narrow for football, but he would have made a fine baseball player, maybe a third baseman with an arm for setting up double plays. He didn't have time for organized sports because he was spending his afterschool hours becoming a mariner. Nonetheless, he was developing a set of muscles. Together, he and Tony spliced lines, a form of isometric exercise rivaled only by pulling torque wrenches with Syd. Then there was the climbing aboard barges and up ships' ladders. These activities earned him the physique of a budding triathlete that none of his video-gaming pals could ever hope to match.

"Follow me," Grover moaned.

They wound through the office, across a wide concrete lot, and into one of the hangar-sized buildings that fronted the dry dock. Inside they found exactly what Beck sought. A piece of heavy plate steel, cut in the shape of a scimitar, hung from an overhead crane. Several frames protruded from it, and a welder in the process of attaching another worked near the base.

"There's the keel," Lawrence proclaimed as the welder looked up from his work.

"Lend me your chalk," Beck said to him. From his apron, the welder removed a piece of chalk and handed it over.

In block letters Hernán recognized from the beginning of logbook entries, a word took shape.

Finished, Beck returned the chalk. "Lend my son your shield and a rod," he said.

The welder took off his helmet, gave it to Hernán, and fitted his stinger with a fresh electrode.

Syd taught him the rudiments of stick welding. Maintaining the arc was the tricky part. The key was holding the end of the rod at a consistent distance from the puddle of melting steel that would glue two pieces together when it cooled. Hernán kept that in mind as he stepped close to the keel. With a snap of his neck he lowered the shield and a split second later tapped the end of the rod. A miniature bolt of lightning flashed, then continued in a white-hot torrent, releasing a stream of bitter smoke into the air. One by one, he scribed the letters.

T-E-N-A-C-I-O-U-S.

The new boat distracted everyone but Hernán. He was eager to visit the shipyard to see the progress, but he was more concerned with Kelly Fisher and his final exams than whether the engines were properly aligned. His tests were important because the grades would affect his ability to enter a specific high school. Sandeep and Phil had applied to The Hill School, as did Hernán. Already Kelly knew she was attending Baldwin.

About thirty miles separated the two prestigious institutions, a distance not spanned by navigable waters. If Hernán wanted to see Kelly he would have to find a ride. That is, if he was accepted. Hernán took it as a sure bet that he would be. His grades were nearly perfect, and they included advanced coursework. He lacked extracurricular activities, but he'd written several essays about his responsibilities aboard *Marlena* that were glowingly reviewed by his composition teacher prior to submission.

"I had no idea that's what you did on weekends," she said after making a few notations in the margin. "I think you'll stand out. That's what admission committees look for, a young man who demonstrates ability in unique ways."

He already knew there were differences between himself and the boys in his class. Certainly all of them were intelligent, applied themselves, and studied diligently. However, outside of academics, they were kind of goofy. They played silly pranks. They bragged about electronic gadgets that served no useful purpose. They talked about girls as if they were describing aliens.

Hernán possessed an odd sort of dignity that left him slightly apart. No more prominently was this trait displayed than at the floating out ceremony for *Tenacious*. The tug was truly a small ship. Her aggressive bow and trim stern, towing winch and forward capstan, her new paint and brass, perfectly coiled lines and unblemished windows, it all came together in a vessel worthy of the name. She was ready to go into harm's way, to stay there for as long as necessary, to come away from danger a victor not a coward. She was Nathan Beck's boat, but it was her youngest crew member who declared her fit for service.

Bleachers had been erected beside the shipyard's wharf. The workers, some of their family members, as well as several dignitaries including the mayor of Philadelphia, took seats. Captain Beck, Hernán, and Grover Lawrence sat in chairs closer to the water. The rest of the crew lined the rail of the boat.

The mayor spoke first, praising the tradesmen, thanking Beck for building his magnificent boat locally, and wishing him the best of luck. The chaplain from the Seaman's Church Institute went next. He gave a short speech, after which he blessed *Tenacious* and her crew. When he finished, there was but one thing left to do.

A set of stairs led to the bow. Up these went Hernán, Beck, and Lawrence. At the top was a bottle of champagne resting on the rail. Before reaching for it, Hernán faced Lawrence and stuck out his hand as if he were congratulating the man for a job well done.

Lawrence narrowed his eyes, studying this son of his customer, then looked up at Beck's company flag, noting the single white star in the middle of a blue field. Nothing aboard *Tenacious* lacked a purpose, and he wondered about the significance of that star. Did it represent a man in the making or someone else? A passage from the *Book of Proverbs* came to him in that moment.

"Train up a child in the way he should go: And when he is old, he will not depart from it."

It occurred to Lawrence that nothing would stop this boy from being a captain, master, and owner. As the thought passed through his mind, he watched Hernán smash a bottle of Dom Pérignon against the hull.

Too many cases of frozen food arrived at the dock. They cascaded from the back of a refrigerated truck into the galley via a human chain that included *Tenacious'* new crewmen. There were additional deckhands, a third engineer, a cook, and a second mate. During a shakedown cruise, these men filled places that didn't exist aboard *Marlena*.

By the time the last frosty box was stowed, another truck waited to be unloaded. This one contained fresh fruit, vegetables, and meat, the kind of provisions first consumed after a boat departed. Hernán managed to escape from his spot, working his way up to the wheelhouse.

The first place he looked was the chart table. It was empty. Next, he switched on the plotter, only to find no course programmed into its memory. Descending the companionway, he searched the bunkrooms for Captain Wilkie. Not finding him, Hernán went looking for his stepfather.

All that food meant one thing: a long trip. It wasn't a short hop to Boston or a week-long tow to New Orleans. The freezers and pantry overflowed with enough grub to put them far away from the opportunity to resupply. He should have guessed this when they stopped at the fuel dock and Syd made sure every tank was topped off. He would have, too, but he'd been spending a lot of time with Kelly. His stepfather treated them to dinners out, during which he sat at a table with her parents while Kelly and Hernán had a place to themselves on the other side of the room. There were movie nights and a trip to the Philadelphia Zoo, all with her parents or Beck a comfortable distance away.

Maybe it's a round-trip to Puerto Rico, Hernán thought, *or towing a mothballed Navy destroyer to Mobile, Alabama, for a refit.* He wouldn't mind a couple of weeks to settle in at Hill. After that, however, he wanted to be aboard *Tenacious* as much as possible.

"I checked the bus schedules," Hernán had told Kelly when they were strolling past the polar bears at the zoo. "It's not easy, but I can get to the dock on Friday night and back to school on Sunday." This solution he discovered soon after receiving his acceptance letter to Hill.

"Why not come visit me at Baldwin?" suggested Kelly. "Phil has a cousin who lives nearby. You could stay with him."

Her reply had forced him to ponder an impossible schedule. He couldn't attend Hill, sail with *Tenacious*, and spend any amount of time with her. Among all his equipment and supplies, the tugboat didn't possess a helicopter to shuttle him around.

Not finding either Captain Wilkie or his stepfather, Hernán returned to the wheelhouse. From the starboard windows he watched a blue sedan roll to a stop beside the last provision truck. Captain Beck stepped from behind the truck to greet the car's driver, Mr. Fisher. Hernán didn't wait another second, nor did he hurry to the car. He knew Kelly was in it, probably sitting in the backseat. He took his time, following the hallways through each level, remaining inside the boat until finally exiting onto the stern via the last watertight door on the weather deck.

"Kelly's come to see you," Beck said cheerfully as Hernán passed him.

Marching forward without meeting his stepfather's eyes, he reached for the door handle. Too late he realized he should have gone for the driver's seat. After a snort, he silently admitted he might have been able to make an escape had he paid closer attention to those driving games Sandeep and Phil liked so much.

The thought was as stupid as the imaginary world displayed on Phil's giant TV.

He sat down next to Kelly, who never looked happier. She waited until her father exited the car, then took Hernán's hand in both of hers and kissed his cheek.

"I came to invite you to a party on Saturday night," she said.

"A party?" he queried, thinking that he misread the situation. His stepfather had told him they were going somewhere Saturday but withheld the details.

"It's for all of us going away to school," Kelly said. "My parents are hosting. They already have the tent set up in the backyard."

"Sounds like fun," Hernán put in. He looked across the dock at *Tenacious*. Tony supervised the other deckhands as they stretched lines for inspection.

"What's the matter?" Kelly asked. "You don't sound excited."

He'd been thrilled to be accepted to Hill. Upon opening the letter and feeling the heavy paper with its embossed seal, he shouted loud enough to be heard on the street. He kept a copy in the drawer beneath his bunk. The original Captain Beck had sent to his mother. He figured he would spend less time on the river but never considered he might have to live permanently ashore.

"Phil and Sandeep are making all kinds of plans," Kelly was saying. "They don't even know what their dorm room looks like and already they're out buying stuff."

Hernán flashed back to his first days with his pals. They looked up to him, his adventures on a tugboat, his stepdad, the captain. Now it was different. They were bound for an undertaking of their own, and this time Hernán wouldn't be there. Wherever *Tenacious* was going, he would be aboard. The problem was how to tell Kelly.

"I won't be there Saturday," he said abruptly.

"Why not?"

Hernán did not emerge from his room until after eleven that night. He went to the stern where he crawled onto the towing bit. It was broad and wide enough for him to lie down. He must have dozed off because when next he opened his eyes Captain Beck was there.

"Mr. Fisher called. Kelly's been crying all afternoon. She told him you're—"

"Where are we going?" Hernán interrupted.

Stunned at being cut off, Beck shifted his stance. Then he said, "*Tenacious* is bound for Norfolk, where there's a dead ship to be towed to the breakers in India."

An old ship, bound for India to be scrapped, as opposed to the Hill School, was Hernán's next step toward the future. "I'm not going to Hill," he said.

"You worked hard for that opportunity," Beck countered. "If you do well, you can go to any college you want. You can pick your profession and make a great life for yourself."

Sliding off the bit, Hernán said, "I already have one." He'd seen his stepfather do extraordinary things, including carry Tony, unconscious and bleeding, up a ladder, but he'd never seen the man speechless. There he stood, his radio hanging from his hip, both hands flexing at his side, and his eyes staring blankly past the rail.

Finally, Beck said, "Do you want to give up one of the best

prep schools in the country? Are you telling me you'd rather leave Kelly and your pals and drag a ship across the ocean?"

"That's what we do," Hernán replied.

Water sloshed between *Tenacious* and the pier. The row of shackles hanging under the towing bit clanked together like out-of-tune bells. Captain Beck stepped closer to the fast-growing boy who spoke with remarkable confidence.

Hernán felt his stepfather's hand on his shoulder, but it was the weight of his gaze that pressed down on him. He sensed he had simultaneously disobeyed and pleased the man. While this was true, it was not the only reason he told Kelly he was leaving with *Tenacious*. He'd been uprooted from Colombia and Aruba, only to form a tighter bond with a group of strangers than he ever had with his relatives. Tony, Ramirez, Syd, and Captain Wilkie were cousins, brothers, and uncles. He wasn't ready to trade their care and affection for something less certain. Not yet.

"It's not what we do," Beck said in a mild tone, "it's who we are."

Who we are, Hernán thought. *We are people who leave our friends and regular families for places unseen or unknown.* Nothing could have better prepared him for this life than leaving his mother the way he had.

Meeting his stepfather's eyes, he said, "We better get underway."

Years later, Hernán was still underway, this time to a place he could barely remember yet never forgot. Having finished with the logbook, he pushed it to the side of the chart table. Tony came in with his rags to clean the windows.

Hernán focused his attention on the console. All the gauges indicated proper temperatures, pressures, and speeds. His eyes scanned past them, stopping at the builder's plate. He polished it regularly, along with the compass housing and the bell. Ever fastidious, Tony ran his rag across the plate, wiping off nothing more offensive than a speck of dust.

"I always liked the name of this boat," he said.

21

CHIEF CALENDA MET the building inspector, a young Dutchman named Arjan Herzog, on the sidewalk in front of Charlie's. They made small talk about Herzog's training in Holland until the towing company packed up their equipment. Neither of them had any doubts about what happened. Yes, the truck was stolen from a construction site. No, the driver was not found among the wreckage, which was amazingly light considering the condition of the building. Surely Herzog's report would recommend extensive repairs before the building could be reoccupied.

What was done mattered much less to Calenda than who did it. He needed no further clues than those he already had, and in this instance, he abandoned his regular intuition for science. A technician collected a blood sample from a few dried splotches on Minchi's floor less than a meter from where the truck stopped. The same technician found no fingerprints on the steering wheel, the shift lever, or the door handle. She did obtain several very distinct ones from a bottle on the truck's floor. This evidence Calenda would ultimately bring to bear on the culprit when the time was right.

Yesterday, after leaving Garrett Turner in the custody of immigration officials at the airport, he paid a personal visit to Montoya.

"This puts an end to it," Calenda said, handing over the check that should have been Turner's severance pay.

Montoya opened the envelope, examined the check closely, and said, "What about *her*?"

"She had nothing to do with what Turner did," Calenda replied. "Cash the check, fix your bar, and move on."

"Just like the last time," Montoya spat.

"You know Marcela broke the law with no help from Luz. Be glad you've made your money. Find a worthy cause to spend it on."

Clearly, Montoya had not followed orders, though he was quick to say he had. His alibi placed him in a poker tournament at the Stellaris Casino, then at a rum shop in Noord, and finally at a Chinese bar in Paradera. There, he supposedly got into an argument with a friend about the Little League World Series. The friend shoved him off his stool. Impact with the floor caused facial bruises and a small cut. He and the friend made up, as friends often do after such incidents.

"Ask the bartender if you don't believe me."

"I believe you," Calenda told him at the end of the interview. That didn't mean Montoya hadn't driven the truck backward through Minchi's front wall. He was lucky none of the girls were present, which was another curious matter Calenda was in the process of pinning down.

"I'll get started now," Herzog said, ducking behind the barriers set up to keep pedestrians at a safe distance.

In a single week, Luz descended from San Nicolaas royalty to island pariah. Main Street's business owners and employees gawked at the remains of her bar. They cast wary glances at China Clipper, then at Minchi's, then at each other, indicating they expected things to escalate sooner or later. She knew they didn't blame her for what happened. Still, they had their superstitions, and bad luck in whatever form was to be shunned.

Luz and Angela waited for Herr Diedrik in the corner booth at Charlie's Bar. Herr Koch served them Coca-Cola, adding a dish of snacks in case they were hungry. They'd already spoken with Chief Calenda. Angela gave him a description of the men who took Maria and Julia to the Marriott. Luz accepted his assurances of a thorough investigation and the prompt administration of justice.

"Difficult times," Herr Diedrik said as he slid into the booth. "But there is a silver lining."

At this point, Luz politely asked Angela to wait at the bar.

"Sanchez is still interested in the deal," Diedrik continued. "Of course, now he is buying damaged goods so the price is greatly reduced."

"Is it enough to cover what remains of the mortgage?" Luz asked.

Diedrik drew a few sheets from his jacket, then replied, "Barely." He laid the papers flat on the table.

Seeing the numbers, Luz immediately calculated how long she could live on her savings.

"There may be proceeds from the insurance company," Diedrik put in. "Given the circumstances, their determination will take time."

"I understand," Luz said. She seethed over the predicament Garrett Turner left her. He was probably sitting in a place more comfortable than Bungalow 58, thinking he had done her a favor.

It left her wondering about her own choices. Should she have asked Mr. Kim for a new house? Should she file suit against Montoya? Should she leave this island once and for all?

The voice of reason spoke to her through Diedrik. "Take some time to make a decision." He was speaking of the Sanchez counter offer, but he moved on to a generous proposal of his own. "You're welcome to stay in my villa. Bring Angela if you're lonely."

In light of her financial position, this was particularly appealing. However, she wanted to be close to San Nicolaas, and San Fuego was too far. In a few days, Hernán and Captain Beck would be tying their boat to one of the docks at the refinery. Hopefully, the port captain would be able to tell her in advance. If not, she didn't want to be lounging in the pool while someone told them about the feud that ricocheted across Main Street.

"I'm comfortable at Astoria," she said.

"The pool is in San Fuego whenever you want it." He kissed her cheek, promised to call her with an update, and left his seat empty for Angela's return.

Sliding out of the booth, Luz said to her one employee, "It's time to find you a new place to work."

Just as they left through the side door, Luis exited the kitchen. He followed their progress until they were out of sight.

"I know what you're thinking," Herr Koch said.

"That I need a date for the gala?" Luis replied without shifting his eyes from the doorway.

After a chuckle, Koch warned, "It'll hurt if you do more than dance."

Black & White Bar stood across an alley and three doors down from what remained of Minchi's. José enjoyed being a bartender, didn't mind working as a maintenance man, and tolerated janitorial duty. He was also the proprietor and thereby empowered to make all operational decisions, including the hiring of personnel.

Of the four rooms behind Black & White, only two were occupied, so when Luz brought Angela to the bar, José promptly took her on. He was happy to increase his rental income and thrilled to have three nights paid in advance. Angela's good looks didn't hurt either. There was a stool just inside the door where her presence would be a better advertisement than a full page in the *Diario*. That being the case, he would like to have Luz herself, if not in one of the rooms, behind the bar. He lacked the audacity to pose the offer so soon after a tragedy. Still, it was on his mind as a task for the future.

"What about the other two girls," he asked Luz. They had just finished helping Angela move into her new room, where she remained to put away clothing Luz had given her. The building inspector wouldn't allow anyone into Minchi's until an engineer determined it was safe.

"Chief Calenda is dealing with them," Luz answered.

"I could use one more," José muttered.

After recommending Maria and warning him about Julia, Luz shrugged and said, "You can make up your own mind."

"I think I'll let them find another bar." He was a little sad to pick up some of Minchi's business, but such was life in a boomtown possibly going bust. "There were some Americans in town," he went on. "Important types."

"They spend the most," Luz reflected.

"This bunch didn't stay long. They looked around the refinery and left. Have you heard anything?"

From the purchasing agent to Garrett Turner, Diedrik to Frankie, everyone in San Nicolaas believed a project of some sort was in the works.

"*Nunca se sabe*," Luz said. By the time her denial faded, Angela came from the back to join them.

"I'm going to the botica to buy a few things," Angela said but didn't take another step.

Luz believed she'd grown too close to Angela. The night before she'd been thinking about a daughter, and she'd also felt guilty about steering the girl toward a potentially unintentional future. These were dangerous emotions, ones that weighed too much for her to carry. She wasn't going to abandon Angela, but nor would she dabble in another person's fate.

"Botica San Nicolaas has the best prices on hair products," Luz advised. She felt Angela's uneasiness but resisted the temptation to comfort her by spending the rest of the day helping her settle in. Already, Luz had outfitted her wardrobe and allowed her to stay at the Astoria. It wasn't easy to dismiss her, but continuing that level of generosity would only spoil the girl. If Angela wanted to run a business of her own, she would have to learn how to function independently.

"*Gracias, señora*," Angela said and left the room.

Luz took her sunglasses from her purse and wished José good luck.

"Come have a drink one night," he said. "On the house."

Stepping outside, Luz saw Minchi's boarded-up façade. Her initial reaction was to walk around the block so as to avoid it. Then she chastised herself for being childish. What was good for Angela was good for herself. She strode forward, head up and shoulders back, confidently greeting the people on Main

Street the way she always had.

Minutes later, she was able to put her feet up and relax, which she did in her room at Astoria. She stared at the photo of Hernán side by side with his girlfriend. As much emotion as she felt for her son, she also thought of the girl. Was she still in contact with Hernán? Did she go to the same school as him? What kind of job did she have?

Turning the photo over, she read, "Hernán and Kelly, 4th of July."

She wondered if her son currently had a woman in his life. Part of her hoped so, and yet another part longed for him to wait. Luz considered herself a good judge of character. Fifteen years contending with girls at Minchi's, plus the tutelage of Carlotta, Charlie, and Herr Diedrik taught her how to gauge people. In her heart, she wanted him to marry a Colombian girl, which wasn't fair. He should be free to choose his own mate. Nonetheless, there was an ample supply of pleasant, caring, and devoted young women from the nation of his birth.

"I've met a few," she said to herself, setting the photo aside.

Taking up her phone, Luz called Herr Diedrik. "Can we meet Sanchez at the notary tomorrow?" she asked.

22

THE MONA PASSAGE, which separates the islands of Hispañiola and Puerto Rico, is ten times wider than the Strait of Gibraltar, which divides two continents. With the storm behind her, *Tenacious* maintained cruise speed through the passage even as her captain was thinking about the more narrow strait. He'd never set foot in British-controlled Gibraltar, but he had been to the part of southern Spain bordering it. He recalled the industrial city of Algeciras where they laid up for supplies and repairs. More memorable was Tarifa, to which he'd driven a rented van out of pure curiosity.

He had taken a winding highway with peeking views across the strait. Africa was over there, but he didn't care. He was interested in the Spanish side of that avenue of water. It was as *Tenacious* passed Tarifa that Hernán observed the windsurfers. Using a pair of powerful binoculars, he watched them racing along the coast, some jumping off wave tops or doing complete flips. As much as he was impressed by their ability, he was reminded of Aruba, where, as a boy, he'd seen windsurfers enjoying perfect conditions for the sport.

There were repairs to be made over the next two weeks, and Captain Beck worked out a rotating schedule to give the crew time to relax ashore. Tony wanted to see a bullfight in Seville and convinced a bunch of others to go with him. Hernán, who spent most of his waking hours with these men, decided to take advantage of a few days alone.

He got stuck with the van because Tony needed all the seats in the sedan. The van had only two up front, the back being open for the supplies and provisions that were shuttled to *Tenacious*. Only drivers over twenty-one were supposed to be at the wheel, but Captain Wilkie solved the problem. He rode with Hernán as far as the center of Algeciras before leaving the vehicle to his 17-year-old mate.

"Go find her," he said, getting out. "Just don't get arrested or miss the boat."

Since leaving Philadelphia and Kelly Fisher, Hernán found himself spending more time with Wilkie than Captain Beck. It was a natural fit. Wilkie treated him more like a grandson than a crew member. With another group this situation would have seriously disrupted morale. However, many of them had watched Hernán grow up. Those who didn't quickly saw that he pulled his weight as much as anyone. He was a damn good boat handler, too, and that counted for more than who his stepfather was.

His outings with Wilkie taught Hernán the ways of sailors reared before the computer age.

"I got nothing against gadgets," the man said, "but you can't spill a drink on 'em, you can't kiss 'em, you can't hardly read the book that tells you what they do."

Hernán was good at reading manuals and teaching Wilkie

how to use the sophisticated devices in the wheelhouse.

"Now let me show you something," Wilkie would say when they pulled into port. It didn't matter if it was Oslo or Aberdeen, Sydney or Hong Kong, San Diego or Montevideo, he found a friendly bar with decent whiskey. He might not have had the language skills of Hernán, but Wilkie's gregarious personality set him among instant friends. He downed three or four strong drinks before settling into a comfortable reverie of exchanging stories with his new acquaintances.

"Forget the barmaids and waitresses," Wilkie advised each time they entered a tavern. "Every man with salt on his breath tries to drag his line across them. You want to find the girl around the corner. She's working at the bakery, in an office, a factory. To her, you're something special."

To that end, Wilkie set a fine example. In Bremerhaven, Germany, they were sent to collect cash to disburse to the crew. Wilkie and Hernán, dressed in their best white shirts and polished shoes, arrived at the bank less than an hour before it closed. Wilkie made excuses to the teller that he needed to speak with a manager. Of course, the manager couldn't see him right away, which was exactly the way Wilkie wanted it. He chatted with the secretary, a woman about his age. Upon learning that she'd been divorced, he chimed in that it had been a long time since he had a home-cooked meal. To Hernán's amazement, she offered to make him one at her house. She had a niece, too, a girl named Trudi.

That kind of fun repeated with varying degrees of success around the world. Hernán learned the social skills of a diplomat, picking up pieces of various languages and customs. His manners, physique, and bearing belonged to a man rather than a teenager.

"If you kiss and tell, you're betraying a woman who doesn't deserve it," Wilkie said as they walked to the dock in Bremerhaven. "She's done you a favor, and you owe her one in return."

Hernán had kissed Trudi but kept his hands mostly to himself. Later, he would experience many of the things discussed on the foredeck where Tony and the deckhands recounted their tales of sexual conquest. These stories were titillating but lacked any depth. They might have been describing a pack of dogs, which could be comical, depraved, or scientifically fascinating. It was never romantic and for lack of that angle, Hernán found them boring, like flipping through the same pornographic magazine for the twentieth time.

In Tarifa, he locked the van, crossed the road, and worked his way to a group of low huts where people sat watching the surfers. The wind shouted across the beach, another similarity to Aruba. The sand was darker, though, and the sea climbed to a four-foot chop as opposed to Aruba's leeward calm.

He noticed several surfers chasing each other. They seemed to be in some sort of competition, but it was difficult to discern. Then one of them with an orange sail cut in front of another who was about to pass him. They both went down. Instinctively, Hernán was on his feet, moving toward the water's edge.

"Don't worry," one of the other observers said.

Both surfers clambered onto their boards and caught the breeze again. The smaller one cut away from the guy with the orange sail, raising a middle finger to make the point. Hernán didn't need binoculars to recognize a female shape connected to that finger. She ran onto the beach, dismounted, and dragged her rig out of the sea. On the dry sand, she folded her wetsuit down to the waist, revealing a bikini.

"Can I help with the board?" Hernán said approaching her.

"Where'd you learn Spanish?" she replied.

"First in Colombia, then in an American school from a Mexican guy."

"It sounds like it," she said, shaking out her hair.

The guy with the orange board skated close enough to shore for them to hear his taunting cackle. She gave him the finger a second time.

"Your friend?" Hernán asked.

"My nemesis."

"You take this seriously."

"Competitively."

"That's no reason to crash into each other," Hernán reflected.

"Are you trying to defend my honor, Mr. Colombia-America-Mexico?"

"I'm trying to make a friend."

"Good. I need a ride to town."

Angled across the cargo bay, her board fit in the van. In the process of dismantling the sail he learned her name was Teresa, she was twenty-three and lived in an attic apartment in the middle of Tarifa. She wanted to know his story, how he came to have the oddest Spanish accent she ever heard. He told her the short version.

"This big tugboat of yours is in Algeciras. What are you do-ing in Tarifa?" she asked.

"First, it's not my boat. It's my stepfather's. Second, when we were coming into the strait, I was watching the windsurfers and thought it would be fun to see them up close."

"First, like father, like son," she countered, mimicking his tone. "Second, you said you were looking for a friend."

"I did," he admitted.

"Did I tell you I have a black belt in karate?" she said next.

"No."

"That's for boys who try to be more than friends."

He gave her the point as they rolled into town, her directing him to a shop that sold windsurfing gear. There, they unloaded her equipment. She had a heated discussion with the manager, something about a problem with the sail.

Hernán stayed out of it until he heard her say, "And if you see Enrique, tell him I'm going to send my Colombian-American-Mexican boyfriend to break his nose."

The manager looked at Hernán, who raised his fist on cue.

"*Vamos*," Teresa said, tugging his arm. "I'm hungry."

She ate as much as two deckhands, mowing down a big salad and a grilled chop with fried potatoes. According to Teresa, cold water and straining with the sail burned plenty of calories. Her body proved it. She also talked about an upcoming contest that she intended to win.

"Have you ever been to Aruba?" Hernán inquired. "It's famous for windsurfing."

"Not yet," she said. "Maybe next year for the annual tournament. What about you?"

"My mother lives there."

Teresa held her fork in midair. "You left that part out of your story, and if she's there, you're a long way from home."

His home floated in twenty-two feet of water, had fifteen other residents including a full-time cook, and the scenery around it changed nearly every day. Teresa said she wanted to see it. They drove back toward Algeciras to a scenic overlook where tourists on their way to Gibraltar paused to look across the bay at the giant rock protruding from the sea. On the near side was industrial Algeciras and from this spot he pointed to *Tenacious* moored along the wharf.

"That's a ship," Teresa said.

"Almost," Hernán reflected.

"Let's go back."

"I thought you wanted to see the boat."

"I saw it. I know you're not lying. That's what I really wanted to find out."

He laughed, got behind the wheel, and once more wound through the passes of southern Spain.

Wetsuits, regular clothes, and sport magazines littered her apartment. Upon entering, Hernán stopped dead, afraid he might step on something important. Teresa forged ahead, tossing things in all directions to make a clear path. She stopped at the foot of a ladder pointing up to the sleeping loft. There, she dropped her shorts, climbed up, and called for him to follow.

"What about the karate?" he asked from below.

"Let me show you the moves that feel good."

It wasn't a fight, but it was exhausting physical sex. Teresa liked to be in control. She spent most of the time atop Hernán, pressing him into the thin mattress, dangling her hair over his chest. As quickly as it started, it ended. She twisted off, propped herself against the wall, and tilted her head to the ceiling.

"How old are you?" she asked, catching her breath.

He almost replied that he was twenty-one, but reconsidered. What would be the point of lying to her?

"Seventeen," he said.

"I give you permission to lie to my mother when we meet her tomorrow."

"Your mother?"

She fell over laughing. "You're a serious boy," she said. "Let's have a nap before supper."

The meal was a formal contrast to Teresa's casual lifestyle. They walked to another part of town where the restaurants were expensive and populated by tourists who bore no semblance to windsurfing aficionados. Among her jumbled possessions Teresa found an appropriate dress, shoes, and a silver necklace. With her hair up and Hernán across the table, she looked every bit the older sister. Yet, he was not a kid brother. The waiters deferred to him like he was the patriarch of the family. For all they knew, he was the woman's younger sibling but had inherited the title.

"Where is your next stop?" Teresa wanted to know.

"My stepfather thinks there's going to be another war in the Middle East," Hernán began.

"I read the newspapers," she put in. "It will be the third war in thirty years if Iran attacks Iraq. You have cannons on that boat?"

"No. There will be escort and salvage work," he clarified.

"You could be killed."

"There are lots of ways to die at sea."

She chewed an olive while pondering that comment. "You're not afraid?"

"I'm not a coward."

After the waiter brought their next dish, she told him a story about how she'd let herself stray too far from shore once. "I was at least a mile from the beach," she said. "The wind was rising, and it was nearly impossible to tack. I thought to myself, 'You were stupid. You're going to die.' Part of me wanted to drop the sail and drift, just give up and discover what fate God had planned for me. But suicide is a sin. I kept trying to get back with no luck. Still, I'm here today to tell you I lived."

"How?"

"A fisherman, *gracias a Dios*. He had a problem with his nets and was returning to port early. I must admit that I was frightened."

"Not enough to give up the sport."

"I do what I love," she countered.

Dishes of olives, grilled vegetables, plates of undercooked red meat, and two bottles of wine passed over the table in the course of the meal. By the time they finished, it was well past two in the morning. Unlike Hernán, who was used to the midnight watch, Teresa was exhausted. Rather than climb the ladder to her loft, she cleared the couch and slept there, taking only the time to pull off her dress. Hernán made himself comfortable on a chair, where he sat thinking about what he loved.

Among her many scattered possessions, Teresa did not have a checkbook, the keys to a car, or a television. Nor did she want them. She followed the rhythm of her sport, chasing competitions and working odd jobs in between. It wouldn't last forever, but for as long as it did, she intended to make the most of it.

They separated at the beach where they met. He helped her with the board and sail, going so far as to pull up the zipper on her wetsuit.

"See you in Aruba," she said after a lingering kiss. She waded into the sea and was soon one of dozens skimming across the surface.

Hernán did not miss the boat. He was several hours early, which gave him plenty of time to pack. Unlike Teresa, he had a checkbook, a credit card, too. He also possessed a valid passport. Euros filled his wallet, dollars bulged an envelope in his bag, and his miscellaneous currency from around the world he left in a jar.

The biggest dilemma he faced was how to tell his shipmates good-bye. Unlike the boy who left Philadelphia clinging to his adoptive family, he was close to being his own man. At a minimum, he owed them his thanks. To shove off without properly acknowledging them was beneath his character. Just the same, he wanted to be away from *Tenacious* as rapidly as he could. He decided to do his best with one man, Captain Wilkie. It was Wilkie who would understand better than anyone. He could convey the message to the others.

In the wheelhouse, Hernán found Wilkie updating the logbook.

"Just tell me her name, nothing more," Wilkie greeted him without looking up.

"Teresa."

"You're back early. Did she throw you out?"

This remark Hernán absorbed without reaction. He glanced out the window where Tony and the deckhands were rinsing down the forward bulwarks.

"If you can't look at me, it must be something serious," Wilkie said next. "You didn't get married, did you?"

"No," Hernán replied. "I'm leaving the boat."

"Hmmm."

"I want to live my life."

Wilkie heaved himself into the captain's chair. "That makes sense," he said. "Where are you going?"

"I don't know," Hernán answered, then quickly corrected himself. "First, I'm going to visit my mother. After that, I'm not sure."

"Okay. One step at a time."

"With the skills I have I can get a job anywhere," Hernán said.

Wilkie scratched his chin. "You have everything it takes to be a great captain. As good or better than your stepfather."

Angry at the comparison, Hernán snapped, "He brought me to this life."

"And you lived up to it. You welded the name on the keel of this boat."

"It wasn't the name I picked."

"Yeah? What would you have called her?"

Hernán wasn't about to admit that he wanted to put Kelly's name on such a stout craft. Hers wasn't a bad name for a boat, but it was a crush he had on her, the first taste of feminine charm that sent him reeling. No, he wasn't here to confess.

"I was a boy then," Hernán murmured.

Several seconds passed until Wilkie said evenly, "In some ways, you're still a boy."

Hearing this from a man he trusted devastated Hernán. His initial rage was displaced by a deep ache. He expected Wilkie to understand, to wish him luck and send him on his way.

"You're leaving your boat, your crew, the men who raised you, and until I tell them what you're up to, they're expecting one day you'll sit in this chair and give the orders. It's a damn shame to see a job left three-quarters finished."

"What do you mean by that?"

"Stand up straight when you hear this because I'll not repeat myself."

Was Wilkie angry or sad? Hernán couldn't tell, but he did as he was told, facing the man with squared shoulders, his hand resting on the console. "Before we left Aruba, I had a long conversation with your mother. She wanted to know something, my opinion on a decision she was struggling with."

Surprised by this revelation, Hernán nearly blurted out a dozen questions.

"Some of her worries were the usual kind about trust and so forth that every woman frets about," Wilkie continued. "Finally, she told me she was thinking of sending you with Captain Beck. She was going to ask him to raise you so that you'd have the chance to be a man like him."

Nearly losing control, Hernán asked, "Why?"

"You can ask her yourself when the time comes," Wilkie answered. "Far as I know, she still lives in Aruba, and you won't have much trouble finding her on that little rock. I ask you to do one thing when you get there. If you don't measure up to what your mother thought you'd become, then you take the blame yourself. You tell her you walked out on Captain Beck, not the other way around."

Hernán hadn't walked out on Captain Beck. Instead, he'd taken his place, a position fate handed him, but one he looked back on as inevitable. Wilkie predicted it before issuing his warning, and Hernán gleaned the sense that he would be much less than his mother expected if he were to return without Beck's blessing. Would she accept him as he was or dismiss him as an unworthy disappointment? In the end, he decided not to take the chance.

That was four years ago, and the question no longer bothered Hernán. He was proud of who he was, ready to be judged by anyone, including his mother. Still, he had some explaining to do. In twenty-four hours, he would be within sight of Aruba, and he realized this homecoming was supposed to include Captain Beck.

❦23❧

INSTEAD OF TEO, Herr Diedrik was at the wheel, and Luz was in his BMW not her sedan. They were en route from the notary's office to San Nicolaas. Half an hour earlier, she signed the transfer of ownership at Bert Eman's desk and shook Kiko Sanchez's hand. He was the next owner of Minchi's, the mortgage was satisfied, and Luz was officially a tourist. She lived in a hotel and ate meals at a restaurant. She was also out of work, which gave her an opportunity to make a call.

"I'm sorry, señora, but I do not have that vessel on my list," the port captain informed Luz. "There is only one ship here, *Athos*, and it has engine trouble."

"It won't cause a problem for *Tenacious*, will it?" Luz asked struggling to pronounce the English name of her son's tugboat.

"There are other piers," the port captain assured her, "all of them vacant."

She rang off, grinding her teeth. At the airports in Bogotá and Aruba, there were giant video screens displaying the expected time of arrival for each flight. Apparently, a ship's schedule was not as certain as an airplane's. On a positive note, nothing more exciting than a fender bender happened on Main Street during the previous night. With the exception of plywood covering Minchi's façade and trash barrels full of debris in front of China Clipper, things appeared normal.

"We should have a party for your son," Herr Diedrik suggested.

She liked his idea, but how could it be organized without knowing Hernán's schedule?

"Something reasonable," the lawyer continued. "Perhaps twenty-five people around the pool at my villa. What do you think?"

"*Tan bueno,*" Luz said, aware that he had not mentioned Captain Beck. Luz didn't know Diedrik to be the jealous type, but he was used to having her on his terms. Beck had raised her son as a father, which put him in line to be a husband of sorts. A man as intelligent as Diedrik would have grasped this connection and calculated his relative standing. With these thoughts swirling in her head, Luz realized she may have sold Minchi's, but she still dwelled in the realm of San Nicolaas.

"We have a gala to attend tomorrow night," Diedrik said lightly as he stopped in front of Astoria. "Would you like to dress here or at my place?"

"Pick me up at a quarter to eight," Luz said, alighting from his car.

Entering the hotel, she was stunned to find Jerry Frazer seated at the bar in the courtyard.

"Hey, Luz!" he called waving his arm in the air as if he were hailing a cab. "My flight was canceled. I'm stuck here another day."

"*Lo siento,*" she replied.

Moving close, he leaned in to kiss her, a move that caused her to put up both hands.

"What?" he asked, shocked by her rejection. "You have another guy on the way?"

"No." Scrambling for an excuse to dismiss him, she added, "I'm going to Charlie's."

"Charlie's? Why would you want to go there when you can spend the day with me? Let's go to the beach for a couple of hours. Then we'll, uh … check out the balcony, have a great supper, maybe try the balcony again, and before you know it, the morning flight will be waiting."

"I can't," insisted Luz.

"Tell the other guy you have a headache. He'll understand."

"Carolina's is open. There are some very nice girls there."

He looked sideways, rocked his head a few times, and said, "Is this about the money?"

Yes, it is about the money! Luz almost shouted.

"How much do you want? Tell me." He reached into his pocket, took out a wad of hundred-dollar bills, and held it up. One by one, he paged off five. When her expression didn't change, he counted off five more.

"No," she said.

"A thousand dollars? You must have a high roller on the hook, Luz. Did this guy hit it big at the casino, because if he did, I'm going to have to reprogram those machines?"

She heard this for the joke it was but took it as the insult it concealed. A man more than ten years her junior was treating her like a disobedient servant, a position she took long ago out of necessity and presently no longer held. Although Frazer was ignorant of those realities, Luz did not have to tolerate his boorish behavior. To make her feelings inescapably clear, she slapped him. The sound of her palm connecting with his cheek brought René out from behind the bar.

"Okay, okay," begged Frazer. "I don't know what I did, but I'm sorry."

"Let's go," René ordered with a finger pointed toward the street. "Before it's my turn in the ring."

Upstairs, Luz took a few minutes to calm down. Only after she stripped out of her clothes, washed her face, and started reapplying her makeup did she realize she was following her old routine. This is exactly what she would have done had she serviced Frazer. She would have cleaned herself, changed clothes, taken a little break, and thus been ready for her next client. Why was she following this ritual on the way to nowhere?

She had said she was going to Charlie's Bar, and it was there she went, wearing the same dress she put on that morning. A crowd of rowdy Americans filled the place. The music was rock and roll, the beer plentiful, and the clothing disheveled. The fun was also contagious. One man put on his snorkel gear and spread himself over a table with his arms out to paddle. His pal poured a drink down the snorkel that sent him into a fit of sputtering and coughing.

Herr Koch shook his head at the revelers and gave Luz a wink. He automatically brought her a Baileys over ice, which she took seated at the end of the bar where she used to sit with Charlie. She resolved to visit the cemetery on Sunday afternoon to place flowers on his and Samito's graves.

At that moment, Luis passed by. "I think my uncle would have loved this," he said, gesturing toward a bunch of tourists downing a row of shots. "As long as they don't block my toilets."

She agreed with his sentiment. There was a downside to merriment that went too far.

"Let me see your shoes," he said next.

"My shoes?" Luz questioned.

"*Por favor,*" he prodded.

Unfolding her feet from beneath the stool, she revealed a pair of low pumps, the kind of practical footwear she wore when she didn't have a client to meet.

"Perfect," Luis said. "I'll be right back."

She couldn't imagine what her shoes had to do with whatever he was up to. Koch refilled her glass, and she looked over the crowd. A few men stole looks, but the rest ignored her. By the time she finished the second drink, Luis returned. He wore a linen Guayabera shirt, snug pants, and a devious grin.

To Luz's surprise, Luis leapt onto the bar, nearly knocking down a row of beer glasses in the process. He turned out to be as sure-footed as he was acrobatic and missed every one.

"Ladies and gentlemen!" Luis called out. "Your attention, please."

The noise faded, and Herr Koch turned down the music. Two women from the kitchen peeked through the door to see what was happening. They either saw this act before or were clairvoyant because they waved dismissively and returned to their work.

"For the same low price you've already paid for your drinks you're about to see a famous dancer in action, someone known from Tierra del Fuego to her hometown of Bogotá, Colombia." With a look to Herr Koch, he added, "Maestro! Music, please."

Koch hesitated, then scrambled to the computerized jukebox that funneled music into the room. With a few clicks, the sound of punchy trumpets playing a rousing salsa burst from the speakers.

"Please join me in welcoming Luz to the World Famous Charlie's Bar dance floor!"

Startled by the sound of her name, Luz turned around at the exact moment Luis jumped off the bar. He landed with his arms out, awaiting her to join him. Everyone in the room and several peering in the door stared at her, which was more unnerving than being naked in front of a stranger in her room above Minchi's. Someone started clapping, followed by others until she could no longer hear the music.

As the applause faded, she slipped off the stool and moved toward Luis. Rather than join hands with him in the traditional style, Luz kept her arms close and began rocking her feet. Luis took the cue. He synchronized his motion with hers, moving backward to draw her toward the center of the room. People cleared the way as Luz rotated through several fast spins, passed Luis, and framed herself against the doorway. Taking his turn in the burgeoning drama, he repeated her steps, ending up on the opposite side. They were only inches apart but not looking at each other. In perfect rhythm with the music, they turned back to back, their feet and arms moving in unison.

Luis decided to take the lead. He caught her left hand in his, tugged at the right moment, and spun Luz into a side-by-side embrace. Immediately, he turned her out again without letting go. It was too much fun to be in contact with Luz. Plus, that was his style. He liked to be close, to feel the heat of a woman's body while they still wore their clothes.

"Dancing is the most effective form of foreplay," Charlie maintained. "Make it last as long as you can." He was a fine dancer himself, though prone to more tranquil versions of the activity. They ranged from one corner of the bar to the other, back and forth, until the song ended. Herr Koch had ice water waiting, and after they each took a sip, the show continued. This time, they began in each other's arms, which was appropriate because the song was a melancholy bolero.

Through the open window, Luz glimpsed the plywood covering Minchi's. An odd sense of déjà vu settled over her. She felt a stranger to that place, as if she had never worked there, never lived within its walls, yet somehow had seen it before. She allowed herself the illusion. Besides, who in Charlie's Bar knew who she was or wasn't? Only Luis, Herr Koch, and the ladies in the kitchen. The audience was benignly clueless and outnumbered the others twenty to one.

"More! More!" chanted the crowd as they bowed at the end of the second song.

The music continued, giving the dancers no choice. A pair of tour buses released a new wave of tourists who were forced to watch from the street. To give them their money's worth, Luis wove in and out of the bar, making sure everyone had a front-row seat at one point or another. He and Luz strutted through a pair of tangos, then a merengue, and finally one more salsa.

He would have loved to keep going, but Luis knew he was denying valuable space to thirsty customers. There was nothing wrong with breaking routine so long as it didn't cut into the profits. Having reached that point, he ended the show.

After a final bow, Luis said, "*Gracias, danki,* thank you." He pointed to Luz, clapped his hands, and then spoke again to the crowd. "Autographs will be available for the next half hour only."

This bit of English escaped Luz. It wasn't until she was back on her stool that she found herself at the head of a line. They wanted something from her, but she didn't know what. Luis stepped up with a stack of Charlie's Bar brochures and a brand-new pen.

"I told them you would sign autographs," he explained in Spanish.

"Seriously?" she gasped.

"Of course," he said, uncapping the pen.

She not only signed her name on the upper corner of the brochure, but held it up as husbands took photos of wives standing with her. Then the husbands wanted their own picture or one with both of them, taken by the next person. The stack of brochures descended with the level of Baileys in her glass. Herr Koch and Luis refilled both until everyone took a turn and Luz was too drunk to feel guilty about deceiving them.

As the bar emptied, Luis came over. She wagged her finger at him. "Famous dancer," she mocked.

"They all wanted your autograph, didn't they?" he replied.

"You're lucky Father Dario wasn't here."

"I should have called him. He would have enjoyed the show."

The effects of the Baileys hit full blast. She felt her head swim and said, "I need to take a nap."

"Let me walk you to Astoria."

She was grateful for the company and kept her arm locked in his all the way to the hotel. Between the dancing and the alcohol, she was less than steady on her feet. They arrived in the courtyard without incident. It was there that Luis voiced another proposition.

"I don't have a date for the gala," he hinted.

Once again, Luz was stuck between what she would like and what she had to have. A night with Luis would no doubt be more exciting than one with Herr Diedrik. Luis was her own age, he was fit, and he was energetic, all qualities Diedrik could not match. However, just as she wouldn't tolerate Frazer's coarseness, she would not provoke Diedrik, who expected only that she accompany him to the ballroom. While the lawyer never overtly stated his physical desire for her, he allowed her to satisfy him at her discretion. Just as this was the moment to deny Luis his request, soon she would have to tell Diedrik that her professional services were no longer available.

"Angela is a better dancer," Luz said, simultaneously acknowledging his invitation and politely declining it.

Upstairs in her room, Luz opened her cell phone, stared at the screen, then closed it. The port captain had her number. In the event *Tenacious* arrived at one of his piers, he would surely call to end her nagging. She set the phone on the nightstand, let her shoes fall to the floor, and swung her legs up onto the bed.

Wow, the tourist life, Luz thought, delighted by the afternoon at Charlie's. What a thrill it was to be carefree, to not worry about opening Minchi's or collecting for the casa or wondering if the girls were following the rules. Years ago, her first client gave her a glimpse of that life when he paid the *molta* in order to have her all to himself at the Hyatt. It was the client's fantasy to have a young woman on his arm, and she fulfilled that role as much as her own delusion of a luxurious existence. She lounged by the pool during the day, dined in one fantastic restaurant after another, and at times, actually believed she was having sex with a boyfriend she genuinely cared about.

Rolling onto her side, Luz realized Inez's assessment of her had been correct. She had been young, cute, and basically ignorant. No, she hadn't been stupid, just underexposed and less informed than someone who chose to work in San Nicolaas should have been. How quickly she learned! That first client ditched her for another chica, which put Luz back at Minchi's competing with every other girl, including Inez, for the less-polished men who came through the door. She taught herself to court them, to tease them, to lure them into her room where they paid to use her. With Inez's help, she went beyond the typical to the extraordinary, performing lesbian shows the price of which astounded her. Luz hadn't known it at the time, but these experiences had been on-the-job training for her future career, the one she terminated after her last coupling with Garrett Turner.

The question was not what she had done, but what she was going to do. She could not stay in San Nicolaas and not only because Montoya had destroyed her house. The townspeople would not speak maliciously of her to Hernán. Nonetheless, she wanted to be his mother not the woman who climbed the stairs at Minchi's, which meant she would have to leave this island.

Her cell phone chimed. Thinking it was the port captain, she snatched it off the nightstand. Making the connection, she was disappointed by the sound of Luis on the line.

"I need a dress," he said.

Thinking he was up to his uncle's hijinks she replied, "What about stockings?"

"It's for Angela," Luis answered.

"Lucky for you we're the same size. Do you want to pick one out?"

"I trust your judgment."

After agreeing to bring the dress to the bar, she hung up and went to the wardrobe. The one Herr Diedrik bought her stood out from the others. Running her hand over the fabric, she surged with excitement. Certainly the party for Andrés would be more glamorous than an afternoon at Charlie's Bar. It was another chance to live a regular life, the very thing she had been contemplating before Luis called.

She paged through the other dresses, pulling several out for closer inspection. Angela's figure was a little larger on top than Luz's and this requirement helped determine the final selection. She hung the garment on the wardrobe door and returned to bed.

Staring at the ceiling, Luz imagined herself at the gala. The music wouldn't be coming from a jukebox, nor would the food be something out of a Styrofoam container delivered by a harried Chinese. La Familia Arends would be on stage while jacketed waiters served a chef-prepared meal. Her designer dress would be one of dozens, and every man would be wearing a tuxedo.

Unlike her early foray to the Hyatt, the gala would not be someone else's fantasy. Her invitation came directly from Andrés. Herr Diedrik was as much her date as she was his. The fact that his sister would be throwing around sour glares and ugly comments made the event that much more real. If things became unbearable, Luz need only mention her discomfort to Inez. If anyone wanted to tangle with Inez, Luz would let them. One word to Mr. Kim and he might release a dozen imperial warriors. None of this came from people like Garrett Turner or Jerry Frazer, who were out to protect the literal investments they'd made in Luz. It was provided by people who saw her as someone deserving the same respect to which any citizen was entitled.

This was the life she imagined living, one with common annoyances like picking the right dress for a party, tolerating the cattiness of other women, and finding a decent wife for her son. After fifteen years, it was about to be hers. She vowed not to make any more decisions until Hernán and Captain Beck arrived. On that pleasant thought, she closed her eyes.

24

THE ACRID STENCH OF CRUDE OIL wafted
through the open window. Hernán raised the glass, backed
down both throttles, and nudged the rudder a few degrees to
starboard. Ahead he noted the channel markers leading into
San Nicolaas Harbor. It occurred to him that through these
waters his stepfather had drifted, eventually coming ashore a
few miles away. This much of the past Hernán learned only a
month ago.

Beck told the story of washing up in Aruba over the course
of several sessions. Hernán sensed an odd despondency in
Beck's voice, which was a strange emotion coming from a practically fearless man. There were plenty of reasons for him to
be in a better frame of mind. Not the least of which was the
fortune he'd made on the periphery of a war he predicted. A
few tragedies balanced the ledger, including the retirement of
Captain Wilkie, who suffered a debilitating stroke earlier in the
year that left him half paralyzed and mute.

Upon Wilkie's departure, Hernán officially took the title of
first mate. To this point in his life, he'd done every job aboard

the boat as needed. If the engineers wanted help fixing something, he was there. If an extra hand was required on deck, he grabbed a line. If Wilkie decided to take a catnap, he steered the boat. Things quickly became more formal, and as they changed, Hernán fully grasped the poignant lecture Wilkie had given him years ago.

No longer could he vault down from the wheelhouse to lend a hand at the forward bit. Nor could he remain in the engine room turning wrenches or minding gauges through the night. No one offered to help with a judgment that was his to make. He was at the helm, alone, but with more than his own interests at stake.

In Algeciras, when he wanted so badly to leave this life, he believed he was ready for anything. He'd seen much of the world. He'd argued and lost. He'd fought and won. He'd made mistakes and gotten lucky. He'd had his share of minor joys and heartbreak, easy afternoons and months of hard work. He thought life would be more of the same. Why not live on his terms?

The reason was that the people who had once taken care of him were now his responsibility. Tony no longer talked about history, and Ramirez didn't coach him through algebra. Syd reported the state of the tug's machinery as opposed to asking him for a screwdriver or to fetch a quart of oil. Captain Beck looked over the logbook, then added his own entries immediately below without editing the ones above. To the uninitiated, this transformation would have seemed unremarkable, a logical progression from journeyman to master. However, Hernán realized it was trust that they were investing in him. With it came a tall measure of expectation, and that phenomenon changed him.

The crew sought his approval as much as his guidance. They

counted on him to settle their differences and punish their disobedience. He imagined it was not unlike being a father. This realization gave him a keen appreciation for what Wilkie had told him in Spain. More important, who Captain Beck was and what he had done for him became increasingly clear.

Life was not limited to a series of jobs, a string of ports, or random couplings with agreeable women. All those things and more were part of the bargain, but how you dealt with what came over the bow spoke to who you were regardless of the title on the door to your bunk. Were you panicky and reckless, desperate and grasping? Or, were you judicious and mindful, deliberate and wary?

At the risk of being arrogant, Hernán was anxious to demonstrate his ability to answer whatever questions arose, including ones he could never anticipate. He enjoyed the challenge of authority not for the power it engendered but for the rewards bestowed. To that end he was eager to reunite with his mother and show her how the right choice had been made in Algeciras as well as fifteen years ago in Aruba.

And now Captain Beck was telling him the story of his dramatic first arrival in Aruba. Not Syd, nor Ramirez, nor Tony, all who served with Beck aboard *Patricia* when she went down east of Curaçao. None of his shipmates revealed anything beyond their own rescue at sea. Whenever Hernán asked them about Aruba, they shrugged and directed him to Beck. Wilkie also stuck to his word and never again mentioned the encounter with Luz.

"Before your mother found me on the beach, I'd been drifting for days," Beck had started.

Had Captain Wilkie been in the wheelhouse with them,

he would have injected one of his sorry bastard comments, but he'd flown home months ago.

"It can take a long time to die. That's why I insist on a lookout no matter where we are or what we're doing."

Hernán thought of Teresa, who nearly gave up after a few hours but was rescued by an alert fisherman.

"The current carried me around the southern tip of the island, past the oil refinery, to a little sandbar off the coast of a village called Savaneta."

As a boy, Hernán roamed along that coast with Beck aboard the launch *Huntress*. He recalled only the refinery flares, which at the time he thought were fire-breathing dragons.

"We're going back there," Beck said. "We'll lay up in Philadelphia a few days then head south."

It wasn't to be. Not for Beck. Surely he couldn't have known that soon he would be dead, his body committed to the deep. No, he wouldn't have seen that as a possibility. He was a man who survived a shipwreck. He avoided personal injury, disease, and the hazards of war. A survivor with that kind of fortitude ignores death's sudden reality. He makes plans for an uninterruptible future.

Beck's plan was to follow the shortest route between the Persian Gulf and Philadelphia. He followed it, too, through the Suez Canal and into the Mediterranean Sea. From midnight to eight in the morning, he guided *Tenacious*. During the half hour overlap between his watch and Hernán's, he parceled out his story of shipwreck and Aruba.

"Savaneta," Beck said. "It's the oldest settled part of the island."

Centuries later, when he made his fateful arrival, it was a

fishing village with a few rental cottages, tourist restaurants, and a seaside pavilion owned by a guy named Charlie.

"He was a character," Beck said. "Your mother saw me first, then Charlie and his pal, Sam, got me to the hospital and showed me an interesting time after I recovered."

Apparently Charlie had good connections on the island.

"He used to relax on the balcony above his bar with a glass of rum and his cat. Sometimes the chief of police, a guy named Calenda, would stop by. We'd have a few drinks together and talk about life. Through Charlie, I came to understand who your mother really was. I want you to keep that in mind when we see her next month."

When we see her next month. It was said with the same confidence Beck lent to every statement and for good reason. He plotted the course, informed the crew, and settled in for the trip, the next leg of which was to be a two-week journey across the Atlantic after a brief visit to Malta. What could stop them? There were several thousand tons of steel under their feet, two massive engines, the latest navigation equipment, plenty of food and fuel, and a crew of professionals with the combined experience of a century at sea.

"Unless you want a day in Algeciras to visit Teresa," Beck chided Hernán.

"Tarifa," he corrected his stepfather.

"Too shallow for us there," Beck remarked.

Perhaps she'll be in Aruba, Hernán thought, wondering if it was the time of the year for windsurfing.

The layover in Malta lasted barely six hours. Together, Beck and Hernán went into Valletta to handle some minor business with a ship owner. Among their errands was a visit to the post office.

"I'm sending this to your mother," Beck said, holding a regular envelope in his hand. "It's the last one from me. You'll see her soon, and the rest will be up to you."

Four years ago Hernán might have made the mistake of returning to his mother a capricious teenager, an error he avoided thanks to Captain Wilkie. However, for all the experience he accumulated, Captain Beck was hinting that there was more to learn and not about tugboats, either.

The Atlantic was ahead of them, first the crossing, then the trip south to the Caribbean. There was no rush. Fifteen, twenty, possibly thirty changes of the watch were ample time to discuss whatever secrets had been kept. Hernán did not expect any startling revelations. He remembered his mother as a working woman, who always seemed a bit tired but cheerful to see him.

"The rest will be up to you."

It was, too, because when Hernán kneeled beside Beck's broken body, he recalled what had been different about him in the Valletta post office. The memory was triggered by his stepfather's final words.

"The Feast of Saint Michael."

These words Hernán had heard as clearly as he felt the weight of Beck's slackening body in his hands, but he saw not the man who was about to die. Rather, it was the one handing a letter to the postal clerk who appeared to him. The only thing missing from the apparition was the medallion that hung around his neck. It had been there from the day Ramirez gave it to him until that moment in Malta at the post office. A flash of gold should have hung between the edges of his open shirt. Hernán hadn't noticed the change at the time. Why would he?

It was as regular a day as any other.

Beck's last words Hernán shared with no one. On the way down the Delaware Bay, en route to the burial ceremony, he asked Ramirez, whose wife was deeply religious and knew all the holy days, about the Feast of Saint Michael.

Ramirez had been startled by the question. "The captain asked me about it when we pulled into Malta," he said. "I told him it's on the 29th of September."

Ahead of the winking channel markers, the refinery flares provided ample illumination to see the reef protecting San Nicolaas Harbor. From behind Hernán, the clock struck ten. Looking at the chart plotter, he noticed the small block in the upper right corner displaying the date.

27 SEPTEMBER.

He took the microphone off its hook and depressed the transmit button. "Tug *Tenacious* calling San Nicolaas Harbor."

25

THE SOUND OF SOMEONE whispering her name woke Luz. Unsure if she'd been dreaming, she lay still for a few seconds. There was tapping on the door, and "Luz, are you in there?" filtered through.

"*Momentico*," she said, heading across the room.

"You're okay!" Inez gushed on her way in. "What a crazy thing to happen."

Unsure of the subject, Luz shrugged.

"*¡Por favor!* Someone drives a truck into the bar. You could have been killed. Andrés showed me the photo in the *Diario*. The article didn't mention injuries, but I wanted to see for myself."

"*Gracias*," Luz said.

"Andrés was going to come, too. I managed to escape by telling him …" Distracted by the dress hanging in the open, Inez stopped short then said, "That's beautiful."

"It's for a friend."

"Don't be too generous. People take advantage."

Luz might have said the same of Inez, who filled the sedan's trunk with clothes, shoes, and accessories for a person she hadn't seen in more than a decade.

"I'm glad to be away from the hotel," Inez continued. "Andrés is giving interviews to the media. Mr. Kim plays the noble benefactor. It's stuffy and boring, the same questions over and over. Why would I want to be there when I can have a nice evening with *mi amiga?*"

Luz was pleased to have company, if only to pass the time.

"What are your plans?" asked Inez.

"I have an errand to run, and then I'm free."

"*¡Perfecto!* Let's have a crazy night out away from those stodgy people with their big opinions about art and politics."

Refreshed by her nap, Luz was a willing partner. If Andrés could have a gala to show off his new paintings, why couldn't she have a going away party for herself in San Nicolaas?

Just before nine, Luis served the last beer of the night. Already he had the chairs atop the tables and the floor mopped. He shut off the music, locked the back door, and closed out the cash register. After securing the money in the safe, he returned to the bar for a final look around when Luz and Inez walked in.

"*Buenas noches,*" he greeted them.

"*Buenas noches,*" they replied.

Holding up a garment bag, Luz added, "This is the dress for Angela."

"*Muchas gracias,*" Luis said. "It looks like you're headed to a before-the-party event."

"Just two women out to have a good time," Inez commented provocatively.

"In that case, I'll dare to join you."

Luz and Inez each took a glass of Baileys while Luis showered. In short order, he returned from his apartment upstairs with wet hair and fresh cologne. He ushered them to the sidewalk, where they paused for him to lock the doors.

"What about the windows?" Inez asked, referring to the open shutters.

"My tiger guards the palace," Luis replied, pointing to Screwball poised atop the parapet above them.

Seeing the cat dozing up there, Inez chuckled and took his arm. "Any man with a tiger knows where to find the circus," she said.

They found it at Black & White, where José presided over a multicultural train wreck without injuries. A dozen middle managers from the refinery, men who lost their jobs that afternoon, loaded the jukebox with a handful of florins. A bunch of Colombian hotel workers squeezed in a few coins, too. Then there were a smattering of Arubans, a couple of Dutch marines, and a random Chinese guy or two, all of whom were looking for nothing but booze and temporary female company. As a result, the music ranged from rock and roll to vallenato to a few old French ballads that had one drunk ready to put his foot through the speakers. With the help of the Dutch marines, José threw him out, issued a serious warning, and returned to slinging bottles when someone shouted, "Shut up and pour me a shot of Jack Daniel's!"

Luis might have been jealous of all the money flying across the bar, but he was on a noneconomic mission. His first task was to cut Angela out of the crowd before this gang of louts took the shine off the apple. He paid José the *molta*, which entitled him to her company exclusively. It was not a favor he was doing for her; it was an ounce of prevention to keep him from getting stupid ideas about Luz. Charlie would have recognized this act as a grand gesture of simultaneous class, improvisation, and self-preservation. Luis made the most of it the way a tourist might of his last day of vacation by asking Angela to accompany him to the gala, adding that he had a dress, too. His invitation sent her flying. Her joy enhanced his satisfaction in having made a young woman happy. She hadn't been his first choice, but she was a good one. In the face of scarcity, asking for more would have been greedy and dangerous.

Delighted by Luis' invitation, Angela immediately embraced Luz. "I'll be careful with the dress," she whispered.

"Enjoy it," Luz told her, "and meet my friend Inez."

"You're married to the man who bought the paintings from—" Angela cut herself short.

"*No importa*," Inez told her. "Let's have a good time with these guys before they run out of money to buy us drinks."

Initially, Luz was shocked at how Inez waded into the crowd, picked the tallest guy, and asked him to buy her a drink. However, as the hour unfolded, she did nothing more tawdry than kiss a cheek, pat a thigh, or press herself against a guy when reaching for her glass. She rotated among the men, waving Luz in to join the dancing. There was plenty of contact, but everyone had their clothes on and nobody's hands wandered beyond acceptable limits.

A powerful sense of relief came over Luz. It was similar to her first return from Aruba to Bogotá. All the tension and disgusting acts of a three-month immersion in San Nicolaas were behind her. She had cash to pay the mortgage on her family's home. She was thinking about finishing high school even as her son was scheduled to begin elementary. Nothing could compare to the moment when he rushed into her arms. She looked forward to doing it again in a couple of days. Then she would be celebrating in a way that would make this night look like a slumber party.

Luz enjoyed herself with Inez, Luis, Angela, and the mixed group around them. The Americans sang along with their rock music and slipped away with José's other two girls when they thought no one was looking.

"I'm telling you, boys," the tall fellow Inez approached hollered, "I'm gonna cry a river of tears all the way to my next job."

"Unless you run out of money tonight," someone called out. "Then we'll drown right here."

They raised their drinks for a toast, boohooing like carnival clowns.

On cue, a sad Spanish song came from the speakers. Angela danced with Luis. An Aruban guy moved cheek to cheek with Inez. José leaned against the wall, taking a well-deserved break. Halfway through the song, the tall fellow found Luz standing at the end of the bar.

"Luz," he said, "*bailamos ahora.*" He lifted her off her feet like a child. His shoulders were so far above her that she had to hold on to his arms. He was a clunky dancer, not able to stay with the beat, which gave her a giggle fit. Thankfully, the song wasn't a long one.

In a final dramatic move, he hoisted her into his arms as he took a bow for his comrades. Luz yelped, pulled her skirt down, and playfully swatted his cheek. He kissed the air between them, then set her down gingerly.

"Garrett Turner was a lucky man," he said and rejoined his pals.

For all the fun at Black & White, less than a block away things were not the tiniest bit cheerful. So upset was Frankie that he retreated to his secret lair in the unfinished hotel at the end of Main Street. This was a place where no other choller bothered him. All the entrances to the building were blocked, but he chiseled an opening through a wall that was invisible from town. Inside, he outfitted a room with discarded furniture. He had a couple of mattresses and pillows secured from the Las Vegas Bar remodel job. Two sturdy packing crates served as a nightstand and kitchen table respectively. A broken mirror he fitted to the wall, and on a rope strung across what should have been a closet, he hung his uniform.

The uniform itself he'd worn only twice and both occasions had been funerals. The first one was for Samito, the Crown Prince of San Nicolaas, whose lighter Frankie carried everywhere. The second was Charlie's, the man who gave him the drum major's outfit that used to be found among the junk decorating his bar. For a long time Frankie thought the worst of life was behind him. Then this business got started with the paintings in Luz's house. China Clipper was busted up. A truck crashed into Minchi's. All the while those tourist officials were eyeing the refinery the way he stared down a half-eaten platter at Pueblito Paisa's back door. Didn't they know he would never beg enough money to fix his teeth if the refinery closed?

It would take years to build hotels and shops and restaurants. Even if this miracle of renewal happened, the touristas wouldn't find him the least bit entertaining, not the way the refinery workers did, not the way the guys who frequented the bars did. He'd end up hauled away to some halfway house like his old pal Speedy. Look what happened to him! He ended up sorting trash at a recycling center but wasn't allowed to take any of it home. What kind of life was that?

Depressed and out of sorts, he leaned on the sill of his private suite and looked out at the refinery. Soon it would fade away like the old Lago Colony: a bunch of streets with nothing but weeds growing out of the cracks. How did he know this? Well, there were a couple of prissy-looking guys who showed up today in a rented sedan. From his hideaway Frankie saw them walking about the refinery in new white hard hats. He'd seen the type before. They came like undertakers in fancy cars and shiny shoes, leaving behind limp handshakes and phony smiles. Had they shut off the car? Hardly. It idled outside the main office building before their driver hauled them away. Soon after, a needle-nosed jet sprinted overhead. Was it theirs? Who else could it have been?

At least Garrett Turner had the gentlemanly countenance to engage in a little street-side banter before he went bonkers, tore up China Clipper, and got a courtesy ride from Chief Calenda. These other guys? They'd kick a dropped guilder down the drain to protect it from a choller's filthy hands.

Wiping his face with his arm, Frankie scanned the refinery's piers. Only one tanker was there, a smallish one that made the docks seem lonely. Then he noticed an odd-looking ship angling in from the channel. It was too big to be a tugboat, but it had similar characteristics, a high bow, a wheelhouse positioned forward, and a low stern. Upon touching the dock, her crew dropped lines to the bollards and extended a narrow gangplank.

Frankie's already growing disappointment sunk him to

despair as he noted the vessel wasn't another tanker. No tankers, no oil. No oil, no refinery. No refinery, no money. Still, there were people milling about, sailors to be more precise. He kept his eyes on the discussion they were having until a couple of them headed toward the main gate, which was his cue to stop feeling sorry for himself and get to work.

As he jogged to the main gate, luck gave Frankie two loaves as both men continued toward town. There should have been half a dozen potential donors to his cause, a whole gaggle of men excited to have a drink, meet a woman, and maybe drop a guilder or two into his palm for witty comments. Still, he was happy with two as opposed to none.

As his targets passed beneath a streetlight, Frankie pulled up short and slammed himself against the wall. It was a ghost who came from that ship, and now it was coming for him. He shimmied along the chalky concrete, and dared not come out of the shadows for fear of being exposed.

It was the radio that caused Frankie to panic. It hung on the one man's hip, holstered in a leather contraption with a strap that ran diagonally across his chest. Only one man in San Nicolaas had worn something like that, and he had not been seen in more than a decade. This wasn't him. Not exactly. This was a younger version, someone with all the correct traits but as if the clock had run backward.

Fearful but eager for more facts, Frankie padded along like a cat burglar, thankful for the shoes Luis gave him, but worried that one of his regular contributors might stumble along and reveal his position. The subject stopped at Charlie's Bar. Something through the window caught his attention. He pointed at it and asked his companion a question.

26

"FIND A DECENT TAVERN to glean information and establish a base of operations." This was how Wilkie made his initial forays into a new port town, and Hernán intended to do the same in San Nicolaas. He didn't expect to find his mother, not on his first pass through town, nor did he expect to find the house where they had lived. In the morning, he would go to the police station. The chief Captain Beck mentioned might be in, and if not, his successor would be. It was the easiest way to find someone. Presently, he wanted to see if he found anything that might trigger a memory or two.

Satisfied that *Tenacious* was secure, Hernán had put on a fresh shirt, strapped his radio fast, and made a final trip through the wheelhouse. Syd was there, transferring some of his notes into the logbook.

"*Athos* has engine trouble," the engineer explained, pointing his pen at the ship on the next pier to the west.

"Do they need help?" Hernán asked.

"Tony spoke with one of the deckhands. They're waiting for parts."

"I'm going to have a look around town."

"You've been to places like this before," Syd put in. "It may be better to see it during the day."

Looking through the window at the colored lights in the distance, Hernán recalled several comparable locales. Day and night made little difference in port towns aside of the type of functioning commerce. As eager as he was to find his mother, he was uneasy about having to tell her what happened to Captain Beck.

"Can't hurt to have a drink or two," he said to Syd.

"In that case, I'll go with you."

Exiting the refinery complex Hernán noticed the guard dozing over his desk. *How exciting could this place be?* he wondered. As a boy, he'd walked through here with Captain Beck any number of times. He didn't remember anything particularly compelling. As for excitement, running about in *Huntress* was the greatest thrill to that point.

He and Syd walked past the line of bars on Rodgerstraat. All of them featured neon signs and solid doors with illuminated buttons. None of them interested him. He made the first right and immediately saw Charlie's Bar. Crossing the street, he found the doors locked but a few windows open to the breeze. The assorted novelties hanging from every conceivable place reflected light from a few dim bulbs.

A patch of faded orange stuck out near the back. He immediately recognized the color and shape of the object. It was a life preserver. Allowing his eyes a few minutes to adjust, he made out a few of the letters stenciled on it.

P-A-T-R-I

There could be no doubt where it had come from. It was the same one that saved Captain Beck's life. It kept him afloat from where *Patricia* sank all the way to Savaneta. There it was, testament to the truth of the story.

"See that?" he said to Syd.

The engineer peered inside, recognized the life jacket, and made the sign of the cross.

Stepping back from the window, Hernán raised his eyes. There on the parapet above his head was a grumpy-looking cat of indeterminate breed.

It was a real live man, Frankie decided. Perhaps Captain Beck had discovered the fabled Fountain of Youth. It would explain where he'd been all these years. Far-fetched but certainly as plausible as the goat herder who found a six-ounce gold nugget just over the hill by the old golf course.

In light of the astounding possibilities that lay ahead, Frankie made a run for his hideout. He wanted to look his best when he asked for a few drops of the elixir that would restore his teeth.

Hernán didn't remember so many bars on Main Street. Turning away from Charlie's balcony, he was within a block of at least a dozen. Each one seemed to have a theme judging by the neon lights and painted signs. Doors opened, men went in or out. Cars rolled by, the drivers and passengers calling out to friends.

Having been in similar places around the world, Hernán understood what this street was all about. As if he needed further proof, a young woman exited a bar wearing an outfit more appropriate for a day at the beach than a night on the town. She saw him coming up the street, cocked her hip, and waited.

"*Papi, venga,*" she cooed.

"*Gracias, pero no,*" Hernán replied.

"*Sí,*" she drawled, "*a mi habitación.*"

Catching his hand, she gave a gentle tug but let go when he failed to slow down.

"*Hasta luego, guapo,*" she called after him.

There were those members of the crew who patronized prostitutes. Hernán was not among them. However, he didn't let their trade stop him from having a good time. As Wilkie taught him, he looked for nonprofessional company, although that was not his purpose tonight. Moving along, he realized Syd had been correct. This wasn't the type of place to meander alone. It wasn't dangerous, but Hernán knew from past experience that a single man in this environment received an annoying excess of attention.

Looking through the glass door of a closed bar, he saw that the interior had been demolished. At his side, Syd stood transfixed by a boarded up building with a sign that read Minchi's.

"Do you remember the name of the restaurant where my mother worked?" Hernán asked.

A few seconds passed before Syd answered with a quiet, "No."

They crossed a narrow alley fronting a hair salon, Internet café, and a women's clothing shop. Arriving at the next corner, they had nearly completed a full circle. Looking back at Main Street, Hernán struggled to recall where his mother's house had been. It was somewhere beyond this particular group of buildings because he and Captain Beck used to walk this way to the refinery.

"Let's have a drink and then head back to the boat," Hernán said.

"Good idea," Syd agreed.

The nearest bar was only a few steps away. Syd took the lead, reaching for the door to Black & White.

"There will be moments when you won't believe your eyes."

Luis couldn't remember when Charlie issued this particular warning. It seemed like every day his uncle was proselytizing on one subject or another to the point where Luis wondered if instead of being an amateur painter the man was working on the next installment of the Book of Proverbs. Then a random event would occur, validating his missives in a way that left uncle and nephew exchanging a knowing glance others around them didn't understand.

This is exactly what happened at Black & White Bar. A song had just ended, and there was a few seconds of relative quiet. A tall guy who had been dancing with Luz set her down and said something that made her smile. She was on her way to joining him at the bar when the door opened behind her. Luis clearly saw two men about to enter.

This was the point when he didn't believe his eyes. He turned to order another round, then did a double take. Luz was still coming toward him, the door remained open behind her, and the two guys on the street were poised to cross the threshold. Luis remembered Captain Beck. There was no forgetting someone like that, and like Frankie, Luis thought the man was back in a different body because a younger version of him was on his way into Black & White. Unlike Frankie, Luis had a firm grip on reality, even after he'd had quite a few glasses of rum. He'd seen this young man's face in a photo among Luz's things when he helped transfer them to Hotel Astoria. He was her son.

Luis forgot about ordering drinks in lieu of verifying this apparition. He was on his way, but the door suddenly slammed shut in his face and the floor shook beneath his feet.

Next, the liquor bottles fell off the top shelf, then the room went dark. José cursed in three languages but was happy when the emergency lights came on. They provided enough illumination for him to see a puddle of costly beverages on the floor, which set him off again. With the jukebox silent, the sounds of sirens drowned his tirade, especially the klaxon warning people to evacuate.

Luis was the first out, because he was on the way to see if it really was Luz's son on the street. Stepping outside, he joined a growing crowd spilling from the other bars. The fire beyond the refinery wall meant this was not a drill. He worked his way back inside Black & White where the party came to an abrupt end.

Strutting across the empty parking lot outside the unfinished hotel, Frankie was dressed for greatness. He wore his uniform, epaulets and all, like a visiting general on his way to inspect the troops. In a way he was. Greeting Captain Beck, whatever form he'd taken, required proper attire. Unfortunately, Frankie didn't have the correct shoes, only the sneakers Luis had given him.

The strangest feeling came over Frankie, as if he were flying. A second later, he realized he was off his feet, but only briefly, because he landed hard on his left side. His head met the asphalt, leaving him dazed and struggling to get up. The sky above him glowed bright as daylight, again, only for a moment. Not only did the sky go dark, but all the lights in San Nicolaas went out as well.

Kneeling on the ground, the choller turned toward the main gate. Beyond its pillars a column of fire pointed upward, emanating from the larger of the two ships he watched earlier. The flames spread down over the side, where a series of pipes ignited like Roman candles. Two figures ran past the security guard who had evacuated his booth. Frankie recognized them as the pair he'd been following. Without hesitating, he chased them into the refinery, knowing that this would be his last chance to sip from the Fountain of Youth.

In the same moment he pulled the handle on Black & White's door, a screeching hiss drew Syd's attention. It was a man-made sound, loud enough to drown out the noise on the street. A second later, a roll of thunder swept over him, which would have been nothing to fear had it not been accompanied by a growing fireball bright enough to outshine the neon above his head. The sidewalk jumped, sending the engineer tumbling into his captain.

Getting to his feet, Hernán helped Syd up, then charged toward the main gate. Flames and smoke poured from *Athos*. In seconds, the fire leapt to the nearby equipment on land. There it paused, but gained strength as was evident by the height of the blaze. If not intercepted, the conflagration was bound to destroy the entire western portion of the refinery.

Hernán understood the danger ahead of him. He'd seen

devastating fires both aboard ships and ashore. He knew the potential of *Athos* disintegrating in a catastrophic explosion. If that happened, it would take a large portion of the refinery and part of the town with it. There was also the possibility of rescuing the ship's crew and preventing a greater disaster. Above all, he grasped that he was one of the few people in a position to do something.

Sprinting toward *Tenacious*, he recalled words said to him on a calm August night when the last thing he wanted was to leave his girlfriend behind.

"This is who we are."

27

CHIEF CALENDA, LIKE THE REST of San Nicolaas, felt the explosion. It wasn't as pronounced in his office as it had been at Black & White, but a few framed photos rattled on the wall. He immediately radioed his patrolmen, instructing them to implement the evacuation plans for the businesses and residences closest to the refinery. Donning his hat, he glimpsed the flashing red lights of fire trucks leaving the station next door.

On his way downstairs, he wondered if San Nicolaas wouldn't be better off with hotels, shopping malls, and cruise ships. There would still be problems: drunk tourists falling from balconies, car crashes, stealing, and fights over palapa huts on the beach. However, an awful case of food poisoning was about the worst thing that could happen on a mass scale.

He chided himself for being lazy. If he wanted the easy life, he should have been a college professor. The hours were short, the pay decent, and the company stimulating. Then again, there was very little excitement other than a rare instance of plagiarism or an affair with a student. That kind of existence was as boring as traffic duty. With an oil refinery, there was a chance the whole town might be destroyed.

Driving toward the main gate with the largest fire he'd ever seen reaching toward the sky, he considered something biblical might be happening.

Hotel Astoria was beyond the evacuation zone. Dozens of San Nicolaas residents crammed into the bar where René and Harold were happy to sell beer and food that would spoil if the electricity wasn't soon restored. Luz was fortunate to have a room upstairs. She lit several candles and distributed them among various safe places, remembering a careless girl who left a candle too close to her bed, a mistake paid for with severe burns.

"*¡Dios mío!*" Inez said, exiting the bathroom. "It's almost too dark to pee."

Luz forced a chuckle. She wasn't feeling as giddy as her friend. Inez took the fire as another zany incident in a string she recalled from her own early visits to the island.

"I'll never forget the explosion that happened when we were working together at Minchi's."

Luz nodded.

"All those men sad about their dead friends, looking for a woman's comfort. The money we made! Imagine if we were working there now. *¡Por favor!* We would need an escort to the bank."

No doubt the brothels of San Nicolaas would be busy as soon as the fire was extinguished. Unlike Inez, however, Luz did not enjoy reminiscing about her past success as a prostitute. She was more concerned about the present, specifically how the fire might affect Hernán's arrival.

"Ah, look, my cell phone works," Inez announced from behind the glow of the screen. She dialed a number, then spoke a few quick words of Chinese to Mr. Kim before switching to Spanish for the rest of the conversation. Luz heard something about how they were safe, not to worry, and that she would return to the hotel as soon as she could, which may not be until morning.

"Why do men treat us like little girls?" Inez huffed upon ending the call. "We may be a little drunk, but we know how to take care of ourselves."

Although not helpless, the adrenalin that propelled Luz out of Black & White began to wear off, leaving her woozy from the many rounds of drinks bought by Luis and the recently unemployed Americans. She tapped a glass of water in the bathroom before easing herself gently onto the bed, where Inez sat with one of the pillows over her lap. A thin line of sweat formed above her lip. She wiped it with her hand and took a long drink.

"Are you going to repair Minchi's?" Inez asked.

"I sold it," Luz said in a tired but clear voice. "This morning."

"Perfect timing."

"*Gracias a Dios*," Luz acknowledged, raising her glass.

A fire truck siren whined past the window. Neither Luz nor Inez had a desire to look in the direction of the refinery. They remained on the bed, surrounded by Minchi's old ledgers, Luz's belongings, and multiple flickering candles.

"Are you going to stay in Aruba?" Inez asked in a quiet voice.

Having prepared herself for freedom, Luz realized the time to go was imminent. The only undetermined factor was the arrival of Hernán and Captain Beck. They might want to have a look around the island, but she would prefer to depart for Barranquilla without delay. In the silence that hung between her and Inez, she wondered if Inez was as self-reliant as she thought. It was Mr. Kim's jet on which Inez flew. At the same time, Captain Beck's boat might affect her own timing.

"I can't remain here," Luz finally answered.

"Before I met Mr. Kim, I worked in Panama, Curaçao, and Spain. Every time I returned to Colombia, I put money in the bank. There's still money in that account. I keep it in case something goes wrong."

Thanks to the repercussions of Garrett Turner's chivalry, Luz was not in the same position. "*Nunca se sabe,*" she whispered.

"It would be hard to live like we did as chicas. Always scrambling to pay the rent, skimping at the grocery, secondhand clothes, old shoes."

For these reasons many girls sold themselves into prostitution. Others did it to hold on to what they had after suffering an unfortunate event or to advance to the next level as in the case of Angela.

"I could do it if I had to," Inez reflected. "You can always make more money. You can find someone to pay you to work, buy something to sell. I see it happen everywhere I go with Mr. Kim. Still, I hide cash here and there in case one day there isn't any."

This made sense to Luz, who had done the same throughout her life as she expected anyone who flirted with poverty would.

"The biggest mistake I made was not having a child," said Inez. "After my stay in Panama, I went to a doctor and got myself fixed. What did I want with a baby? What if I got pregnant from one of the guys who came into the bars? What if I fell for some man in Bogotá who left me and his baby to fend for ourselves? You know this happens every day."

She knew all too well as it was exactly how Luz ended up without a husband.

"At least your husband died in an accident," Inez was saying.

He hadn't been her husband, but Luz didn't clarify the point. She was shocked Inez remembered that bit of her personal history.

"I wish I had a son or daughter. They're your flesh and blood. They give you a reason to dream."

It wasn't sweat that wetted Luz's cheeks. Rather tears formed at the corner of her eyes, finally beading large enough to roll down to the pillow.

"Every place I worked, girls like you and me would post little photos of their children on a mirror, beside the bed, or on a wall. Some of those chicas left the photos out in the open when men came to do their business. They thought it would make the clients more sympathetic, and then they'd pay more. I thought about getting a few pictures myself. In the end, I found other ways to make them behave generously."

Hernán's photo, the one of him and his girlfriend seated on the front of a boat, was only inches away. It and the others that came every year were never on display at Minchi's. No client, not even Herr Diedrik, had seen them.

"I always wondered how those girls explained to their kids where they were or what they were doing and why. Maybe I was lucky after all. Not having a child, I never had to lie."

Luz bolted to the bathroom where she hung her head over the sink and retched. Nothing came up. She coughed and spit and gagged to no avail. She rinsed her mouth, refilled her glass, then leaned her head against the cool porcelain.

"I didn't mean to accuse you," Inez said from the doorway. "I meant ..."

It was the reality of her life that upset Luz, not an unintended indictment. It was she who bought a brothel and worked there, who did nothing to educate herself for another job. She claimed it was to meet the expenses of her mother and sister, but she could have found another way. Her confession to Father Dario may deliver her soul, but it would not remove the shame her son might feel upon learning what his mother had done.

There was the added embarrassment of the comparison to Inez who had been a hard-hearted whore when Luz met her. Yet, she appeared loyal to Mr. Kim, a dedicated wife who tried to learn his language, tolerated his strange food and customs, and supported him as she could. The worst thing she'd done was have fun at Black & White, which had been more like a high school dance than the alley cat prowl of a former prostitute looking to earn pocket change. She had succeeded in the way Luz should never have failed.

No man had been good enough. Samito, Herr Diedrik, and the ones in between, Luz turned them away. Who was she waiting for? Did she really believe Captain Beck was going to show up with a ring in a box the way it happened for the tourists on Palm Beach? And if not him, who? A tycoon who owned a jet? A young guy with a trust fund and good looks?

The problem was she couldn't answer the question, which led to another query. Why did it matter?

Luz leaned back from the sink, took a deep breath, and

looked at Inez. "I never lied to my son," she said. "I haven't spoken to him in fifteen years."

In accordance with the official evacuation plan, the homes and businesses closest to the refinery wall were deserted. All but one. Luis, Angela, and Screwball watched the refinery burn from the balcony above Charlie's Bar.

He was certain he'd seen Luz's son outside Black & White, but when he investigated, Luis saw no one but the San Nicolaas regulars. Finding one man in that crowd would have been nearly impossible, especially with everyone rushing about. Luis returned to the bar for Angela, Luz, and Inez. They were all headed to Astoria when he stopped short at Charlie's, where he invited the women to join him on the veranda. Luz and Inez politely begged off.

"Will we be safe here?" Angela said nervously as they climbed the stairs.

"The dragon will stay on his side of the wall."

The view from the second floor left Angela feeling less confident than her host. She gathered Screwball into her arms, sat down on the recliner, and scratched the cat's chin.

Luis' first order of business was to unpack his uncle's binoculars. The rig was more like a pair of miniature telescopes than something to be used for bird watching. He set them atop a tripod, tightened the mounting screw, and aimed over the parapet.

Looking through the eyepieces, Luis saw a fuzzy scene of orange, yellow, and black. Rotating the focusing dial the image resolved with incredible detail. A line of fire trucks bisected the complex. Water streamed from every nozzle. Men unrolled hoses for more connections. Their efforts did more to prevent the spread of the fire than to beat it back. Tilting up, he found *Athos*. Her wheelhouse was invisible behind a wall of flame rising from the deck. Panning the ship's length he arrived at the bow.

Another vessel entered the frame. Incredibly, it was maneuvering closer to *Athos*. Adjusting the angle, Luis closely examined this other boat. Men hauled cables across the stern seemingly unconcerned about the inferno growing around them. One level up, a man stood at a control station. Black streaks marred his shirt but did not disguise his identity. It was Luz's son. Beside him was a tall mast with several lights and three flags. At the top was the Stars and Stripes.

"God bless America," Luis said, noticing that the second banner, which hung just above the Aruban flag, was a solid blue field with a white star in the center.

It might have taken Hernán and Syd a minute to run from Black & White to *Tenacious*. However, Andy, Ramirez, Tony, and the rest of the crew were already at work. The lines were cast off, the gangplank was up, and two fire monitors sprayed water toward *Athos*, which at this point was on the verge of becoming a floating bomb.

Hernán had to make a choice: put the fire out aboard the ship, tow it clear, or flee the area. He figured she must contain crude, which was a plus. Chemicals or gasoline would have detonated by now. Just the same, crude eventually boiled, released volatile compounds, and subsequently exploded, especially when in the confined space of a ship's hold.

Taking over the aft control station, Hernán directed his men, issuing orders through the radio and by shouting. For all her horsepower, *Tenacious* was no racer. The lack of space between the refinery's finger piers further complicated her moves. Hernán eased the stern away from the dock then reversed both engines, effectively backing her toward the channel. All the while, the deckhands maintained steady streams of water on the nearby fire.

His next move, Hernán already had planned. Since he was moving in reverse, he continued around the end of the pier, then entered the slipway beside *Athos* stern first.

"Heads to tails!" he shouted to Tony who supervised the men on the stern deck. The deckhand gave him a thumbs-up, knowing his captain wanted to connect a line from the stern of *Tenacious* to the bow of *Athos*.

They passed below and alongside the fire as Hernán angled into the slip. No one dared stop working for a look at the flames, but they felt the heat. Tony and two other deckhands dragged a steel cable from its rack, joined it to the one on the towing winch with a heavy shackle, then readied another shackle to hook through the line from *Athos*.

As he'd seen hanging from the tankers in Philadelphia and around the world, Hernán spotted the line dangling to the water. It was standard procedure among refineries, chemical plants, and other terminals that every docked ship have a line at the ready should the vessel need to be moved without the assistance of on-board deckhands. Hernán could only imagine what happened to *Athos'* crew. He prayed they made it out of the stern section. If not, they'd been roasted alive.

Steel to steel, *Tenacious* met *Athos*. Hernán kept the stern in tight even as he allowed the bow to wander, thereby putting more distance between it and the fire. Tony leaned over the side, grabbed the ship's line, and hauled it to his comrades. One man looped the waiting shackle through the eye, and the other slammed home the pin. With five twists of the wrist the nut was secure. The three of them cleared the deck.

Glancing forward, Hernán noticed the open space in the slip was diminishing. *Athos'* mooring lines must have burned through, allowing her to drift off the dock. If he didn't act quickly, he would be sandwiched against the other pier like a piece of metal between the furnace and the forge. Now there was no choice; he would have to nose into *Athos* while simultaneously dragging her to the channel, putting his boat stupidly close to danger.

As he manipulated the controls, the stern cable came tight. Easing ahead on the throttle, Hernán waited for the first sign of movement. Half a minute passed, another thirty seconds, ten more. He added power and finally the ship began to slide. Hands steady, he scanned the various stations, making sure each man was doing his job.

Despite being damaged, afire, and crewless, *Athos* cooperated. She exited the slip, leaving a trail of burning oil that eventually broke apart into harmless patches. To keep her from torpedoing into the reef on the opposite side of the channel, Hernán swung *Tenacious* to the south so she was in the proper towing configuration, that is, directly ahead of *Athos* with the cable stretched between them.

"Let's give her some room to breathe," he said into his radio.

Tony released the winch's brake, allowing the cable to slowly pay out over the stern. He knew he would still be killed if the ship exploded, but at least he would see it coming.

In a remarkable display of compassion, Inez did not ask for details. Nor was Luz in the mood to provide them. She was angry with herself for losing control, for blundering into a part of her life she managed to keep private. She mentioned that Hernán had grown up with Captain Beck and they were returning in a couple days. These facts Inez accepted with a gentle hug.

During the early years of their separation, Luz pined for contact with Hernán and Captain Beck, lingering by the telephone, checking the mailbox every day. As time went on, she believed silence was for the better. The packages that arrived were like Christmas gifts out of season. They provided comfort and sustained her through the months ahead. Photographs showed a growing boy, his report cards reflected his intelligence, and Captain Beck's notes praised him like a favorite son. Hernán was on his way to achieving the goal Luz set the night she sent him away. Her son was not going to be a playboy or a bum or a fool.

Had one day she answered a call from her son or sent him a letter, Luz would have done exactly as Inez guessed. She would have deceived him. And why? To protect him from how she worked? Yes, and that would have necessitated another lie to explain why she wasn't with him the way a mother should be. So it would go to the point where she would be trapped. Did Captain Beck understand the dilemma? She had a hunch he did. The distance each package traveled increased after every one of Hernán's birthdays.

Inez interrupted her thoughts. "Soon Hernán will be here," she said cheerfully. "You can start over."

There were women who might have been perfectly happy to continue on without considering what anyone, including their children, thought about what they'd done. Luz wasn't one of them. She clung to a sense of hope and dignity that she would be able to begin anew without the burden of her past weighing on her son. It was possible with a single caveat. She had to maintain the deception that she'd been anything but a puta.

She had the means, not just monetary, but the skills as well. In the shifting glare of reality, Luz pondered how she once considered herself a master of those talents. She used them at will and with the best of intentions, providing for her family and creating a wonderful opportunity for Hernán. However, like the elephant that attacks his trainer, her greatest strength could become a deadly weakness if she inadvertently let her guard down. If she was going to preserve the lies that protected her illusion, she would have to be at the main gate when Hernán and Captain Beck walked through.

With that in mind, she said, "I'm going to miss the gala."

28

RUBBING HIS EYES, Luis sat back from the binoculars and took a sip of rum. Angela had fallen asleep hours ago, leaving him free to watch the height of the catastrophe uninterrupted. He took in the expanse of the refinery, what was left of it. The fire effectively burned itself out, consuming the tanks, equipment, and structures on the west side of the facility. Plenty of twisted metal remained for an ambitious scrap dealer and precious little for a company to process crude.

The ship where it all started was about a mile offshore, half sunk as far as he could tell. In a bold move that would go down in Aruban history, *Tenacious* towed *Athos* out of the harbor. Tugs from Oranjestaad arrived on station later, lending assistance in extinguishing the on-board inferno.

The fire department was in the process of demobilizing their equipment. Drained hoses were rolled up, nozzles stowed, and tired men stripped out of their protective clothing. One of his lieutenants relieved Chief Calenda at the main gate.

Seeing the policeman heading toward his patrol car, Luis hurried down to the street, intercepting him on Rodgerstraat.

"Commandante, how about breakfast?"

"Why not?" answered an exhausted Calenda.

Fortunately, the stove in Charlie's Bar burned gas. In the rising sunlight filtering through the windows, Luis struck a match, found a pan, and scrambled eggs. Bread he toasted in the oven and coffee he made in an old percolator pot that hadn't been used in years. He carried the meal on a tray to the bar where he joined Calenda. As they began eating, the coolers started to whir, indicating the electricity had been restored to San Nicolaas.

"Just in time for sunrise," Luis said.

"Too late for the refinery," Calenda noted.

"There's one more act to this play."

The chief listened carefully as Luis described his plan for both of them. Although he would have preferred to take a couple of days off, Calenda acquiesced to the call of a noble cause.

"Are you sure the rest of the cast is going to cooperate?" he asked after a sip of coffee.

"Of course!" beamed Luis. "We were understudies to a master. It's our turn to take the stage."

"In that case, I better make sure my costume is clean."

"Hop Long has two-hour dry cleaning services, and the electricity is on."

They toasted the endeavor by tapping their mugs together.

With the chief properly briefed and well fed, Luis climbed the stairs to his apartment. There, he found Angela stretching and yawning beneath his sheets. Is there a better sight than a pretty young woman lying across your bed dreamy-eyed and naked? Luis thought that no, there wasn't.

"*¿Qué hora es?*" she asked.

As if on cue, Screwball banged his bowl against the wall on the veranda like the gong for a Chinese emperor.

"Feeding time at the zoo," Luis told his guest.

A big payday can rouse a crew from the dead. The men aboard *Tenacious* were no exception to this maritime axiom, especially when they were within sight of a town like San Nicolaas. They drew lots to decide who went ashore first and anxiously waited at the rail like dogs straining the leash. Their captain shared the sentiment but for different reasons. However, none of them were free to do as they wished.

A prevented disaster is like saving a man's life. The rescued becomes the ward of the rescuer, and so it was with *Athos* and *Tenacious*. The ship hung at anchor with little chance of drifting. Her engine room and several cargo compartments were flooded, her wheelhouse destroyed, and her chances of resurrection looked grim. Thus, it was only prudent that *Tenacious* stand by until her owners made a decision on what to do.

"She'll be one for the breakers," Syd said to Hernán as they sipped coffee in the wheelhouse. "The steel's buckled, all the expensive equipment ruined; what would you do?"

"Call the insurance company," Hernán suggested.

"The crew wants to put the launch in the water and have a night out," the engineer continued.

"As if they couldn't use a rest."

It had taken hours to get *Athos* under control. Once it was safe to go aboard, Hernán, Syd, and Tony surveyed the damage. They learned through radio communications that the crew was accounted for. Two men were badly burned and in the hospital. An overheated pump precipitated the disaster, the exact details of which wouldn't be known until interviews were conducted.

The radio beeped on the house channel. Tony's voice came over the speaker. "Uh ... Captain ... you there?"

"Go ahead," Hernán said.

"We ... uh ... have a stowaway."

"Say again."

"Come to the stern deck," came the reply.

Impossible, Hernán thought on his way aft. They'd been at the dock less than half an hour before the fire broke out. Only someone waiting in the shadows could have gotten aboard in the confusion that followed. Then it occurred to him that the crew had conjured up a clever prank designed to give them a reason to take the launch to town. His suspicions were nearly confirmed when he found Tony chatting with a disheveled bum wearing a drum major's jacket.

Frankie's lips formed into his gap-toothed smile. For a few seconds, he thought he might be stuck aboard a modern version of the *Flying Dutchman*. He remembered Tony and Syd from a decade and a half ago. It made sense that they were older, but the other fellow, the one who resembled Captain Beck in every way but age and complexion, he didn't fit. Then a memory shook loose, and he figured everything out.

"You're not Captain Beck!" the bum exclaimed as Hernán approached. "You're Luz's son."

Of the nicknames, titles, and salutations people used when referring to him, Hernán had not heard that one since he was a little boy. It sounded strange, as if this clown was talking about someone else.

"You know my mother?" More incredible than this joker being on Hernán's boat was the idea that his mother was acquainted with him.

Striking a pose worthy of Napoleon, Frankie replied, "See her every day, sometimes three or four times."

"Where is she?"

"I'm not telling until you put me on dry land."

"No problem," Hernán agreed, expecting Frankie to cooperate. "As soon as the harbor opens, we'll head in."

"Then I'll keep things locked up here until you pay for the key," the choller said, tapping the side of his head.

In a bygone era, a disrespectful moron like this would have been keelhauled for speaking like that to a captain. Frustrated, Hernán looked toward Tony and Syd, who both shrugged. "Okay, what do you want?"

"We'll start the bidding at a new set of teeth," Frankie declared.

Turning to Syd, Hernán said, "Get the port captain on the radio. Tell him we're bringing home one of his own."

"¿Señora?"

Her door opened barely a crack, just enough to let the voice in. Sitting up, Luz searched for her watch. Groggy and having trouble focusing, she couldn't find it. It was bright in the room, too, which meant it had to be well into the day. She remembered talking with Inez until the all-clear siren signaled that San Nicolaas residents should return home. At that point, a minor hangover had set in, giving her a headache and a touch of nausea. Inez took a pill bottle from her purse, saying, "Two of these fix me up every time." She placed the tablets in Luz's hand and fetched a fresh glass of water.

"Gracias," Luz said. "I'm sorry I won't be at the gala tonight.

You understand."

"I'll save a seat in case you change your mind," Inez said, closing her purse. "Call me when you have good news."

When had Inez left? At six? Seven? And what time was it now?

"*¿Señora?*"

"Come in," she said only because it was Harold.

He entered with a tray that he placed on the vacant side of her bed. A club sandwich, a glass of juice, and a thin slice of chocolate cake waited for Luz.

"You must be hungry," Harold said. "It's almost two."

"That late?" Luz groaned. Inez must have given her sleeping pills.

"Or early, depending on how you look at it," suggested a new voice.

She looked up to see Andrés sticking his head through the opening. Not understanding his comment, she took a sip of juice. She immediately felt better and hungrily eyed a wedge of the sandwich.

Harold asked. "Would you like something else? A bowl of soup?"

"No, thank you," Luz replied. The cook left her to Andrés, who was now seated on the other side of the bed.

"The gala," the artist began, "doesn't start until eight. You'll want to be fashionably late, which means you have plenty of time to get ready."

"I don't—"

Andrés interrupted her protest. "You're right. You don't want to miss it. The new paintings. Your friends. The music. La Familia Arends is making a special appearance. Remember when they used to play for Charlie's parties in Savaneta?"

She remembered. Since then, La Familia Arends had become a sensation in South America, traveling the continent for sold-out concerts. They returned to Aruba only twice per year to write new songs and rest. She loved their music but was in no mood for dancing. She needed to contact the port captain and Chief Calenda to find out what was going on in the harbor.

"Is it true that Herr Diedrik bought you a special dress?"

"Yes," Luz answered, shifting her eyes toward the closet. Inez had seen the dress and must have told Andrés that she wouldn't be attending the gala.

"Be careful. There will be plenty of jealous women in the room," he reminded her.

"But—"

"But nothing," he cut her off.

Luz was growing angry. In light of the circumstances, his prodding offended her.

"I regret divorcing you," Andrés said next. "It was the biggest mistake of my life."

She cocked her chin and retorted, "Nonsense. We hardly knew each other."

"I had good advice from Charlie, but since when does a 20-year-old listen to reason?"

He could have been talking about her as a young woman who came to San Nicolaas. She shrugged off the point as he got to his feet.

"The only second chances we get are the ones we find for ourselves," he said.

She ignored his logic with silence.

"See you tonight," he finished and pulled the door closed behind him.

Aggravated, Hernán hung up the microphone and paced the wheelhouse from port to starboard. The port captain declared San Nicolaas Harbor unsafe, denying any vessel access.

"Not even rowboats," he'd said, making it clear that small craft were also forbidden. "There's the possibility of reignition."

Considering nothing remained to burn, Hernán doubted the man's assessment. So as not to challenge anyone's authority, he suggested *Tenacious* berth in Oranjestaad.

"All pier space is occupied with cruise ships," came the reply. "Please stand by your current position with all hands until relieved."

All hands included Frankie, who held court on the foredeck with Tony and Syd, who admitted having met him during their previous stay in Aruba. Despite their cajoling, the choller wouldn't say anything about Hernán's mother.

Stuck with little to do and nowhere to go, Hernán opened the logbook and inscribed a line about the current situation. Flipping back through the pages, he came across several in Captain Beck's hand.

"0450. Approximately twenty miles east of Cape May. Seas four feet. Speed sixteen knots. On course for Philadelphia."

Mundane entries like these were the kind a captain prefers. They indicate all is well.

Staring at the page, it struck Hernán that his stepfather had crossed over his own burial site only days before dying. The irony of this realization gave him cause to gently close the logbook and return it to the corner of the chart table where it belonged.

On the morning of the entry he just read, Hernán had anticipated another conversation about his stepfather's days in Aruba. Unfortunately, Beck, like the rest of the crew, was excited to be in Philadelphia.

"I'm going to look up old Jack Ford," Beck said when Hernán entered the wheelhouse that morning. "I don't know if you remember, he sold *Marlena* to me."

Hernán remembered the story but not the man.

"A brilliant guy," Beck said, adding, "Take us to port, Captain. I need some rest."

They caught the flood tide and rode it all the way to Philadelphia. *Tenacious* was moored at the shipyard where she'd been built. A couple of Grover Lawrence's men looked after her while the crew dispersed to their families. Beck and Hernán went to their brick rowhome, which was full of stale air and nothing else. Mrs. Clarke, the neighbor who looked after the property, was surprised to see them.

Thinking of the house, Hernán turned from the chart table and descended to the next level where the captain's quarters were located. A tug as large as *Tenacious* afforded her crew spacious accommodations compared to the boats Hernán knew as a boy. There had been barely enough space to turn around in *Marlena*'s bunks. Entering the room that had been Beck's, he found what would be considered a large studio apartment in Manhattan. A comfortable bed bordered the far wall and two chairs with a small table flanked the opposite. In between were a desk, shelves, and cabinets for personal belongings. The head was located through another door.

The place had become a shrine with everything maintained as if Captain Beck might walk through the door at any minute.

Most likely Tony, who was the neat freak of the boat, had been working here. Clean and pressed, Beck's shirts and pants waited in the drawers. His coat hung in the closet, which made Hernán smile, considering Aruba's climate. In the desk's center drawer, he discovered the drawing of his mother.

Picking it up, he realized the sketch was of a woman perhaps a few years older than he was now. Time had not stood still since the drawing was made. There was a story to hear, the one about her life since they parted. And he had one to tell about the man who took her son as his own.

His real father may have died in a coal mine, but nothing so dramatic befell Captain Beck. They'd been in Philadelphia two days, spending the time visiting business contacts like Grover Lawrence and Jack Ford. Wherever they went, Beck introduced Hernán as "my son."

"Let's build him his own boat so you'll have some competition," Lawrence said. "I'll bet he comes up with a name quicker than you did."

As it happened, there was no need to fashion any steel into a tugboat. The evening after they spoke at the shipyard, Hernán had been sorting through some childhood memorabilia, organizing it with the idea of putting together a couple of scrapbooks to show his mother.

"I'm going out to buy some trinkets to give away in Aruba. Want to go with me?" Beck had asked.

"Sure," Hernán replied.

They descended the stairs to the rental car parked at the curb. Just as he got to the vehicle, Beck said, "Forgot my wallet. I'll be right back."

Hernán watched him go through the door then started the

car and waited. Switching on the radio to the all-news station, he listened to a report about the final peace treaty between Iran and Iraq. It was a segment full of details that interested him because they had been in the area for several years. When it ended, he looked back at the door and noticed Mrs. Clarke knocking on it. Curious, he crossed the sidewalk to her.

"I heard a shout and an awful thud. Is everything all right?" she asked.

Pushing open the door, Hernán saw his stepfather sprawled facedown at the bottom of the stairs. Behind him, Mrs. Clark gasped and said she'd call 911. He carefully eased Beck onto his back, stunned by the gash on his stepfather's forehead. Blood matted the nearby hair and had pooled on the floor. One of Beck's eyelids fluttered as the other opened wide.

"The Feast of Saint Michael," he said.

This was the moment when Hernán thought of the medallion. He saw it wasn't where it should have been. In the seconds that followed, dozens of memories flashed through his mind: the post office in Malta, Teresa's scent, the floating out ceremony for *Tenacious*, the feel of Kelly's lips against his, and the look on Captain Wilkie's face when he talked about poor bastards. There was the sound of Captain Beck pounding up the stairs after arguing with Nicole and his swearing at having banged his shin. Was it possible that he'd simply tripped and landed at the bottom of the same set of stairs? Was it possible that his oversight of a worn or crooked tread, a condition he never would have tolerated aboard his tugboat, had been his undoing?

Mrs. Clarke was asking if Captain Beck was okay, if he'd fallen down the stairs or if something else happened. Instead, Hernán heard his own mother's voice. She was young and beautiful and spoke in crisp Spanish. Aruba's warm breeze lifted the hair off her shoulders and tugged at her dress. "Go with Captain Beck," she said. "He will bring you back to me soon."

Hernán held her image in his hand, this pencil drawing that appeared from time to time like a welcome ghost. He would have to explain what happened to the father he knew to the mother he didn't.

"Captain?" Syd called in from the passageway. "The San Nicolaas port captain is on the radio again."

"On my way," Hernán said without averting his eyes from his mother's image.

29

THE MARINA HOTEL and Casino's marble lobby welcomed everyone from the Aruban prime minister and members of parliament to prominent businesspeople, a few judges, and a former Miss Colombia. Together with their spouses, adult children, co-workers, and hangers-on, they filled the hallway outside the largest ballroom. Two ATV television reporters struggled to keep up their man-on-the-scene coverage. They awaited Andrés Cortés, reigning Master of New Dutch Realism.

Luis released Angela to the protective custody of a friendly bartender. He lingered near the edge of the lobby with Herr Diedrik, who worried like an anxious father with a daughter out on a date.

"I should have met her at Astoria," the lawyer said. "What if she's done something … irrational?"

Comfort came from Father Dario, who wore his collar and a serene look on his face. "She'll be here," the priest assured him. "On her own terms."

Luis concurred. "An event like this is irresistible. Look at all the people."

It was a sophisticated crowd, but Herr Diedrik did not think of Luz as the type to publicly socialize in these circles. She might encounter a few of the men in her room, at a hotel, or for a quiet dinner in the back corner of a restaurant. Just the same, he'd never seen her openly mingle at one of the other functions attended by Aruba's cultural elite.

"*Damas y caballeros*, ladies and gentlemen," the master of ceremonies intoned over the public address system. "Please join Mr. Yu Kim and his lovely wife Inez in our main ballroom to welcome Aruba's own Andrés Cortés."

The crowd formed a line at the door where Mr. Kim and Inez greeted each attendee. Arranged gallery-style along three walls were the latest works of Aruba's native son. The subjects of the larger-than-life paintings looked down like Greek gods. Some were human figures more than eight feet tall, painted with such realism that they appeared to be oversized actors. The settings they occupied varied from noble palaces to mysterious, stormy shores. A gala attendee couldn't have been blamed if he tried to walk into the life-like scenes for a look around.

While the new paintings were the subject of much scrutiny, there were two others where a platoon of wags gathered. Black cloth disguised the steel frames around them, but the people who pointed and gossiped knew they had once been the walls of a particular house.

Suddenly, sporadic clapping broke out, and then the entire room surged with a round of applause. Andrés had made his entrance. He shook hands with Mr. Kim, kissed Inez on both cheeks, and put his arms up for the adoration of fellow islanders and visitors alike. When the noise settled, he took to the stage where there was a microphone.

"*Danki*, Aruba, *danki*," he began. "It is a pleasure to be home." He took a deep breath then continued. "Every artist has his own vision, the way he sees a picture in his mind before it becomes paint on a canvas. Tonight, you'll see scenes that were inspired by people and events here in Aruba, some from the past, some from the future."

At this point, the crowd turned away from Andrés and looked over his paintings. What he told them made no sense because the paintings resembled scenes from the European Renaissance more than recent Caribbean history. They had names like *The King and His Court*, *The Explorer Returns*, and *The Forbidden Coast*. Whispers circulated as some of the more sophisticated attendees issued quiet opinions to one another.

"Of course, I'd like to thank Mr. Kim and Inez for making this show possible," Andrés said. "I'm very fortunate to have such a generous patron."

Another round of applause rose and fell. Mr. Kim bowed. Inez blushed.

"Finally, I want to say that oftentimes an artist forgets everything to pursue his vision. He ignores what is important, the many things small and large that make his existence possible. There were those people who wouldn't let me quit when I was frustrated and gave me what I needed to continue when I didn't have the money. I am grateful to you all, but there is someone special I want to acknowledge tonight. She supported me during my earliest days, and if she hadn't, I would have been painting your cars instead of the canvases on display."

Muted laughter rippled through the room.

"Luz?" Andrés called. "Where are you?"

People looked from one to the other, past the paintings, across the stage, until their eyes eventually stopped a few feet from the door. Even if she hadn't taken a step forward, one of the judges, a member of Parliament, a few of the businessmen, Herr Diedrik, his sister, and Inez all would have known who Luz was. A couple of wives had their suspicions, too, but for the moment, they were captivated by Luz's dress. The halter style exposed her shoulders and back, giving the illusion that she was much taller than her smallish frame. The fabric hung to her calves in a shimmering blue glow hinting at the figure beneath it.

People around her backed away. A few murmured behind cupped hands to their companions' nearby ears. From the far side of the room came the sound of a single man clapping. It was Father Dario, and he kept going until the others joined him.

"*Muchas gracias, Luz,*" Andrés intoned with a slight bow. When the room quieted, he finished with, "Now, everyone, enjoy the music, the paintings, and the entire evening."

Andrés surrendered the stage to the youngest member and guitarist of La Familia Arends.

"*Bon nochi,*" he said. "*Somos La Familia Arends.*" With a brisk strum of his guitar, the musical portion of the evening began.

The artificial harbor across the street from the Marina Hotel accommodated mostly small craft. There were charter boats available for visiting anglers, modest sailboats, and a few motor yachts. A hundred yards away the water was deep enough for cruise ships and a special wharf had been constructed to receive them. An esplanade connected the two facilities, making it an easy walk for anyone interested in the shops, restaurants, and casinos that stood on both sides of L.G. Smith Boulevard.

Chief Calenda parked his car at the hotel, crossed the street, and strolled toward the last bollard at the cruise ship wharf. No longer did the passenger vessels remain in port until midnight. Their corporate owners wanted money spent in their floating casinos as opposed to on land, which meant they had to depart early enough that the after-dinner crowd wouldn't be tempted to try their luck ashore. The wharf would remain vacant until six the next morning when the tourist flotilla pulled in.

He leaned on the bollard thinking that Charlie would have lit a cigarette to pass the time. Not a smoker, Calenda was left with his thoughts, which could be troubling but not cancerous. He reflected on the changes that came to his island, and not just the relocation of the parliament building or the addition of another hotel at the end of Palm Beach. Aruba suffered through a morning and evening rush hour like the big cities of the world. The island needed to expand its electricity, water, and sewer plants to meet an ever-increasing demand. Hardly anyone fished commercially anymore, especially not like Old Man Juarez who would land his catch at dawn for a line of anxious buyers. Food came in refrigerated containers, except for the delicacies, which shared space with the tourists on airplanes. All of it was bought at huge groceries instead of at the dock or a roadside stand. Gated communities sprawled over large tracks of land, insulating their residents from the inconvenience of knowing their neighbors.

There was more coming, too, because San Nicolaas was a last frontier of sorts, a town protected by its ugliness, a woman who cut her nose to stave off rape. She had a piece of magic in that her belly touched the sea and for this privilege, people doled out expensive charms. He knew he would live to see the day when the only difference between Palm and Baby Beaches would be the signs at the airport: a left arrow or one pointing to the right. After what happened at the refinery, nothing could save her.

Again, if Charlie had been smoking, his cigarette would have been finished by now, perfect timing to step back as a rope was thrown to the bollard beside Calenda. It landed with a thump, then emitted a creaking groan as the weight of the boat pulled it tight. Several more lines were made fast until the vessel was secure. A short gangplank was lowered to the dock.

The first man off was Frankie. "*¡Gracias a Dios!*" he hollered, fell to his knees, and kissed the ground.

"Stay right there," Calenda ordered.

"Yes, sir!"

Next came Luz's son, and this was the first time Calenda had seen him since he was a boy. "Captain," he said, "I apologize for the inconvenience caused by Frankie."

"Inconvenience?" protested Frankie. "We have a deal. He's going to buy me a set of teeth, and I'm going to tell—"

"Wait over there," interrupted Calenda. He then addressed Hernán. "Captain, in the case of stowaways, there's some minor paperwork to be done for the night magistrate. It'll only take a few minutes, and you can be on your way."

"I understand," Hernán agreed. "Frankie was going to give me some information."

"He's going nowhere. These magistrates on the other hand can be fussy about appearances."

"Look at me dressed for a parade," Frankie interjected.

A few minutes later Calenda and Hernán headed in the general direction of Oranjestaad's police headquarters.

"These people look familiar," Inez said to Luz.

They stared at the largest of the paintings, *The Explorer Returns*. Eighteenth-century ships, their sails stowed, occupied the left quarter of the frame. From them, a trail of wagons led to a receiving platform where a monarch greeted his chartered mariner who bore oddities from far-off lands. The clouds overhead cast pools of shadow that muted the lesser figures while bright sunshine illuminated the key elements.

"Their faces," continued Inez. "I've seen them before. Maybe in a magazine?"

She'd actually seen them in San Nicolaas, but Luz was not about to tell her. The monarch, in a velvet robe trimmed in fur, bore a striking resemblance to Charlie. In another life, members of his court tended bar in San Nicolaas. The ladies-in-waiting were young women Luz and Inez had worked with in those same bars. An aging prince with white hair and one upturned jester's shoe stared off in the distance. The real man vowed to build a house by the sea and have Luz live in it with him. The fair-skinned explorer pointed a finger to an unfurled map held open by a boy Luz had watched grow up in a series of photos mailed to her.

"I must be missing something," Inez said and started for the next picture.

Luz remained in place, her eyes fixed on a carriage seemingly exiting the scene. A figure inside gazed at the unfolding ceremony. It was like looking into a mirror.

At last she stepped away, catching up with Inez who was

already several paintings ahead. Herr Diedrik joined them, as did Luis and Angela. One by one they discussed Andrés' work, praising the detail, admiring the imagery, and marveling at how they all knew him when his most famous effort was a set of flames on the hood of a car.

"We're ignoring the music," Inez suddenly said.

They all turned away from the pictures to look at the stage where La Familia Arends was about to begin the next song. The oldest member held up his violin. He drew out the first several measures before the others joined in. His grandson, the one with the guitar, leaned toward the microphone and began to sing.

Just as she recognized the faces, Luz knew where that guitar had come from. It had been the first gift brought back by the captain who had taken her son to America and around the world. The instrument sounded beautiful as the artist took his turn with the lead.

"Let me borrow your date," Inez said, taking Herr Diedrik's arm. "I'd like to dance with a man who knows how for a change."

"*Claro*," Luz said. Seeking a moment to herself, she encouraged Luis and Angela to enjoy the song as well. Alone, she turned back toward the last two paintings in the show, the ones on which Montoya made a fortune worthy of depiction in the others.

Two men stood before them. Luz noted their uniforms and stayed a comfortable distance back. For several minutes they talked, gesturing in various directions. Just as the last chords of the song faded away, they turned around. A voice came from behind her, and it snapped Luz out of a daze.

"Him I know," Inez said with a finger pointed at Chief Calenda. "Tell me, Luz, who is this other handsome fellow?"

Stepping forward, Luz put her hands upon Hernán's shoulders. She squeezed the solid flesh of her only son, then pulled herself tight to his chest. The feeling of his arms encircling her released the tears that for too long she held back.

"This is my son," she replied. "He's a man now."

❧30❧

ASTONISHED BY THE PAINTINGS that adorned his childhood bedroom, Hernán forgot about the circuitous route on which Chief Calenda guided him. He suspected something was amiss when they entered through a nondescript door. Magistrates operated their courts in official buildings and behind this door was nothing but a blank hallway with utility pipes. Still, he followed along until the music grew louder. Then the chief opened another door, revealing the pictures.

Curiosity carried Hernán into the ballroom. He wanted to know how the walls of his mother's house had come to be on display here. Calenda explained the technical details, prudently leaving out Montoya's part.

"The artist is here," Calenda said.

He would have liked to meet the painter, but as Hernán turned, he was startled to find himself face-to-face with the woman in the sketch he held earlier in the day. It was his mother, and she wore the medallion that had been around Captain Beck's neck, the one he must have sent from Malta.

"I wasn't expecting you until tomorrow," she said, pulling

back without letting go of him.

"The Feast of Saint Michael," Hernán affirmed.

Taking her son's arm, Luz ushered him across the room, unaware of Inez calling to her. Nor was she cognizant of Angela, who was bewildered by how everything Luis told her would happen actually did come to pass. Stopping before the window, Luz pointed toward *Tenacious*.

"*¿Tu barco?*" she asked.

"*Sí,*" he answered.

"*Vamos.*"

They headed for the door, where Luz paused to whisper a few words to Chief Calenda. The policeman nodded, then extended his hand to Hernán.

It wasn't until she was closer to *Tenacious* that Luz grasped what was happening. Her pace quickened, her heels clicking along the pavement, her eyes widening at the size of her son's ship. She remembered Captain Beck's tugboat, the one he took Hernán aboard on a night much like this one. It seemed big to her, but the one before her now could have swallowed its predecessor.

The last time she'd been on a boat was during her first trip to Aruba. Because of what happened then, she refused to step on one since. With Hernán behind her and Syd ahead, she didn't hesitate. In three steps she was past the gunwale, standing on solid steel. She looked up at the windows high above. It was there that the captain steered and gave the orders. In a flash, she slipped off her shoes, tossed them to Syd, and mounted the stairs.

As her son did as a boy fifteen years ago, Luz did this night as a woman and mother, eager to greet the person who returned her son a man. She reached the top of the first flight, keeping her eyes fixed on those windows from which came a soft green glow. He was in there, waiting for her.

On deck below, Hernán recalled the events that brought him from Bogotá to Aruba to America and to so many ports around the world before finally landing him here again. What baffled him was why the woman he'd just met had sent him with Captain Beck in the first place. His mother's life was a story he wanted to hear. However, looking at the wheelhouse, seeing her reach for the handle on the aft door, he would have to tell a piece of his own first.

Grasping the handle, Luz started to look over her shoulder. She was ready to leave this place for Barranquilla or another destination. Where she went she didn't care as long as she traveled with her son and Captain Beck. Movement below distracted her before she caught a glimpse of San Nicolaas. Hernán was climbing the stairs. She smiled at him, then pressed her eyes closed and opened the door.

"*Tú vives*," she said.

31

IT WAS JUST AFTER MIDNIGHT and Herr Diedrik, Luis, and Chief Calenda leaned on the bar. The three of them had followed Hernán and Luz's progress to the waterfront. Suddenly, Luz scampered onto the boat where she paused a moment, then raced up the stairs toward the wheelhouse. Soon thereafter, the crew stowed the gangplank, took in their lines, and the boat eased away from the dock.

"What did she say?" Diedrik asked Calenda, the last of them to speak with Luz.

"She said Aruba needs an honest lawyer more than an honest lawyer needs her."

"Classy to the end," Luis observed.

"This leaves me vulnerable to marrying one of my sister's friends," Diedrik reflected.

"There are worse fates," Calenda told him.

"You haven't met these women."

The evening unwound two hours later with the last song from La Familia Arends. Luis returned Angela to Black & White Bar where the girls of Rembrandtstraat wanted to hear all the details. They swarmed her, forming a human traffic jam in the middle of the alley.

"Her son came back?"

"She left with him?"

"Where did they go?"

"What about Minchi's?"

"What about ..."

Luis was grateful to avoid an awkward departure. He parked his truck in front of Charlie's and stepped out to find Frankie waiting on the corner.

"It took me a long time to get here on the bus," the choller grumbled.

"Sorry, Frankie," Luis said.

He handed Luis a fresh copy of *Diario.* "More bad news."

The headline verified Frankie's prophecies.

"REFINERY PERMANENTLY CLOSED."

An article detailing plans for San Nicolaas filled the rest of the front page. An inside spread rendered Main Street as a dressed-up pedestrian shopping district. Another diagram showed condos overlooking Baby Beach, a new golf course, a three-berth cruise ship terminal, and new hotels. A smaller article mentioned demolition of the refinery would begin next month.

"I'm never getting another set of teeth."

"You still live in paradise," Luis said.

"But not forever."

Acknowledgments

For stories told and memories shared, I would like to thank my friends in Aruba. I am equally grateful to all of the readers of *An Island Away* who sent e-mails pushing me to finish this sequel. Your kind words are always appreciated. I enjoyed spending time with these characters again. I hope you did as well. Special thanks to my editor Susan. I am fortunate to work with someone so talented. I thank my wife, Heather, for her honesty and encouragement. And lastly, Mr. Vernon Fletcher is not to be forgotten for his wary countenance.

About the Author

Daniel Putkowski is a graduate of New York University's Tisch School of the Arts. He divides his time between Aruba and a suburb of Philadelphia. His first novel, *An Island Away*, remains the #1 bestselling book in Aruba. *Under a Blue Flag* is his fourth novel.

To learn more about the author, visit
danielputkowski.com

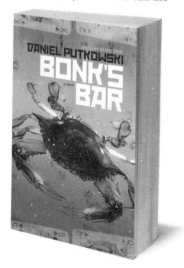

ALSO BY **DANIEL PUTKOWSKI**

"Universal Coverage is the *1984* novel of our era."

—GRACE-MARIE TURNER, PRESIDENT, GALEN INSTITUTE

"Compelling novel in the tradition of *Animal Farm* and *1984*
that shows ... the disastrous consequences of government-run health care."

—NEWT GINGRICH, FORMER SPEAKER OF THE HOUSE OF REPRESENTATIVES

"Terrifying look into our future ... A must read."

—CYNARA COOMER, MD, FOX NEWS MEDICAL CONTRIBUTOR

UNIVERSAL
COVERAGE

BOB SMITH HAD IT ALL. A beautiful house, a happy family, a rewarding career, and a government concerned with his well-being. But when his young son collapses, everything begins to crumble. Suddenly thrust into the world of Universal Coverage, Smith discovers that the ideals he voted for have spiraled out of control. The U.S. nationalized health care system has quickly devolved into a nightmare of unbearable waits, inevitable fraud, and uncertain outcomes presided over by a disinterested bureaucratic class. As Smith struggles to save his son's life, he finds the only hope is *Salvare,* an unauthorized hospital ship providing world-class care to anyone with cash who's willing to make the journey. A miracle at sea awaits aboard *Salvare* if Smith is brave enough to question the dangerous path his country has taken. Time is running out, and in matters of life and death, timing is everything.

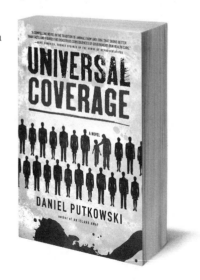

Available wherever books are sold